"No diplomat of his generation has a finer willingness to pierce self-deception or as gifted ... ...ight leaps from every page of this remarkable volume."

—JESSICA MATHEWS
President, Carnegie Endowment for International Peace

"Chas Freeman's important work chronicles a series of American missteps that have immense, multifaceted, and ongoing implications for the United States in the Arab and Islamic worlds—and globally... The book is packed with uncommon wisdom and profound analysis, and laced throughout with bold prescriptions for more effective American positions, policies, and actions."

—Dr. JOHN DUKE ANTHONY
Founding President and CEO, National Council on U.S.-Arab Relations

"[Freeman] is a master of the apt and well-turned phrase—a delight to read. You probably will not agree with every word you read here, but you ought to read every word to understand the challenges and opportunities for American foreign policy."

—Hon. THOMAS R. PICKERING
Former Under Secretary of State for Political Affairs; Ambassador to Jordan, Israel and the United Nations

"Chas Freeman is an old fashioned American patriot.... If I could, I'd get this book on the curriculum of every service academy and defense college and university. Our military will pay the price for our wrong-headed policies unless we change them. Freeman shows the way."

—M.J. ROSENBERG
Columnist, Media Matters for America

"A treasure trove of information and history for those interested in the region...Former foreign service officers rarely speak out as Chas Freeman has done here... We are proud of him, even when we don't agree with his views, because he has found his voice, and speaks compellingly on some of the most difficult issues confronting our nation in this new century."

—Hon. FRANCES D. COOK
Former U.S. ambassador to Cameroon and Oman

Other titles from

Just World Books

"Timely Books for Changing Times"

This title, like most of our titles, is being published first in paperback, and will later be released as a hardcover, in two or more e-book versions, and in a number of overseas editions. Please check our website for updates on the publishing plans, and to buy the books:

 www.justworldbooks.com

Our Fall 2010 schedule includes initial publication of the following additional titles:

Gaza Mom: Palestine, Politics, Parenting, and Everything In Between
Laila El-Haddad
(October 2010)

Afghanistan Journal: Selections from Registan.net
Joshua Foust
(November 2010)

A Responsible End? The United States and Iraq, 2005-2010
Reidar Visser
(November 2010)

JUST WORLD BOOKS
In early 2011 we will publish titles on Pakistan (by Manan Ahmed); on food policy, especially in the Middle East (by Rami Zurayk); on China (by Chas W. Freeman, Jr.); and on issues in Christian nonviolence (by Ron Mock).
Visit the website for more news and to sign up for updates.
Also, follow us on Facebook and Twitter.
www.justworldbooks.com

AMERICA'S MISADVENTURES
IN THE MIDDLE EAST

Other works by

Chas W. Freeman Jr.

Arts of Power: Statecraft and Diplomacy
(1997)

The Diplomat's Dictionary
(Second edition, 2010)

America's Misadventures in the Middle East

Chas W. Freeman Jr.

Foreword by
William B. Quandt

CHARLOTTESVILLE, VIRGINIA

Just World Books is an imprint of Just World Publishing, LLC

Book design by Lewis Rector for Just World Publishing, LLC.

Publisher's Cataloging-in-Publication
(Provided by Quality Books, Inc.)

Freeman, Charles W.
America's misadventures in the Middle East / by Chas W. Freeman, Jr.—1st ed.
p. cm.
LCCN 2010934170
ISBN-13: 978-1-935982-01-2
ISBN-10: 1-935982-01-X

1. Middle East—Foreign relations—United States.
2. Middle East—Foreign relations—1979- 3. United States
Foreign relations—Middle East. 4. United States—
Foreign relations—1989- I. Title.

DS63.2.U5F74 2010   327.56'073
                          QBI10-600164

Contents

Foreword

What should Americans expect from those who shape our foreign policy? At a minimum, I would hope for common sense, historical perspective, intelligence, good judgment, and a sophisticated understanding of the link between power and diplomacy. If we are lucky, we might also get a knack for thinking of the consequences of any action, an appreciation for the role of contingency, and a temperament that values long-term gains over instant gratification. In the real world, of course, we usually have to settle for only a few, if any, of these qualities among our senior statesmen.

It is one of the many virtues of Chas Freeman's book, *America's Misadventures in the Middle East,* that he reaffirms the validity of these qualities of gifted leadership in foreign affairs by incorporating them into these trenchant essays on some of the most challenging issues of our times. The surprise is that his realism and commonsensical approach to matters of strategy and national interest now make him appear—in the eyes of some—to be some sort of radical whose views are so far outside the mainstream that he was forced to resign, shortly after his appointment, from the position of chair of the National Intelligence Council (NIC) in 2009. If we need any further evidence, this incident alone should raise questions about the way in which foreign policy is discussed and understood in the United States today.

Freeman would seem to have been an ideal candidate for the NIC job in an administration that was eager to show that it was ready to rethink foreign policy after eight years of George W. Bush's efforts to refashion the whole world into a compliant American imperium. He had had a distinguished, 30-year career in the Departments of State and Defense, receiving two Distinguished Public Service Awards, three Presidential Meritorious Service Awards, and a Distinguished Honor Award along the way. In 1972, he was the principal American interpreter during President Richard Nixon's path-breaking visit to China; and he later served as director for Chinese Affairs at the U.S. Department of State. He was deputy chief of mission and chargé d'affaires in the American embassies in Beijing, 1981 to 1984, and Bangkok, 1984 to 1986. Moving back to Washington, D.C., to work as deputy assistant secretary of state for African affairs, he was a principal negotiator of the agreement that led to the Cuban troop withdrawal from Angola and Namibia's attainment of independence from South Africa. He was the U. S. ambassador to Saudi Arabia during Operations Desert Shield and Desert Storm, 1991-2; from 1993 to 1994, he served as assistant secretary of defense for international security affairs, where he earned accolades for his roles in designing a North Atlantic Treaty Organization (NATO)–centered, post–Cold War security system in Europe and in reestablishing defense and military relations with China.

After retiring from government service, Freeman wrote two well-received books on the art of diplomacy. In 1997, he became president of the Middle East Policy Council.

In short, Freeman had broad experience, demonstrated analytical ability, and leadership skills that could have been very useful to the Obama administration. But he was also controversial, in particular, because of his views on Israel. As he tells us in chapter 19, once his appointment as chair of the NIC was prematurely leaked to the press, a campaign was launched, primarily from pro-Israeli circles, against the nomination. As he said in a March 10, 2009, statement explaining his decision to withdraw his name:

> I believe that the inability of the American public to discuss, or the government to consider, any option for US policies in the Middle East opposed by the ruling faction in Israeli politics has allowed that faction to adopt and sustain policies that ultimately threaten the existence of the state of Israel. It is not permitted for anyone in the United States to say so. This is not just a tragedy for Israelis and their neighbors in the Middle East; it is doing widening damage to the national security of the United States.

Reading the present collection of Freeman's essays, which span a period from the late 1990s to the present, is both heartening and depressing. The good news is that Freeman demonstrates that it is possible for an experienced diplomat to foresee problems before it is too late to do anything about them. His essays on Iraq and Afghanistan are examples of prescience in the service of policy analysis. He—like many other thoughtful observers—recognized early on that those wars would impose high costs, both material and reputational, on our country. He recognized, too, the serious problems that would face a poorly informed U.S. government that stumbled into massive "nation-building" challenges for which it was totally unprepared. By now, many Americans doubtless will agree with Freeman—after much avoidable damage has already been done to our interests.

Freeman was ambassador to Saudi Arabia at the time of Saddam Hussein's invasion of Iraq in August 1990. Like most others, he did not see that invasion coming; however, once it happened he worked speedily and effectively with military and political leaders to coordinate the international response that led to Iraq's forced withdrawal from Kuwait in February 1991. Freeman is not against the use of force, but he always asks what its purposes are. As the war in Kuwait wound down, he was among the few who saw that the administration had ended the war without a clear idea of what would come next. The war fighting had been managed with great skill, but the diplomacy surrounding the war and its termination was flawed and amateurish. Crucially, it failed to plan for or establish a stable postwar order in the sensitive Persian Gulf region, which has been a locus of continuing tension and instability ever since.

One may ask why the words of an experienced diplomat with a good track record of anticipating and dealing with thorny problems would not be valued by the Obama administration. Why didn't the president and his advisers fight for Freeman's confirmation as chair of the NIC, a perfect spot for his kind of wide-ranging and restless intelligence? I suspect that part of the answer, if one may speak bluntly, is that Freeman coupled his warnings about Iraq and Afghanistan with a politically controversial call for a balanced American policy on Arab-Israeli issues. He also dared to call for engagement with countries such as Iran and Syria. And he insisted that the art of diplomacy means that one should always conduct foreign policy with a tone of respect. He quotes Bismarck to the effect that even a declaration of war should be issued in polite language. The Fox News pundits of today would have a field day with such maxims of power infused with restraint.

It is striking that Freeman, in these essays, sounds a bit like President Barack Obama himself in spring 2009. Freeman today, like Obama back then, believes that the reputation of the United States matters. He wants his country to be respected for its values and principles. He argues that U.S. leadership is essential for solving the Arab-Israeli conflict, and success in that arena would significantly improve America's standing in the Middle East and in the wider Muslim world. In short, he sounds like just the right person to play a key role in an Obama administration. But that would be the politically naive view.

Freeman has stuck to his principles, as shown in these essays. It is less clear that the Obama administration has been able to do so in the face of intense partisanship on almost all aspects of foreign policy. The days of presumed bipartisanship on behalf of an interests-based foreign policy are seemingly long gone.

Freeman has been falsely charged with being on the Saudi payroll. In this volume, he writes intelligently about Saudi Arabia, its history, its role in the region, and issues in U.S.-Saudi relations. He is no apologist for the Saudis, nor is he a Saudi basher. Instead, he shows a solid appreciation for the role that Saudi Arabia—a rich but vulnerable country—plays in the Middle East region.

All in all, there is much to learn about "old-style" diplomacy here and much to regret that Freeman's views seem so "radical" from the perspective of today's politicized discourse. Readers of this volume will learn a great deal and will appreciate the style as well as the content of these essays. They will also be able to look forward to another volume of his essays—those dealing with China and U.S.-Chinese relations. As I have said, this is a man of many parts and broad interests. We are fortunate to have these records of his thoughts.

William B. Quandt
University of Virginia
July 2010

Persian Gulf Region

Zagros Mountains

IRAQ

Isfahan

Basra

KUWAIT

IRAN

Kuwait City

Shiraz

Bushehr

Al Khafji

Persian
Gulf

Bandar-e
Abbas

Strait of Hormuz

Dhahran

BAHRAIN
Manama

OMAN

Doha

Dubai

QATAR

Riyadh

Abu Dhabi

UNITED ARAB EMIRATES

SAUDI ARABIA

OMAN

0   50   100 Kilometers

0   50   100 Miles

Cartography by Lewis Rector and © 2010 Just World Publishing, LLC

PART I

From Desert Storm to the Invasions of Afghanistan and Iraq

About 10 years after the end of the 1990 to 1991 war to liberate Kuwait, I thought enough time might finally have passed for me to write a short but reasonably candid account of how the war had looked from the American Embassy in Riyadh. But as I prepared to seek input and advice from my friend, the wartime commander Norm Schwarzkopf about how to improve what I had written, the 9/11 attacks on the United States by religious radicals from Saudi Arabia took place. I set the piece aside as no longer timely. It has remained unpublished till now.

In a compilation of writings (speech texts and articles) recounting my views about the interaction between the United States and the Middle East, however, this personal account of the Gulf War seems the logical place to start. This was my first exposure to the Arab world; it was also the period in which the seeds of both 9/11 and the Afghan and Iraq Wars were sown. I argued in 2004 (see chapter 2) that the failure of the United States to craft a political victory to match our military triumph over Saddam's army in Kuwait reflected uniquely dysfunctional elements of the American way of war. Our failure to achieve political closure with Iraq led eventually to yet another war with Saddam. Then too, the sociopolitical frictions of the Gulf War of 1990 to 1991 helped launch an angry young Saudi, Osama bin Laden, on his transition to radical anti-Americanism. That also had consequences.

When I wrote the account of the war that follows, however, 9/11 and the American invasions of Afghanistan and Iraq were still unthinkable. I concluded my review of the Gulf War with some thoughts about the lessons that might be drawn from it. I have left these conclusions as they were. I think they hold up pretty well, as far as they go. But, with further hind-

sight, lessons beyond those I mentioned will undoubtedly occur to anyone who reads my words. Some of these lessons have been written about by Christian Alfonsi, in his insightful book, Circle in the Sand: Why We Went Back to Iraq *(Doubleday, 2006), which draws heavily on interviews with key officials as well as things I and others at the American Embassy at Riyadh wrote in 1990 to 1992 to explain the Gulf War's origins and unintended consequences.*

Here is how the war looked to me as ambassador to Saudi Arabia at the time.

Chapter 1

From the Eye of the Storm:

The Kuwait Crisis as Seen from the American Embassy at Riyadh

Written in 2000-2001

Introduction

In April 1989, President George Bush asked me to serve as United States ambassador to the Kingdom of Saudi Arabia. After the now-customary senatorial procrastination over confirmation, I began my actual service in Riyadh in November. The embassy and diplomatic mission I headed were then the largest in the world, staffed by nearly 5,000 American civilian and military personnel and Third-Country national employees, many of them implementing assistance programs paid for by our Saudi hosts and not shown on Washington's books.

Saudi-American Relations: Appearance and Reality

Despite the image of close cooperation between the United States and Saudi Arabia that both countries preferred to present to the world, the actual relationship as I took up my duties in Riyadh was a decidedly mixed picture. On the one hand, the intelligence agencies of the two countries were celebrating the success of their joint venture with Pakistan against Soviet imperialism in Afghanistan (an enterprise in which China played a crucial role as a source of military supplies for the warriors of the *mujahedeen*). Saudi Arabia remained, by far, the largest export market for the United States in the West Asian-North African region known as the Middle East. More than 100,000 Saudi Arabians had pursued higher education in the United States. An equal number maintained second homes in various parts of America.

On the other hand, senior American and Saudi Arabian political, economic, and military officials seldom visited each other. Cabinet-level joint commissions and other institutions created a decade or more before to foster bilateral dialogue and interaction were moribund. Lack of official effort to support American companies' sales efforts had contributed to their loss of significant market share to their European commercial competitors. Israeli-instigated vetoes of proposed arms sales by the U.S. Congress had reduced the United States to fourth place among the suppliers of weapons to the Kingdom, after the United Kingdom, France, and China. There were almost no military exercises or other direct interactions between American and Saudi Arabian forces. As I arrived in Riyadh, a major military sale (of M1-A2 main battle tanks) was in prospect, but neither side had under consideration any significant initiatives to enhance political, economic, or military ties with the other.

As ambassador, I took it as my mandate to put Saudi Arabia back on the Washington policy map and vice versa. I also sought to stimulate more exchanges of official visitors (including congressional delegations), to restore U.S. arms sales and military cooperation to the position of primus inter pares, and to revitalize U.S. exports to the Kingdom. These goals came to seem ironic, in light of Iraq's subsequent occupation of Kuwait (August 2, 1990–March 2, 1991) and the impact of the Gulf War on U.S.-Saudi Arabian relations.

End of the Old World Order

In the last two months of 1989, the tearing down of the Berlin Wall and the overthrow of Romania's Stalinist dictator made it evident that both the Soviet Empire and the international divisions it had created were at an end. This realization stimulated the American embassy in Riyadh to attempt to analyze the implications of the end of the cold war for U.S. interests in Saudi Arabia and surrounding states. Among the implications we perceived was that Moscow might no longer be able to restrain the regional ambitions of its erstwhile client states. We speculated that this could be dangerous in the case of Iraq, which had emerged from its eight-year struggle with Iran as the predominant military power in the Arabian/Persian Gulf. We concluded that, among other dangers, in the new circumstances, Iraq might be tempted to use force to assert its long-standing claims to sovereignty over Kuwait or to intimidate other small countries in the Gulf.

General Norman Schwarzkopf held the position of CINCCENT—commander in chief of the U.S. Central Command (CENTCOM). He had inherited long-outdated cold war–era plans directed at the defense of Iran from Soviet attack. He was determined to redirect his command toward preparation for more likely contingencies. In November 1989, he received approval from the Joint Chiefs of Staff (JCS) to make planning for the defense of the Arabian Peninsula the central concern of his command. When General Schwarzkopf discussed this with me in Riyadh in February 1990, I agreed with him that the most realistic planning focus would be to prepare U.S. forces to cope with the contingency of an Iraqi or Iranian invasion of Kuwait, possibly supported by a Yemeni invasion of Saudi Arabia's southern province of Najran, as had happened in 1934. From July 16 to 23, CENTCOM conducted a command-post exercise of the Kuwait contingency (code named "Internal Look"), providing invaluable operational and logistical planning data for the CINCCENT's response, less than two weeks later, to the actual Iraqi surprise in Kuwait.

In early April 1990, in part at my urging, the assistant secretary of state for Near East and South Asian Affairs (NEA), John Kelly, convened America's Middle East ambassadors at a chiefs of mission meeting in Bonn, Germany.[1] My embassy contributed to this conference our analyses and conclusions about the regional implications of the end of the cold war, in the form of three telegrams.[2] These telegrams speculated, inter alia, about the danger that Iraq might use its military preeminence in the Gulf to commit aggression against Kuwait. It turned out that only the American ambassador at Baghdad, April Glaspie, and I considered this a realistic possibility. Others present dismissed the notion of Iraqi aggression against Kuwait as implausible.

Inadvertent Signals to Baghdad

In late April 1990, I became aware that the U.S. Navy proposed to cut in half or even end the four to eight-ship naval presence it had maintained in the Gulf since the 1940s. The Chief of Naval Operations (CNO) was under severe budgetary pressure to reduce the number of ships in the U.S. Navy, one of which was specially equipped as a command vessel and much in demand elsewhere. He had reportedly concluded that, with the end of the cold war, the Gulf was no longer of sufficient strategic importance to the United States to justify a continuing naval presence of any consequence there. Similarly, the Department of State proposed to close the U.S. Consulate General at Dhahran, the only foreign consulate in Saudi Arabia's Eastern Province (where the Kingdom's oil reserves and production are concentrated), on the grounds that U.S. post–cold war interests there were insufficient to justify a continuing presence there.

Like other concerned ambassadors in the region, I strongly supported CINC-CENT General Schwarzkopf's objections to the CNO's proposal to draw down the U.S. Navy from the Gulf. He, in turn, supported the continuation of the American presence at Dhahran. In June, Chairman Powell agreed that the Navy should stay. In July, my objections to the proposed closure of the consulate at Dhahran won a temporary stay of execution for that post.

1. We ambassadors suspected that the choice of venue was motivated, in part, by the desire to keep us away from Washington. Doing so ensured that we could not inadvertently complicate NEA's bureaucratic life by raising awkward and possibly politically incorrect questions or by pursuing issues directly with other bureaucracies outside NEA's control. The Department of State, was at that time (under James Baker), notoriously unreceptive—even hostile—to ideas from outside the secretary's immediate inner circle.

2. To date, for reasons it may yet explain, the Department of State has refused to declassify and release all but fragments of the texts of these telegrams, nicknamed "the hairy mammoth" series. Christopher Alfonsi opens *Circle in the Sand* with a description of their contents.

Iraq almost certainly took notice both of the comparatively low ebb in Saudi-American interaction and of the Navy's and the Department of State's proposals to draw down the American presence in the Gulf. Both were widely known and discussed within the American community in Saudi Arabia. Baghdad also surely recalled that, notwithstanding the U.S. Navy's escort of Kuwaiti oil tankers during the Iran-Iraq War, Kuwait had long been the Gulf country most critical and least supportive of this presence. The United States had no significant military interaction with Kuwait, still less any shadow of a defense commitment to it. Washington issued no instructions suggesting it was reconsidering this stance. (The Bush administration later found it convenient to make Ambassador Glaspie a scapegoat for the absence of American action to deter Iraqi aggression against Kuwait. Congress chided her for the famous failure to threaten dire consequences should Iraq invade Kuwait when Saddam Hussein unexpectedly summoned her on July 25. But she had no authority to utter such threats and would quite correctly have been severely disciplined had she appeared to commit the United States to war on her own.) All this signaling of apparent U.S. disinterest in the region may have played a role in Iraqi President Saddam Hussein's miscalculation of the American response to his lunge over the Kuwaiti border on August 2.

Inattentiveness and Disbelief

In any event, as great events (like the decolonization of the Soviet empire in Eastern Europe and the reunification of Germany) unfolded elsewhere, Washington's attention was not on the Gulf. Even when Saddam Hussein threatened Kuwait and the United Arab Emirates (UAE) over alleged cheating on oil production quotas set by the Organization of Petroleum Exporting Countries (OPEC), U.S. policymakers essentially ignored him. They focused instead on his threats in the same speech to "rain fire" on Israel—if it, once again, committed acts of aggression against Iraq.[3] (In retrospect, the underpinning for Saddam's bluster was probably his belief in an imminent breakthrough in Iraq's program to build missile-deliverable nuclear bombs. Its motives lay in the fiscal crisis that overproduction of oil and consequent low prices had conspired to produce in Baghdad.)

Nor did the Gulf countries themselves take Saddam seriously when he began to threaten military action against Kuwait. It was an article of faith among them that Arabs did not fight other Arabs. Iraq had received massive financial support from Kuwait (as well as Saudi Arabia and the UAE) when it was in danger of being overrun by Iran in the early 1980s. The notion that Iraq would repay this crucial assistance with a military attack on its benefactors was easily discounted.

As Iraq escalated its threats against the Gulf Arabs, Jordan opened secret negotiations with Baghdad on unification of the two countries. Rumors were also heard, during June and July, that King Hussein was somehow about to reassert his family's

3. Israel had bombed and destroyed nuclear facilities outside Baghdad in 1981.

ancient claim to the Hijaz. (The Hijaz is the old name for the Saudi Western Province, in which the holy cities of Makkah [Mecca] and Madinah [Medina] are located). King Hussein began occasionally to refer himself as "Shareef," the title used by the ruler of Makkah in the pre-Saudi period. The Saudi royal family dismissed this as just more evidence of the well-attested history of mental instability in Jordan's ruling family. Meanwhile, tensions rose on Saudi Arabia's unsettled borders with Yemen. But no one intuited a connection between these events or posited a conspiracy led by Baghdad.

Riyadh's relations with Kuwait were then strained. Among other reasons, Saudi Arabia shared Iraq's suspicions of Kuwaiti cheating on oil quotas. Still, Saudi Arabia's foreign ministry echoed the Kuwaiti position that actions to deter Iraqi aggression were unnecessary and could, in fact, prove counterproductive. Saudi Arabia, like Kuwait, did not put its forces on alert. Only the UAE saw the threat as serious enough to justify deterrent actions.

In early July, Abu Dhabi asked the U.S. Air Force to mount a then-unprecedented joint-air exercise in the Emirates. Despite objections from Saudi Arabia and other Gulf states (which I advised Washington to ignore), the United States agreed. The result was that the UAE was the only Gulf state in a state of military alert and readiness when Iraq invaded Kuwait.

Asked by the United States in May, June, and July whether they had need of deterrent gestures, the Kuwaiti government repeatedly rejected the suggestion. (The highest levels of the Kuwaiti government reiterated this complacent judgment in response to a renewed offer of support from the American ambassador on the evening of August 1, just hours before the Iraqi invasion.)

On July 20, 1990, the Iraqi army conducted a large combined-arms exercise in central Iraq. At the end of July, Iraqi forces deployed near the Kuwait border. Kuwait's forces finally went on alert. The best guess of U.S. intelligence analysts was that the worst that might happen would be an Iraqi seizure of Kuwaiti oil fields south of Rumaila. Baghdad had occupied these fields once, years before, demanding and receiving cash from Kuwait as a precondition for withdrawal. But, even this level of Iraqi military initiative seemed unlikely to most observers. Saudi Arabia had begun a mediation effort between Baghdad and Kuwait. The Iraqis and Kuwaitis were scheduled to meet August 1 in Jeddah.

On July 30, I polled my country team at AmEmbassy Riyadh. They advised me (with one notable dissent from my deputy chief of mission) that they saw no reason I should not proceed with long-standing plans for home leave in August. Washington concurred. Whatever happened between Iraq and Kuwait was expected to be limited and bilateral in nature. No one foresaw anything occurring that would directly involve the United States or become much of an issue in U.S.-Saudi Arabian relations. At most, some speculated, the Arab League might take over the Saudi effort to clean up whatever mess the Iraqis and Kuwaitis produced. At worst, they said, I might have to return early from home leave. Before dawn on July 31, I left Riyadh as long planned.

Shock, Surprise, and Resolve

By August 1, 1990, I was at my vacation home in Bristol, Rhode Island. At 3 in the morning on August 2, I was awakened by jet lag. I tuned my shortwave radio to the BBC, hoping to hear the results of the previous day's Iraqi-Kuwaiti negotiations in Jeddah. Less than four hours after these negotiations concluded with both sides agreeing to reconvene a week later in Baghdad, I learned, Iraq had invaded Kuwait.

Saddam Hussein had combined deception with rapid military movement to achieve total surprise. It later appeared that he had been secretly planning his attack on Kuwait for at least five years. The convening of talks in Jeddah led Kuwait and others in the Gulf to discount Iraqi military deployments and preparations for invasion. The July 20 Iraqi army exercise, when reexamined with the benefit of hindsight, turned out to have been a full rehearsal for the August 2 invasion. The actual movement of Iraqi forces, guided into Kuwait by a visiting basketball team from Baghdad composed of Iraqi commandos, was massive and overwhelming. By August 3, the Iraqi Republican Guard was digging in along the border with Saudi Arabia.

It took Washington a few hours to realize that Iraq had not just seized a few oil fields but all of Kuwait. By happenstance, British Prime Minister Margaret Thatcher had long been scheduled to join President Bush at the Aspen Institute in Colorado on August 2. As a fortuitous result of this encounter, the American and British response to Iraq's aggression was jointly concerted. The Anglo-American response, soon joined by France, was also more resolute than it might otherwise have been.

By August 3, it had become clear that Baghdad had acted without preconcertation or backing from Moscow. The USSR seemed ready to join France, the United Kingdom, and the United States in opposing Iraq's seizure of Kuwait. Simple lack of objection from China would permit the United Nations Security Council (UNSC) for the first time to act as the guardian and enforcer of international law its founders had hoped it might become. Iraq had attempted to inaugurate the post cold war world order with an assertion that "might makes right." But the defining characteristic of this new world order might instead, I hoped, be collective repudiation of such lawless behavior and effective action by the international community to reverse and punish it.[4]

As August 4 began, two divisions of the Iraqi Republican Guard along the Saudi border were observed making preparations for a further advance.[5] Iraqi reconnaissance patrols were identified deep inside Saudi Arabia. What had been seen as a local issue suddenly began to take on much wider strategic implications.

4. To my knowledge, the phrase "new world order" was first used in a highly restricted telegram I sent from Riyadh in mid-August. This—not the hegemonic gloss that others subsequently put on it—was the sense and context in which that phrase was employed by President George H. W. Bush and his senior advisers.

By August 5, President Bush had made a firm decision to offer U.S. forces to defend Saudi Arabia.

The U.S. interests at stake were clear. Neither the United States nor the global economy (on which American prosperity depended) could afford to allow Iraq to gain the ability to dictate oil prices either directly, through conquest, or indirectly, through intimidation. There was no assurance that Iraq's appetite for territorial expansion would prove limited to Kuwait. Allowing the post–cold war era to begin with the precedent that larger states could with impunity swallow up their smaller neighbors would severely damage the prospects for stability and the peaceful settlement of international disputes in the new era. Indeed, allowing Iraq to get away with its aggression would put at risk all of the gains the international system had made since the 1930s. And, of course, the United States could not allow our long-standing strategic partner and friend, Saudi Arabia, to be overrun without severe damage to our credibility.[6]

I returned to Saudi Arabia with Secretary of Defense Richard Cheney and other senior American officials. Late on August 6, we met in Jeddah with Saudi King Fahd bin Abdulaziz. After studying overhead photography of the Iraqi buildup on his border and the Iraqi patrols 20 kilometers inside his Kingdom's desert territories, Fahd's only question was whether the United States was willing to deploy more than purely symbolic forces. General Schwarzkopf outlined plans[7] calling for the deployment of 220,000 troops to the Kingdom. The King asked that this deployment proceed. Advance units of the 82nd Airborne Division arrived in Kingdom on August 7.

U.S. Deployment and Its Implications

Both General Schwarzkopf and I were acutely aware of the potential for serious friction between U.S. forces and their conservative Muslim hosts.[8] Before he left Jeddah, we discussed the outlines of what became General Order No. 1, banning access to alcohol by U.S. forces deployed to the theater and requiring them to undergo indoctrination in Arab culture and Islam.[9] We also agreed that we would have to reach an understanding with the Saudis on the legal status of U.S. forces to

5. The pattern of deployment and resupply of these two divisions was identical to that which had typically preceded their renewed forward movement for attack during the Iran-Iraq War of 1980 to 1988.

6. U.S. interests with regard to Saudi Arabia are often summarized as access to energy supplies, continued moderate management of the Islamic holy places, and transit. The point about oil is self-evident. One has only to imagine the use of Makkah as a pulpit for the dissemination of radical anti-Western ideas among the world's billion Muslims to understand the second. Finally, the Arabian Peninsula sits athwart the sea and air routes between Asia and Europe. It is one of the great choke points in the world's lines of communication.

7. These plans (for the operation later named Desert Shield) were made possible by the entirely fortuitous scheduling of the command-post exercise of Kuwait-related contingencies referred to above.

8. Saudi Arabia is the only non-Western kingdom to have survived the era of colonialism with-

be deployed to the Kingdom. Our soldiers, sailors, airmen, and marines would have to have the right to practice religions other than Islam. Women in their ranks[10] would need exemption from the religiously sanctioned strictures imposed by Saudi custom. We would need to work out procedures for close cooperation between my embassy and consulates and the general's civil affairs officers to handle disputes speedily and to solve them before they got out of hand.

I stayed in Jeddah for the next few days to respond to Saudi insistence on establishing a valid legal framework for the U.S. deployment that had already begun. This was a frustrating process. Officials in Washington neither shared the sense of urgency of their Saudi counterparts nor their (and my) apprehensions about the political implications of subjecting U.S. forces to Shariah (Islamic law) procedures and penalties.[11] They were understandably preoccupied with efforts to establish an international basis of political support for opposition to Iraq's actions. Consultations with the capitals of UNSC member states, briefings of members of Congress, and efforts to arrange access for aircraft, ships, and troops in Egypt and the Gulf Cooperation Council (GCC) states gave them more than enough to do. Or so they thought. The exasperated Saudis finally ordered their ambassador to Washington, His Royal Highness Prince Bandar bin Sultan Al-Saud, to force the issue with the White House.

U.S. military leaders, for their part, including especially those with whom I was dealing in Saudi Arabia,[12] were acutely aware that it would be five to six weeks before the United States and our coalition partners had enough forces in Kingdom to contain an Iraqi attack. It would take even longer to build a force capable of repelling such an attack and mounting a counterattack.[13] In the interim, both the Saudi capital of Riyadh and the oil fields of the Kingdom's Eastern Province were vulnerable. The danger of an Iraqi attack on both had to be rated as high. Once the

out penetration by Western missionaries or soldiers. Many Saudis interpret their religious tradition as banning the presence of non-Muslims, especially the armed forces of nonbelievers, on the Kingdom's soil. Alcohol is considered a dangerous drug in Saudi Arabia and sale or possession of it is a serious criminal offense, often punished by public flogging. Saudi tradition cloisters women, does not allow them to drive, and requires that they be veiled in public.

9. A surprise result of this was that several thousand American soldiers became sufficiently intrigued by Islam to continue to study the Quran on their own and ultimately to become Muslim.

10. Women were already an integral part of the U.S. armed forces. A disproportionate percentage of military truck drivers, loadmasters, and other logistics specialists were female.

11. In the end, the two sides agreed that U.S. forces deployed to the Kingdom would be considered assigned to my embassy and enjoy the privileges and immunities of technical staff. As the U.S. deployment ballooned, I came to head the largest embassy in history, with some 550,000 heavily armed "diplomatic staff" assigned to it.

12. Lt. Gen. Charles Horner, the commander of the Central Command's air forces (CENTAF), remained in Saudi Arabia to establish a forward headquarters in Riyadh to which CINCCENT could relocate, to direct the use of air power (U.S. Air Force and Navy) against Iraqi forces that might invade Saudi Arabia, and to manage the huge airlift of troops, munitions, and equipment that the deployment entailed.

Arab League had condemned Iraq, the Saudis ordered the Iraqi embassy at Riyadh closed. (Military attachés from several countries friendly to Iraq quickly emerged as surrogate collectors for Iraqi intelligence. My embassy helped the Saudis make life difficult for them.) Jordanian King Hussein's, Yemeni President Ali Abdullah Salih's, and Palestine Liberation Organization (PLO) Chairman Yasir Arafat's active support for Saddam Hussein led to the expulsion of Jordanians, Yemenis, and Palestinians from Saudi Arabia and most of the rest of the Gulf. The Saudis also shut down the clandestine Iraqi military logistics base on their Red Sea coast through which supplies had flowed to Iraq during the Iran-Iraq War. (The Iraqis shifted their logistics operations from Saudi Arabia to Aqaba, in Jordan. The result was mounting strain between Jordan and the U.S. Navy, which was enforcing the newly enacted UN embargo on Iraq.)

Iraqi propaganda focused on inflaming Arab and Muslim passion against the presence of infidels in the Islamic heartland.[14] Despite its secular character, the PLO, which could tap into a wide network of Palestinian intellectuals involved in news media throughout the Arab world, helped Iraq push this message of "Islam in peril." My embassy and consulates (at Jeddah and Dhahran) set up 24-hour information centers to deal with concerns about possible acts of terrorism against U.S. troops or the more than 25,000 American residents of Saudi Arabia. Large numbers of refugees (and not a few Iraqi agents) followed the Amir of Kuwait (whom I visited shortly after his arrival in Dhahran) in flight over the desert into Saudi Arabia. My embassy deployed consular officers on the border, well forward of U.S. and Saudi forces, to assist American citizens as they arrived and to do initial visa processing for non-Americans eligible for refuge in the United States.

The embassy and consulates also worked closely with CENTCOM and the relevant Saudi ministries and state-owned enterprises to arrange logistical support for U.S. and other foreign forces arriving in Kingdom. (Ultimately, these arrangements produced a forward-positioned 90-day supply of fuel and water for the counterattack and made Saudi Arabia the world's largest importer of jet fuel!) We also helped link CENTCOM's various component commands with key institutions requiring protection, like Saudi Aramco, the world's largest oil company. As the build-up proceeded, we worked with CENTCOM to find places to accommodate its huge demands, particularly for aircraft bed-down.

---

13. The 82nd Airborne, a light infantry division, privately described its function vis-à-vis the Iraqis during this period as to provide "speed bumps." The expectation was that the 82nd would be barely able to slow an Iraqi advance, even one subjected to attack by all available U.S. air power.

14. One result of Iraqi propaganda alleging that bars and brothels had been set up in Makkah and Madinah for the U.S. troops supposedly occupying Islam's holiest cities was a spate of calls to me from residents of those cities eagerly asking directions to these establishments, which they wished to patronize. It was sometimes difficult to convince them that it was all nonsense. No coalition forces ever entered either Makkah or Madinah, though some Muslim Americans and others were given leave to perform the pilgrimage.

Our major concern at the embassy, however, was to reassure the American community that they should stay at work. The Saudi Arabian economy relies in very large measure on expatriate labor. Every other nationality was watching the Americans for guidance as to whether to stay or flee, on the not unrealistic assumption that the U.S. government would be better informed than others about the danger of Iraqi attack, especially with chemical or other unconventional weapons.[15] An American departure would have set off a stampede, shutting down everything from oil production to weapons system maintenance by defense contractors. Throughout the seven months of the conflict (August 2, 1990–March 2, 1991), we constantly had to balance our assessment of the risks of civilian casualties against the requirement to fuel and sustain the war effort. Concerned about press leaks,[16] the Department of State forbade us to brief the American community about the Iraqi chemical weapons arsenal and how to cope with it. But, with hysteria on this subject very near the surface, we were able to control it only by ignoring our instructions. Embassy staff conducted more than 100 community briefings. By and large, despite agitation by corporate counsel in the United States seeking to avoid litigation in the event of tragedy, the American workforce stayed on the job. There was not a single leak.[17]

Meanwhile, the several U.S. armed services began to compete for the honor of early and decisive participation in the defense of Saudi Arabia. General Schwarzkopf, once he took up residence in Riyadh, was usually able to deflect most such requests, but sometimes I had to front for him (and vice versa). This was the case, for example, with instructions I received from steadily escalating levels of the U.S. government to obtain Saudi cooperation for the "bed down" of B-52s at King Abdulaziz International Airport in Jeddah.[18] Schwarzkopf had not requested these aircraft and did not want them. An informal discussion with the Saudis by his deputy, Lt. Gen. Horner, had convinced him that, while their deployment would be marginally helpful in military terms, it could be very costly in political terms. Since

15. I spent a great deal of time, in close coordination with my exceptionally able British colleague, Ambassador Sir Alan Munro, damping down panic among ambassadors from other countries with limited access to information. This task became particularly arduous once Riyadh's nights (and diplomatic swimming pools and gardens) were filled with shrapnel from exploding Scud and Patriot missiles, and civilians began to be killed by this.

16. Saudi Arabia, traditionally closed to the foreign press, temporarily opened itself to some 1,600 American journalists and countless others from other nations.

17. This issue produced more than its share of comedy (fortunately, not tragi-comedy). In December 1990, the human rights bureau at the Department of State denied the Saudi Ministry of Interior permission to buy U.S. gas masks for distribution to foreigners, including Americans, in the Kingdom. The denial was based on their finding that the ministry was a human rights violator and hence ineligible to buy military-related equipment. Meanwhile, the Department of State assured the embassy that there was no danger of chemical attack and denied the embassy's request to be supplied with gas masks and suits for contingency stockpiling. But when Iraqi SCUD attacks began against Riyadh, the department ordered the embassy to distribute the gas masks and suits it had prohibited us from stockpiling!

18. Jeddah fit the requirements for these ancient but potent bombers well. Its port was near its

the issue was political rather than military, however, he did not feel he could object to what, he correctly discerned, was a pet project (calculated to gain funding for another extension of aircraft life span) of the Air Force Chief of Staff. Not until the president read my politely reiterated objections to the instruction he had been persuaded to send me, ordering me to approach the king about B-52 deployments in Jeddah's Hajj Terminal, did the U.S. government seem to accept that what might be marginally useful in military terms could produce a major political setback.[19]

General Schwarzkopf was the first war-fighting commander in chief (CINC) to be co-located with an American ambassador in theater. Both of us were determined to avoid the frictions that had hampered relations between American military commanders and ambassadors in the past. We quickly established an excellent working relationship, based on respect for the division of labor between us, coupled with readiness to help each other bureaucratically in the common interest of getting our jobs done. Our staffs cooperated well from the grassroots level (where civil affairs and consular officers quickly intervened to smooth over problems with our Saudi hosts) to headquarters (where each of us had representatives at the other's staff meetings and where we carried out a number of planning projects together). Still, the mismatch in our assignments affected my ability to help him.

Schwarzkopf was responsible for what happened in many countries throughout the region, including Iraq, Iran, Jordan, Yemen, Egypt, Sudan, and all the GCC states. Though often consulted by him on regional matters, my staff and I were always acutely aware that our responsibilities and expertise related solely to Saudi Arabia. We did not feel authorized or qualified to offer advice about the internal dynamics of Iraq. And with the closure of the U.S. embassy at Baghdad, there was no one in theater with the mandate and stature to question the conventional wisdom in Washington and other capitals about the political effects of our actions on Iraq.[20] Since the conventional wisdom turned out to be wrong, this proved to be a serious organizational omission.

---

airport, so shipment of heavy bombs to the airfield would be relatively easy. While its commercial side was overused, the part of it set aside to handle the huge volume of air traffic during the Hajj was empty and therefore, theoretically, available.

19. A single photograph of a B-52 in the Hajj Terminal at Jeddah, the gateway to Makkah and Madinah, would have given Saddam Hussein's propaganda apparatus the match it needed to ignite Arab and Muslim rage against the alleged presence of infidels in the holy places. Moreover, to the layman, it would be hard to explain how B-52s, not normally regarded as a defensive weapon, were consistent with the defense of Saudi Arabia, the declared mission of U.S. forces in the Kingdom. Finally, I argued, deployment was not necessary. It would be possible to obtain agreement to preposition munitions and support equipment at Jeddah. If use of B-52s became necessary as a result of an Iraqi attack, they could launch from elsewhere and recover in Jeddah. If Iraq attacked, few would notice, and no one would care that B-52s were operating out of the area normally reserved for the Hajj. In the event, permission for prepositioning of bombs and so forth was obtained from the Saudis, and B-52s were based in Jeddah during the counterattack on Iraqi forces in and around Kuwait. Amid all the other air activity at an airfield temporarily closed, like others in Saudi Arabia, to civilian traffic, no one remarked on the presence of B-52s.

Saddam's Gamble

It was easy enough to understand Iraq's motivations for occupying Kuwait. It owed Kuwait about $16 billion (and another $28 billion or so to Saudi Arabia) for aid during its eight-year war with Iran. Iraq had been nearly bankrupted by the war, but Kuwait had begun to press for repayment. Baghdad believed that Kuwaiti cheating on production quotas set by the OPEC was part of the reason for the low oil prices that were keeping it on the verge of financial ruin. Iraq had long claimed sovereignty over Kuwait. The Kuwaitis had few sincere admirers in the Arab world. As noted earlier, Baghdad had some reason to believe it could take Kuwait and its riches and get away with some or all of both. If Iraq held Kuwait, it would control a potentially decisive share of the world's reserves and production, and be in a military position to intimidate Saudi Arabia and other Gulf Arab oil producers. If Iraq were able to continue its advance through Saudi Arabia to the UAE (which it had also publicly threatened), it might hope to control as much as two-thirds of the world's oil supplies and ultimately dominate all of West Asia and the Arabian Peninsula.[21]

Those of us in the path of a possible Iraqi offensive beyond Kuwait were initially puzzled (though pleased) that Baghdad did not press its attack before U.S. and other forces could arrive in sufficient strength to oppose it. The best answer seems to be that Baghdad was surprised and deterred by the speed and strength of the international reaction to its seizure of Kuwait. Iraq's Jordanian and Yemeni allies argued strenuously in the UN and elsewhere that what had happened was an intra-Arab problem in which the United Nations and other outsiders had no business meddling. Other Arabs saw, however, that the Arab League could not hope to impose a solution on Iraq and that relegating the matter to a process designed to produce an "Arab solution" would simply play into Baghdad's hands. By the time it became apparent to Baghdad that this would not work and that time was therefore not on the side of its diplomacy, Iraq had lost the ability to achieve decisive victory over the United States and other forces already in theater. Nor was Baghdad persuaded by the argument that an attack on U.S. forces undertaken to inflict maximum casualties would accomplish anything other than provoke an even larger U.S. intervention.[22]

The initial reliance on sanctions to dislodge Iraq from Kuwait, quite predictably, had no effect. Sanctions are widely seen as a substitute for the use of force.[23] Ironically, however, the signal they send to a determined opponent is that

---

20. The Department of State had, of course, assigned a political advisor to CINCCENT, and this very able officer was soon supplied with assistants to cope with a burgeoning workload. But the focus of this job was not Iraq, nor did the officers assigned to advise Schwarzkopf have any special expertise on Iraq.

21. The prospect that Iraq might be able to dismember Saudi Arabia, taking its oil-producing areas while turning over other provinces to their Hashemite and Yemeni claimants, is thought by some in the region to explain Jordan and Yemen's diplomatic (and logistical) support of Iraq throughout the war.

those imposing sanctions do not care sufficiently about the issues at stake to go to war over them. Baghdad had already determined that Iraq's national interests justified the use of force to seize Kuwait and the risk of a wider war. Iraq was understandably not much impressed by the sanctions imposed on it. Moreover, sanctions usually take time to be made effective and to have an impact on the target economy. It took time to curb sanctions busting by Jordan and other allies and friends of Iraq. Although the sanctions against Iraq ultimately became the most effectively enforced in history, the immediate consequences for the Iraqi economy were limited. (Even the longer-term effects of sanctions on Iraq were limited, as the success of Baghdad's game of "cheat and retreat" with regard to the UN monitoring effort on weapons of mass destruction [WMD] illustrated.)

The greater puzzle to many is why, when confronted in January 1991 with a choice between withdrawal from Kuwait under a UN-set deadline or counterattack by more than 700,000 well-equipped U.S. and Saudi-led coalition forces, Saddam Hussein chose to risk his armed forces by remaining in Kuwait. I believe that Saddam judged that he could not survive in power if he backed down without substantial gain in the form of money or territory. Neither was on offer. In the end, faced with a choice between possible political death through military defeat and certain political suicide through withdrawal under pressure, Saddam saw risking the lives of his armed forces as preferable to risking his own. Given the way things worked out for him,[24] it is hard to fault his judgment about how best to secure his primary objective—his own survival.

Saudi Arabia's Calculus

King Fahd's motivations for inviting U.S. (and later British and other) forces to Saudi Arabia were simple. There was no possibility that Saudi Arabia's armed forces could successfully resist an Iraqi assault.[25] Faced with a choice between the permanent loss of independence or even sovereignty that the success of Saddam's gamble would entail or the substantial political risks involved in admitting alien forces to defend his Kingdom,[26] Fahd chose to make the short-term compromises necessary to guarantee Saudi Arabia's survival. For the same reason, despite the severe financial strain involved, the King saw funding the coalition,[27] both in its defensive and offensive stages, as preferable to risking the loss of his Kingdom's oil-rich eastern province or accepting Iraqi domination.

22. As the Japanese attack on Pearl Harbor in 1941 and the North Korean attack on U.S. forces in Korea 1950 illustrate, the main consequence of such casualties historically has been to rally American public opinion behind an expanded war effort.

23. As I have put it less charitably elsewhere, "sanctions are military cowardice tarted up as moral outrage."

24. Saddam Hussein remained in power. Margaret Thatcher, George Bush, and Mikhail Gorbachev were all deposed. King Fahd was incapacitated by a series of strokes. Saddam outlasted John Major, Bill Clinton, and Boris Yeltsin in power.

25. When Iraq invaded Kuwait there were more men under arms in the Iraqi armed forces than

Some of the negative political consequences of military cooperation with infidels against another Arab state could be and were mitigated by the creation of a parallel Arab and Islamic coalition, nominally co-equal with the "international" coalition led by the United States. King Fahd named his nephew, Prince Khaled bin Sultan bin Abdulaziz Al-Saud, commander of the Royal Saudi Arabian Air Defense Force, as Supreme Commander of the Arab and Islamic coalition. The presence of trip-wire forces from other Arab and Islamic states on Saudi soil had the added merit of complicating Iraq's politico-military calculations by putting it potentially at war with the very peoples its propaganda sought to rally to its support. So Saudi Arabia financed, transported, and equipped contingents from a wide range of Muslim countries (such as Bangladesh, Chad, Egypt, Pakistan, Senegal, and Syria), despite the limited ability of some of them to contribute much militarily.[28]

Just as the Kingdom's financial resources had their limits, however, there was always an implicit limit to its willingness to tolerate a foreign military presence, especially a non-Muslim presence, on its soil.[29] This factor, working in tandem with the religious and climatic calendars, set a limit on how long the various coalitions seeking to reverse Iraq's occupation of Kuwait could afford to wait before taking military action. In April 1991, the Muslim holy month of Ramadan[30] and the onset of Saudi Arabia's scorching summer heat[31] would more or less coincide. Schwarzkopf and I saw that both the political and the natural climates could become significantly less congenial for the U.S. and other forces deployed in Saudi Arabia.

there were men of military age in the Kingdom of Saudi Arabia. Saudi Arabia maintains small professional forces equipped with high technology weapons systems. By contrast with its neighbors, it is a remarkably unmilitarized society. The Kingdom has no conscription and attempts no military training of civilians.

26. In the event, astute compromises by the king and his ministers and empathetic efforts by U.S. and other foreign forces managed to contain political reaction within the Kingdom. After the end of the fighting, there was a brief upsurge in pseudo-religious militant opposition to the monarchy and its policies. This opposition was decisively suppressed.

27. The extent of Saudi financial sacrifice for the war effort is little appreciated abroad. At the time, the Kingdom had a gross domestic product (GDP) of around $100 billion, about the size of GDP for the U.S. state of Georgia. After adjustments for oil-price windfalls and so forth, Saudi Arabia's net outlay for the war came to about $55 billion. To put this in perspective, one must imagine that the United States, with a GDP at that time of about $7 trillion, had suddenly to make unbudgeted expenditures of nearly $4 trillion.

28. Egypt, the most populous Arab country and a long-standing U.S. military partner with strong ties to Saudi Arabia, contributed very substantially to both the defense of the Kingdom and, ultimately, the liberation of Kuwait. The Syrian presence, though substantial in numbers, was more politically symbolic than military and much more relevant to the defense of Saudi Arabia than the liberation of Kuwait. Pakistan's fractious domestic politics limited its forces to relief of Saudi forces normally dedicated to defense of Makkah and Madinah and to positions blocking possible Yemeni attack in the South.

29. As noted, Saudi Arabia was proudly unique among non-Western societies in never having permitted foreign forces, religions, or ideologies to enter its territory—until the Gulf War.

30. Ramadan is a month of religious reaffirmation. As the Islamic calendar is lunar, rather than solar,

Many Coalitions

The U.S.-Saudi and U.S.-GCC relationships were, however, merely among many that President Bush, Secretary of State James A. Baker, III, and Secretary of Defense Richard Cheney had to worry about. The Gulf War was directed by a coalition of domestic political and international diplomatic coalitions brilliantly orchestrated by Baker on behalf of Bush.

First among these coalitions from Baker's point of view was the relationship between the White House and Congress. Congress was concerned to protect its constitutional prerogative to declare war. If it felt slighted or fell out with the president's policy, it could, as it ultimately did in Indochina, deny funding or set crippling restrictions on the duration of deployments. Saudi Arabia, therefore, became a vast military theme park, with a general and ambassador as park rangers, in which every member of Congress could tour and be photographed, posing patriotically, with troops in desert camouflage uniforms.[32] This was a very useful form of education and helpful in sustaining the domestic political coalition behind the U.S. intervention in the Gulf. As they toured, members of Congress (who are, contrary to popular belief, mostly hardworking and much above average in intelligence) learned why offensive military action would almost certainly be necessary. But it was not at all clear that Congress would support a decision by the president to counterattack Iraq, if that became necessary, and the danger that Congress might thwart decisions concerted with other coalitions was ever present.

Among such "other coalitions" the grandest was the "international" coalition, grouping the United States (and its NATO allies), the Arab-Islamic coalition, and the United Nations. In the case of Kuwait, the UNSC was acting as a sort of court, issuing writs of mandamus to Saddam Hussein's regime in Baghdad, demanding withdrawal under threat of sending a posse to compel it. But there was little congruity of view among the UNSC's member states and its consensus was always in danger of flying apart. From time to time, Baghdad's long-standing arms suppliers, the USSR and France, launched uncoordinated diplomatic initiatives to save Saddam Hussein from the consequences of his folly in Kuwait.[33] The position of others, like China, on the use of force to expel Iraq from Kuwait, was uncertain. And the UNSC, in addition to being a participant in the various coalitions seeking

Ramadan shifts its position by eleven days in each international (solar) year. Ramadan is when feeling against behavior that contradicts the tenets of Islam, as understood in Saudi Arabia, reaches its peak.

31. By law in Saudi Arabia, employers have to release their employees when the temperature climbs above 45 degrees Celsius (113° Fahrenheit). During my time in the Kingdom, the temperature never officially exceeded 44° C. As an employer, I was gratified by the restraint shown by the Saudi meteorological authoriti0es. The thermometers at my residence in Riyadh routinely recorded highs of 58 degrees Celsius (137 degrees Fahrenheit) in summer.

32. During the seven-month war, the embassy and United States Central Command (CENTCOM) managed the visits of 2,010 official VIP visitors.

33. Soviet votes in favor of key UNSC resolutions tended to be preceded by large grants orloans from Saudi Arabia, the crucial paymaster of the diplomatic and military coalitions alike.

to restore Kuwait to independence, was also, of course, a committee, with all of the indecisiveness and tendency to drive for the lowest common denominator position that committees exemplify.

Meanwhile, back in the theater itself, there were the two military coalitions operating side by side, each with its own complex internal dynamics.[34] Schwarzkopf commanded a coalition initially made up mainly of NATO member countries but later joined by Eastern Europeans and others. Many countries were represented by token forces recruited by Secretary Baker to demonstrate the international breadth of the coalition against Iraq.[35] Some of those participating were, however, doing so in no small measure to showcase weapons or military logistics systems they hoped to be able to sell in the region once the crisis had passed.[36] This competitive economic motivation made them unusually insistent about the part they should play in any conflict.

France presented a special problem in this regard. The equipment of its air and ground forces was virtually indistinguishable from that of the Iraqi forces (to whom France had sold its top-of-the-line armaments). Fear that French forces might be misidentified as Iraqi and attacked by other coalition members resulted in their restriction to areas of the battlefield where this risk could be minimized. An added complication emerged, as it became apparent that France's withdrawal from active participation in NATO had left it at an initial disadvantage in operating as part of a multinational coalition.[37] Military jealousies often found their reflection in political bickering far from the theater as the French sought first to attach themselves to the Arab and Islamic coalition and then to reassign themselves to CINCCENT's direct command.

In contrast to General Schwarzkopf's "international" coalition, His Royal Highness General Prince Khaled bin Sultan Al-Saud's "Arab and Islamic" coalition was less united politically, and the level of military competence of its members varied much more widely. In addition to Saudi forces, including a first-class air force and Chinese-manned intermediate range ballistic missiles, Prince Khaled com-

---

34. Generals Schwarzkopf and Khaled bin Sultan have each written of the difficulties of coordination they experienced. I admire the restraint they showed in their comments about both each other and their respective allies.

35. Saudi Arabia and other Gulf states paid all deployment costs and then some for some of these forces (e.g., the Argentine navy contingent).

36. Few ministers of defense have the exclusively military policy focus of the U.S. Secretary of Defense. In many countries, the defense minister is the chief arms salesman for the national defense industry (often made up of state-owned enterprises), and his success or failure is measured by how much he manages to sell abroad. Sweden's decision to send a field hospital unit to Saudi Arabia, for example -- the first foreign deployment by Swedish troops in two centuries—was justified in Stockholm, in part, by a desire to show off and sell military medical equipment and systems.

37. NATO operating doctrine, procedures, and standards constitute the world's first and still its only system of multinational coalition warfare management. The NATO system was also perforce adopted and applied by the Arab and Islamic coalition as well as neutrals and non-NATO members in the "international" coalition.

manded small and well-equipped air and land forces from other GCC states, including most of the Kuwaiti air force (which had managed to fly out to Saudi Arabia before Iraqi forces could capture it). He also had a very large and "heavy" Egyptian expeditionary force fully committed to participation in whatever ensued.[38] The commitment of his Syrian forces to more than defense against Iraqi attack on Saudi Arabia was doubtful, and efforts to coordinate Syrian units with broader military planning by the two coalition commanders proved difficult.[39] Some very competent small contingents, like the Senegalese, could not communicate in either Arabic or English, the working languages of the coalitions. Others arrived with little more than the clothes on their backs and had to be issued with everything from underwear to artillery.[40]

Finally, there were delicate coalitions at work among Saudis and other Gulf Arabs.[41] The presence of Kuwaiti refugees throughout Saudi Arabia meant that virtually every Saudi had heard firsthand about the suffering visited on Kuwait by Iraqi forces. There was essential unanimity among Saudis and others in the Gulf that Iraq should leave Kuwait. But some continued to doubt the propriety of using non-Muslim, non-Arab forces to force the Iraqis out. Almost no one envisaged an attack on Iraq, as opposed to Iraqi forces in Kuwait. As the early sense of danger of Iraqi attack faded into memory, objections to the expense of the foreign forces began to be voiced. When some Saudi women conducted a public demonstration calling for the right to drive cars, conservatives in the Kingdom erupted in outrage. More and more ordinary Saudis began to question King Fahd's decision to invite foreign forces into the Kingdom.[42] The King and other senior members of the Saudi royal family began to ask when and how their U.S. and other coalition partners proposed to bring the stand-off over Kuwait to an end.

38. In practice, however, the Egyptians quite understandably looked for guidance mainly to CINCCENT and the American and British commanders of armor and mechanized infantry forces alongside whom they would fight.

39. U.S. Special Forces liaison officers were finally accepted by the Syrians as necessary to coordinate with other elements of the coalition and to manage air-to-ground communication. Every other coalition element had long since welcomed these officers.

40. All of which they carted away with them after the fighting, much to the distress of those charged by the U.S. Congress to monitor and prevent the retransfer of U.S. military equipment to third parties without explicit U.S. permission.

41. Traditionally, the smaller Gulf states have feared domination by Saudi Arabia. This is, however, one of the few things on which they agree. Despite their cooperation in the GCC, the Gulf Arabs remain divided from each other by territorial disputes, disparities in living standards, political and sectarian differences, personal animosities among rulers, and varying geopolitical perspectives.

42. Some religious radicals, like Osama bin Laden, argued that an Afghan-style jihad could liberate Kuwait and that reliance on United States and other foreign troops to do this from Saudi soil was unnecessary as well as sacrilegious. They were put under surveillance but nobody took them seriously.

U.S. Planning and the "Second Deployment"

By early October, Schwarzkopf had in place sufficient forces to hold and ultimately repel an Iraqi attack on Saudi Arabia. President Bush had, however, initially assumed that the forces he had deployed would be sufficient to mount an offensive to liberate Kuwait, if one became necessary.[43] He was reluctant to accept the fact that the huge force he had placed in the Gulf did not give him an option to counterattack Iraqi forces. But coalition strength in theater was, in fact, far short of the 3-to-1 ratio used by military planners to guestimate requirements for taking the offensive against well-entrenched forces. CINCCENT had been given the task of defending Saudi Arabia. He had no authority to plan to liberate Kuwait. Indeed, political sensitivities within the multiple coalitions overseeing operation Desert Shield made it imperative that he avoid any indication of planning for offensive action to dislodge Iraq from Kuwait. As it became apparent to even the habitual partisans of sanctions that these were unlikely to succeed and as the impatience of Gulf Arab rulers with coalition inaction against Iraqi forces in Kuwait mounted, however, Schwarzkopf could foresee being asked for a plan to do just that.

In early October, I learned that, off-line, with a wink and a nod from General Powell, CINCCENT had begun to examine how to assure success in a counterattack on Iraqi forces occupying Kuwait. I was struck by three of Schwarzkopf's conclusions: (1) It would take a prolonged bombardment from the air to reduce Iraqi forces to numbers and morale conditions at which they could be assaulted with any assurance of success. (2) As much as three times as many coalition forces as were already in theater would be needed to mount a successful assault against a determined Iraqi defense. (3) It would take four to six months to accomplish the necessary build-up, even if our logisticians wrought a minor miracle (as they, in fact, did). March and April—Ramadan and the hot weather—were just four and a half months away. If March were taken as an informal deadline for the realization of a realistic option for a ground offensive, further deployments would have to begin at once. In coordination with Schwarzkopf, I put this argument forcefully to Washington. A week later, in late October, I heard that President Bush had decided to authorize the additional deployments necessary for a possible counterattack on Iraq.[44]

There had still been no decision to counterattack Iraq. But the option to do so was now being prepared. Visits by Secretary of Defense Cheney and Joint Chiefs of Staff Chairman Colin Powell helped nail down the battle plan. Secretary Baker obtained commitments from King Fahd, the Amir of Kuwait, and the president of

43. It is not clear who misled the president on that. Schwarzkopf had made it clear from the outset that the initial deployment of 220,000 would not be enough to take the offensive against Iraqi forces that so greatly outnumbered them.

44. The decision involved recalling much of the U.S. reserve to active duty, and would entail considerable personal and economic dislocation and political controversy. No official decision was, therefore, made or announced until after the midterm (congressional) elections of November 6, 1990, had taken place.

the UAE, Sheikh Zayed Al-Nahayan, to finance an offensive. On November 29, 1990, UNSC Resolution 678 set a deadline for Iraqi withdrawal from Kuwait. By early December, a time for the opening of the air campaign phase of the counterattack, should one be necessary, had been proposed for planning purposes. The deadline for Iraqi withdrawal from Kuwait was midnight on January 15, 1991. The time contemplated for attack was 2:40 in the morning on Thursday, January 17, 1991, when the moon would be at its dimmest and the use of stealth bombers and special forces against Iraqi air defense and communications facilities would be most likely to achieve surprise with minimal casualties.[45]

War Aims and War Termination Strategy

Now that a counterattack on Iraq seemed almost certain to be necessary, I was increasingly bothered by the absence of any statement of U.S. or coalition war aims or any evidence of planning for a process of war termination or for the elaboration of postconflict security arrangements in the Gulf. These were subjects that Schwarzkopf and I had discussed on numerous occasions and that our staffs were jointly engaged in studying. Schwarzkopf felt strongly that it was not his role to define policy. He complained that he was not getting the policy guidance he needed.

As ambassador to Saudi Arabia I felt that I could put forward ideas about the issues Schwarzkopf and I were concerned about, even though they were regionwide rather than limited to Saudi Arabia. I did not believe I could properly insist upon my own view of these issues or demand answers to the questions I had with regard to them. Answers, I believed, would have to come from those in Washington charged with managing U.S. policy toward the region as a whole. So I sent in a series of telegrams attempting to prod a response from Washington to some basic questions: (1) What were we trying to accomplish beyond the removal of Iraqi forces from Kuwait? (2) What terms did we intend to impose on a defeated Iraq, and how did we propose to impose them? (3) What arrangements for a more stable and secure peace in the Gulf did we believe a war could and should produce? In short, how would we define victory and secure and consolidate it?

These questions were answered with deafening silence from Washington, though several people with access to my telegrams, including on one occasion Secretary Baker, commented that the questions I was asking were certainly good ones. As the deadline for military action against the Iraqi occupiers of Kuwait approached, neither Schwarzkopf nor I had seen a statement of U.S. or coalition war aims. We found ourselves speculating about what U.S. and coalition war aims

45. I was aware of the date and time of the proposed offensive sometime in the first week of December. It became apparent in January, when Secretary Baker visited just before the UN deadline, that he had not been briefed on either the battle plan or the timing of the offensive. I judged that, if President Bush had wanted him to know the details of military planning, he would have arranged for him to be briefed and that it was not appropriate for me to usurp a decision only the president, as commander in chief, could make. So I said nothing.

were, beyond the liberation of Kuwait and the reduction of Iraq's military capabilities to a level at which Iran might once again balance Iraq. Finally, in consultation with Schwarzkopf, I wrote a telegram outlining the minimum objectives that Schwarzkopf would pursue unless he was instructed otherwise. This frankly unimaginative and unambitious statement of war aims[46] apparently met with approval from the limited group that had access to it. The only acknowledgment of it I received was informal feedback from General Powell to the effect that it was a good statement of what we were trying to do.[47]

What I had failed to understand was that concern about the possible disruption of the various coalitions Secretary Baker was managing made it impossible for anyone to put down in writing anything beyond what had been stated publicly at the UN and in testimony to Congress. Fear of leaks thus became the enemy of specificity about war aims. The inability to be specific about objectives, and the fact that diplomatic and military planning were going on in different compartments, made it impossible to devise a war termination strategy. And this, in turn, made it impossible to define the postwar order we wished to see in the Gulf.

Desert Shield Becomes Desert Storm

The January 15, 1991 deadline set by the UNSC passed without an Iraqi withdrawal. On the evening of January 16, I was authorized to inform King Fahd, using a code preconcerted with Foreign Minister Prince Saud Al-Faisal, of the time of the proposed counterattack.[48] At 2:40 in the morning, as the Iraqi radar and communications nets were taken down, I went to the embassy and began notifying key members of the coalition diplomatic community that air strikes against Iraqi forces and installations had begun.[49] By 3:45 in the morning, based on a conversation with Schwarzkopf, I was able to add that the wave of American, British, Saudi, and Italian bombers that had swept across Iraq at 3 in the morning had suffered almost no casualties. Thus began an assault by 2,000 coalition aircraft that dropped one

46. Stripping aside details, what those of us in the field intuited Washington to want of us was to (1) expel Iraqi forces from Kuwait while otherwise preserving Iraq's territorial integrity; (2) maim the Republican guard and eliminate Iraqi nuclear, chemical, and biological facilities, reducing Iraqi war-fighting capabilities to a level at which they could, once again, be balanced by Iran and other neighbors; (3) make sure that Arab and Islamic forces, rather than ours, were the ones actually to liberate Kuwait City and to get public credit for doing so; and (4) ensure that Baghdad recognized and demarcated its borders with Kuwait.

47. I had hoped that the decidedly modest war aims I outlined would be seen as inadequate and would provoke some useful guidance. I was deeply disappointed and apprehensive about the absence of such guidance for Schwarzkopf.

48. The King had earlier indicated that, for security reasons, he did not wish anyone in Saudi Arabia to be informed in advance of the proposed timing of the counterattack and that he would accept U.S. military judgment about when military operations might most advantageously begin.

49. There was considerable initial surprise that the counterattack attack had not been limited to Iraqi forces in Kuwait. It was easy to explain, however, why such a restriction would have been militarily nonsensical.

bomb on Iraqi forces every minute for 42 days.

Iraq responded by firing Scud missiles, first on targets in Israel and, shortly thereafter, on Riyadh and Dhahran. In both Israel and Saudi Arabia, the result was widespread alarm by civilians.[50] Their alarm was all the greater because the best estimate of the intelligence community had been that Riyadh was at the extreme range—or out of range—of Iraq's modified Scuds. Military briefers correctly disparaged Scuds as militarily ineffective and speculated that their only purpose was terror.[51] That was certainly their main effect.[52] Anxiety about chemical weapons usage by the Iraqis reached new heights among Saudi and expatriate civilians alike. In both Israel and Saudi Arabia, there was mounting popular pressure to respond with comparable savagery against Iraq.

The Israelis demanded that CENTAF destroy the launchers in western Iraq from which Iraqi gunners were striking Tel Aviv. CENTAF responded by diverting substantial resources to the task, chasing down will-o'-the-wisp targets provided by Israeli intelligence. When this failed to halt Iraqi gunners' attacks, Israel demanded that its air force be permitted to take its own direct action against targets in Iraq.[53] This resulted in some very ugly verbal exchanges, during which CENTAF made it clear that it would shoot down any unidentified aircraft it found flying over Iraq.[54] Israel backed down but sought a direct communications link with CENTCOM Forward, in Riyadh. The United States sensibly rejected this politically unworkable suggestion. CENTAF redoubled its efforts to find and kill the Iraqi gunners targeting Israel, even as other Iraqi gunners continued to strike at coalition forces in Saudi Arabia.

On January 29, 1991, Iraqi tanks crossed the borders of Saudi Arabia and seized

50. Although Iraqi warheads slew no one directly in Israel, they killed nearly 100 people in Riyadh. To the undoubted delight of Iraqis charged with preparing battle damage assessments, the Israelis reveled in their suffering, publicizing every warhead landing site and incident of death by anxiety or accident connected with it. The Saudis said and revealed nothing about what the 41 Scuds that struck them did or where they did it. The fact that the huge Western press contingent in Riyadh and Dhahran failed to notice and report the deaths of as many as 28 people—in one incident in Riyadh—does not speak well for their ability to report on a war in an Arabic-speaking environment.

51. I question this widespread assumption. The pattern of Scud attacks suggested a sustained but unsuccessful effort by the Iraqi rocket forces to strike military targets with a weapon that was simply too inaccurate to achieve what they wanted. A prime target in Israel was clearly Dimona, the site of Israel's long clandestine nuclear weapons fabrication facility. The targets in Saudi Arabia were manifestly the Riyadh and Dhahran Air Bases, and later tankers based at King Khalid International Airport outside Riyadh and the military facilities at Hafr Al-Batin (where Senegalese troops were struck).

52. In Dhahran, American women and children were evacuated on aircraft that repeatedly came under fire from Scuds as they attempted to load. This was not an experience that anyone involved is likely soon to forget.

53. This would have required the Israeli Air Force (IAF) to violate Jordanian air space, obliging Jordan to abandon its nominal, if pro-Iraqi, neutrality to enter the war, or to violate Saudi air space. The IAF could do nothing CENTAF forces were not already doing, even if it could be kept out of the way of the huge number of sorties being flown by coalition aircraft in the space it proposed to invade.

54. CENTAF found the Israeli imputation that the IAF could do a better job at Scud-hunting than U.S. Air Force and carrier-based aircraft irritating, to put it mildly. The priority assigned to

the oil town of Al Khafji, the center for Japanese offshore oil operations in Saudi Arabia. A nearly simultaneous amphibious assault on the town from ships of the Iraqi Navy was halted by coalition naval patrols. In the ensuing battle, the Saudi Arabian National Guard, a tribal levy of light infantry (with U.S. Army advisers), showed conspicuous bravery. After some days, the invading Iraqis were dislodged and taken into custody. Saudi morale got a big boost from this symbolic local victory. But Iraqi Scuds continued to land on civilians in Riyadh and Dhahran.

The Saudis, unlike the Israelis, were already involved in bombing Baghdad and other Iraqi targets. But their participation was much overshadowed by that of the U.S., U.K., and other coalition members with aggressively parochial press contingents. Popular pressure built on and within the royal family to launch the missiles Saudi Arabia had acquired from China some years before. On two separate occasions, the missiles were fueled and said to be only twenty minutes or so from being fired at Baghdad. On each occasion, Schwarzkopf and I managed to talk King Fahd and Minister of Defense Prince Sultan bin Abdulaziz out of these attacks.[55] The Saudis assigned their own briefer to CENTCOM's daily sessions to ensure that their public had a better sense of their very significant contribution to the air campaign.

The Gulf War was the first conflict in which substantial numbers of tactical missiles had been fired at U.S. forces. It was also the first conflict since World War I involving U.S. forces in which there was a serious risk of large-scale use of chemical weapons being used against us. It was the first conflict in which biological weapons posed a real threat to U.S. forces and the first war we had fought with forces that might possess nuclear weapons. There was little concern on the American side that Iraq might use nuclear weapons. Even if Baghdad had such weapons in deliverable form, which many doubted, long-standing U.S. doctrine was well known to justify devastating retaliation in kind against nuclear attack. Iraq was effectively deterred from the use of nuclear weapons.

The United States had, however, destroyed its chemical and biological arsenals. Neither it nor its coalition allies could respond in kind to Iraqi attack with either kind of weapons.[56] The United States toyed with the notion of communicating to

Scud-hunting on behalf of Israel had already diverted aircraft from targets that CINCCENT considered vital for the war effort, including WMD sites in Iraq, Scud sites threatening U.S. and other coalition troops, as well as the general bombing campaign against Iraqi forces. More important than that, however, was the essential impossibility of integrating Israeli forces into air tasking orders coordinated in Riyadh and involving up to 2,000 aircraft, not a few of them from nations technically at war with Israel. There was also, of course, concern that an Israeli attack on Iraq might hand Saddam Hussein the coalition-breaking propaganda weapon for which he had been looking.

55. We argued that (1) Saudi Arabia was already precision bombing carefully selected targets in Iraq and could do even more; (2) attacks by missiles no more accurate than Iraqi Scuds would kill civilians, about whom Saddam Hussein cared nothing; (3) Saudi Arabia and the coalition would lose the moral high ground if we responded in kind to Saddam's actions; (4) if there were targets in Iraq important to Saudi Arabia, the Royal Saudi Air Force could hit them, with no need to fire missiles at them; and (5) the deterrent value of the Chinese missiles might actually be impaired rather than enhanced if the inaccuracy of their targeting became known.

Iraq that it might respond to chemical or biological attack with nuclear retaliation but never made the decision to do so. Fortunately, President Bush and his principal advisers, who agonized over the question of how they might respond to an Iraqi attack using unconventional weapons, never had to answer the question. In the end, uncertainty over how they would decide, coupled with the severe degradation of Iraqi forward-positioned chemical stockpiles cut off from replenishment by the coalition bombing campaign, seems to have been enough to deter Baghdad's use of chemicals. A lot of hard work by the U.S. embassy, backstopped by CENTCOM, kept panic within the American community in hand and American expatriate workers on their jobs in the Kingdom.

A much greater concern to me and to other U.S. personnel in Riyadh, frankly, was the possible use by Baghdad of biological weapons, specifically various persistent strains of highly contagious anthrax, which Iraq was known to have produced in abundance. Biological weapons can contaminate an area against human habitation for hundreds of years. They do not require sophisticated delivery systems.[57] It was never clear to Schwarzkopf or me how we would respond to a biological attack. Perhaps the Iraqi inference, never contradicted by us, that the United States would respond to biological attack with nuclear weapons was enough to deter the use of biological warfare by Baghdad.

In the event, Iraq surprised the world with the first use of calculated environmental warfare, setting fire to oil wells in Kuwait to create a black cloud that covered much of the country and dropped soot up to 500 miles away. Iraq also released huge quantities of crude oil into the Gulf in an apparent effort to sabotage the vulnerable desalination facilities on Saudi Arabia's Gulf coast. These facilities were protected from the threat of catastrophic shutdown with only considerable difficulty.

Meanwhile, the so-called second deployment of forces authorized by President Bush in early November "closed" (was brought to completion) on February 11, 1991, three days ahead of schedule. Shortly thereafter, hundreds of thousands of ground forces completed their movement to positions far to the northwest of Kuwait. U.S. Marines and British troops staged diversionary maneuvers, suggesting an intention to attack Kuwait from the sea. The original plan had called for the coalition ground attack on the Iraqi forces dug in along Iraq's and Kuwait's borders

56. Iran did so in response to Iraqi chemical attacks during the Iran-Iraq war, convincing Iraq that chemical weapons should be used sparingly on the battlefield. No one has ever used biological weapons in war, though—years after the Gulf War—Israeli Prime Minister Netanyahu had to admit that his government had used biological agents in an embarrassingly unsuccessful assassination attempt in Jordan. This remains, to date, the only confirmed use by a state of a biological agent against its opponents.

57 An aerosol can, carried in a car or truck to its destination and set off there, will serve well. Ironically, ambiguous evidence suggested that, as it became apparent that it was going to suffer decisive defeat by the coalition, Baghdad may have attempted to bomb Riyadh with biological agents. The Iraqi aircraft that were allegedly carrying these weapons never made it to their target. They were shot down over the Gulf. On the other hand, there is no proof that any such attack was actually launched by Baghdad. Perhaps deterrence worked.

with Saudi Arabia to take place on February 21. The attack was delayed by two days, while the Russians, supported by the French, made a last-ditch (and, by then, from the Saudi and American points of view, highly unwelcome) effort to persuade Saddam Hussein to cut his losses by withdrawing from Kuwait before his forces there were annihilated.

At 4 in the morning on February 24, 1991, the ground attack finally got under way. Demoralized and much reduced in numbers by the 38 days of aerial bombardment to which they had been subjected, Iraqi troops along the frontlines put up little resistance. As coalition forces poured into Kuwait and the areas just west of it, their principal problem was how to cope with the astonishing number of Iraqis seeking to surrender.[58] Most Saudis are devotees of the especially austere Sunni school of Islam known as Wahhabism. They tend to regard the largely Shiite Iraqis with all of the affection that Irish Protestants reserve for their Catholic brethren. Given the speed of the Iraqi collapse, I found myself having to persuade them that they should take in hundreds of thousands of Shiite refugees.[59]

The drama of the coalition campaign, with its huge sweep around Iraqi forces and its annihilation of them in the largest tank battles in history, is best related by those who actually participated in it. I was no more than an admiring observer of one of the most disproportionate military victories in the annals of warfare. Like everyone else in Saudi Arabia, I celebrated the end of the war 100 hours after the onset of its land warfare phase, at 8 in the morning on February 28, 1991. A few days later, I toured Kuwait.[60] Like everyone else who had forgotten the lessons of Gamal Abdel Nasser's apotheosis after his Suez debacle, I imagined that a military triumph of the magnitude achieved by the UN coalition forces would almost automatically be translated into the fall of Saddam Hussein's regime and a political victory for those who had stood up to him.

58. Crucial to this success was a very effective but last-minute psychological warfare campaign designed and implemented by CENTCOM in cooperation with the U.S. intelligence community. The delay in approval was caused by the fact that, by contrast to possible conflicts in Europe and Asia, the United States had had no approved contingency plans for military operations in the Gulf. JCS Chairman Powell had to intervene, at my urging, in the interagency process in Washington to gain approval for CENTCOM to mount its psychological operations campaign.

59. Saudi Arabia's amazing generosity to the Iraqi prisoners of war and refugees it took in after the fighting ended is yet another insufficiently known act of Islamic charity by the Kingdom.

60. The country was under a black pall of smoke so thick that, on the ground, it seemed like night, with the main illumination coming from the huge columns of flaming oil from wells that Iraqi forces had lit before their retreat. Those forces paid a heavy price for their vandalism and

Triumph without Victory

The Gulf War was, however, highly unusual. Its war aims were ex post facto. General objectives vis-à-vis Iraq were not stated officially by the U.S.-led coalition until three days after fighting had ended. UNSC Resolution 686, containing a generalized list of war aims, was passed March 3, 1991, the same day that Generals Schwarzkopf and Khaled bin Sultan met two Iraqi generals of lower rank for a purely technical military discussion at the southern Iraqi town of Safwan. Definitive terms for ending the fighting were not approved until April 4, 1991, when the UNSC passed the immensely complex (34-clause) Resolution 687.[61]

This cavalier approach to war termination dismayed me, for it is a commonplace that wars end not when the winner declares victory but only when the loser admits defeat. Yet the fighting was unilaterally halted by the coalition after 100 hours of ground war.[62] No negotiation or other process was ever devised, that would compel Iraq to accept that its actions had constituted aggression, and had been justly punished by the international community.[63] Saddam Hussein never admitted either that he had been wrong to do what he did or that he had led his country into catastrophe. So, the UN's resolutions notwithstanding, the war never ended. It continued, as low intensity conflict punctuated by feckless efforts to drive Saddam from power by measures short of war.

The failure to translate military triumph into either a domestic political humiliation for Saddam Hussein or the "more perfect peace" that is the object of war,[64] not—as is sometimes postulated—the failure to press onward to Baghdad, is the main reason Saddam's dictatorship remained in power. His political survival was also inadvertently aided and abetted by a sanctions regime that funneled Iraq's food and medical imports through him — a grant of privilege for which any politician aware of the power of patronage would be deeply grateful.

the looting of Kuwait. I saw some 16,000 of them lying dead along the highway to Basra, phosphorus-blackened corpses stretched out amid the toys, women's clothing, and toilet fixtures they had stolen and were seeking to take home with them.

61. This resolution had so many demands on Iraq hung from it that it became informally known in New York as "the Christmas tree." In the Arab world, in ironic wordplay on Saddam Hussein's threats to offer the coalition the "mother of all battles," Resolution 687 was called the "mother of all resolutions."

62. The main reason was that the White House thought that "the 100-hour war" was a catchy phrase that would serve the president well in the upcoming 1992 election. And, since Kuwait had been liberated, the Republican Guard maimed, and Iraq's military-industrial base devastated, no one at a decision-making level in Washington could think of anything else that needed to be done.

63. It is true that Baghdad (though not Saddam Hussein personally) belatedly announced that it "accepted" the "mother of all resolutions" two days after it was passed by the Security Council. As the Iraqi government did so, however, it protested that the resolution was "unjust," laying a basfor the policies of resistance and negation of the UN truce terms it subsequently pursued.

64. William Tecumseh Sherman, 1882.

Postwar Tristesse: Stuck in the Gulf

Another reason for the survival of the Saddam regime may be found, however, in the absence of an agreed vision for a postwar order in either Iraq or the Gulf. Having liberated Kuwait, U.S. and other coalition forces clamored for immediate withdrawal from the Gulf. Their Arab hosts were happy to see them go, expecting that the region would soon return to the comfortable, foreign force–free environment that had preceded Iraq's aggression.

As the triumphant troops made their victory parades back home, however, rebellion broke out everywhere in Iraq outside the Sunni Arab-dominated central region around Baghdad. The Kurds rose in the north. Iraq's Shiite majority sought to overthrow Saddam Hussein's control of the south. It had been expected that Iraqis would rebel against Saddam; this was no surprise. The Iraqi army swung north to suppress the Kurds, setting off a stampede of refugees into Turkey.[65] Meanwhile, in the absence of contrary instructions, coalition forces occupying southern Iraq did not aid, still less facilitate the Shiite rebellion. Instead, they treated all armed Iraqis—even those involved in rebellion against Saddam—as hostile, confiscating their weapons and interning them.[66] Iraqi weapons captured by the coalition from the Shiite rebels, like weapons taken from the Iraqi armed forces, were destroyed.

A key coalition concern during the war had been to preserve the territorial integrity of Iraq. The conventional wisdom presumed that Iraqi Shiites would seek to establish a state similar to the Islamic Republic established by their fellow Shiites in Iran or that they would subject themselves to Iranian influence.[67] Similarly, it was assumed—and frequently stated by pundits in Western newspapers—that Saudi Arabia and other Gulf states with sometimes restive Shiite minorities would oppose assistance to Iraqi Shiites.[68] The fact was, however, that Washington and other coalition capitals were busy celebrating victory. They had no interest in being reminded of unfinished business or taking on another struggle in the Gulf. In the United States, President Bush and his advisers had shifted focus to the 1992 election campaign. Willy-nilly, the coalition ended up cooperating with Baghdad to

---

65. Turkish protests and threats of refoulement ultimately led to repatriation of these Kurds. They were returned to a hastily established "no-fly zone" in northern Iraq (Operation Provide Comfort).

66. Many more Shiite refugees for Saudi Arabia resulted from this policy.

67. These assumptions would not withstand scrutiny. Iraqi Shiites had fought loyally for Iraq during the Iran-Iraq War, proving that, in political terms, they were Iraqis first, Arabs second, and Shiites last. The Iraqi Shiite leadership, despite efforts to suborn it (and a considerable aid effort to their rebellion) from Iran, was not oriented toward either secession or the establishment of an Islamic Republic.

68. In fact, the Saudi Arabian government was vigorously urging support for the Shiite rebellion in the interest of overthrowing Saddam Hussein and offsetting Iranian assistance to the rebellion with its own.

suppress opposition to Saddam's regime![69] By September, it was clear that, barring an unforeseen event, Saddam Hussein's regime was going to remain in power for some time to come.

With Saddam still defiantly in power in Baghdad and with no relations between most coalition members (including the United States and Saudi Arabia) and Iran,[70] there was no possibility of return to the prewar pattern of balancing Iraq against Iran.[71] Although it fell to the Clinton Administration to announce it, a policy of "dual containment" was, in effect, the only alternative available to the United States, Saudi Arabia, and Kuwait.[72] This policy, like the enforcement of UN sanctions and WMD inspection activities in Iraq, required the continuing presence of substantial coalition forces in the Gulf. But there was no longer a common sense of threat from Saddam Hussein to hold a coalition together. The Arab and Islamic coalition dissolved almost immediately. The "international" coalition took longer to melt away but, as time went on, Americans plus an essentially symbolic British contingent were all that remained of it. Thus, much as the U.S. armed forces shared the desire of their Gulf Arab hosts that they remain visitors rather than permanent residents of the region, they could not. And, more than a decade after the outbreak of the Gulf War, U.S. forces remained stuck in the Gulf.

69. Once the coalition forces withdrew from southern Iraq, the Iraqi military put a quick and bloody end to the Shiite rebellion. By the time Washington and London finally agreed with the Saudis on a program of support for rebellion in Iraq, it was too late.

70. Iran had many opportunities to hamstring coalition operations against Iraq during the fighting. Its behavior was nevertheless exemplary. But, as the saying goes, "no good deed goes unpunished." Any Iranian notion that forbearance would be rewarded, as it was lavishly rewarded in the case of Israel, was quickly rebutted by the resumption of enmity as usual between coalition members and Iran after the fighting ended.

71. CINCCENT and the American embassies in the Gulf had envisaged a three-tier security system for the Gulf. The three tiers were defined as (1) working with the GCC to strengthen the collective defense capabilities of the Gulf Arab states and raise the threshold at which they would have to seek outside assistance; (2) implementing the Damascus Declaration, by which Egypt and Syria pledged to help defend the GCC in the event of a renewed threat to the independence of its members; and (3) maintaining a robust exercise schedule and sufficient prepositioned military equipment and munitions in the Gulf so that U.S., British, and other extraregional forces could quickly and effectively intervene, if required. The underlying presupposition for this three-tier system was a resumed balance of power between Iraq and Iran. The concept became announced policy but was, in practice, stillborn.

72. Balance of power strategies demand freedom of diplomatic maneuver by those who practice them. The rigid hostility toward both Baghdad and Teheran that the war bequeathed to the coalition allowed no such subtle flexibility.

Afterthoughts: A Few Possible Lessons to Be Learned

In this chapter, I have dealt with only those parts of the war in which the American embassy at Riyadh was most actively involved, and incompletely even with those.[73] Human history is now long enough that it can produce few pedagogical surprises for those familiar with it. And, as General Robert E. Lee remarked a few years after another war, "The time is not come for impartial history. If the truth were told just now, it would not be credited."[74] Still, I think the embassy's experiences may provide some instructive instances of ancient truths. Let me list a few possible examples:

- "At any moment of the day or night, two-thirds of the world's people are awake, and some of them are up to no good."[75]
- "There is only one thing more fatal to statesmen than the failure to collect and analyze intelligence: the failure to heed it."[76]
- "The idea of using commercial restrictions as a substitute for war... is a persistent and mischievous superstition in the conduct of foreign affairs."[77]
- "Diplomacy has an important part to play at the onset of a war. When no adjustment can be found which satisfies all the parties, and they are left with the decision to resort to force, the role of the diplomat is to look to the future, to the conditions in which after the clash of arms the effort to compel can once again give way to the dialogue of persuasion .... Wise statesmen ... will ... bear in mind the future settlement with the enemy, and will see the advantage of making their demands on him as palatable as possible, so that he will be more easily brought to accept them and easier to live with in international society afterwards."[78]
- "Diplomacy must be judged by what it prevents, not only by what it achieves."[79] (The absence of an explosion or even visible friction between non-Muslim forces and their Arab hosts stands as an example. This was a hard-won achievement of close and effective embassy-military cooperation with host governments.)

73. My two books, *Arts of Power: Statecraft and Diplomacy* and its footnotes, published as *The Diplomat's Dictionary*, contain fuller reflections on the transition from peace to war and back again to peace. (The United States Institute of Peace published both in 1997.)

74. But see the excellent account of the crisis from my British counterpart, Sir Alan Munro, published in the United Kingdom as *An Arabian Affair: Politics and Diplomacy behind the Gulf War* (London: Brassey's, 1996).

75. Dean Rusk.

76. Chas. W. Freeman Jr., *Arts of Power*, p. 31.

77. Dean Acheson, 1969, cited in Chas W. Freeman Jr., *The Diplomat's Dictionary*, 2nd ed., p. 262.

78. Adam Watson, 1983, cited in ibid., p. 317.

79. Abba Eban, 1983, cited in ibid., p. 73.

6 • Coalitions are a form of committee. Committees ratify but do not make decisions. They do not even ratify decisions that exceed the lowest common denominator of their members' interests unless a leader inspires them to do so.[80]

7 • "States seek to join coalitions for many motives: to share the burden of advancing or defending national interests, to court the protection or favor of potential patron states, to gain economic support or military equipment and training, to make money by hiring out their capabilities, to share in the spoils, or to be in a position to profit from the resolution of issues in dispute. Coalitions serve the common denominator of such disparate interests for as long as that common denominator exists. Once a coalition attains its political, economic, or military objective or finds it impossible to achieve, the coalition dissolves, leaving little but nostalgia behind it…. Victory and defeat are equally fatal to coalitions."[81]

8 • "When you strike at a king, you must kill him."[82] "Stay your hand or strike to kill; half measures leave walking enemies."[83]

9 • "For war to end, the vanquished must accept both the military reality and the political consequences of their defeat. Those who would resort to the use of force must therefore consider not just whether they can prevail over the enemy and bear the cost of doing so. They must ask whether and how they can obtain the enemy's surrender or capitulation to the terms they would impose. The enemy must be brought to accept and respect a resolution of the issues that gave rise to the war on terms it originally considered inadmissible. If the use of force fails to produce such adjustment in relations between belligerents, it is more likely to complicate and embitter these issues than to advance them toward resolution. Future war will be more, rather than less, probable."[84]

10 • "Do not enact conditions which will compel your former adversary to await his time for revenge."[85]

11 • "We are unlikely to get what we want unless we know what that is."[86] "If a man does not know to what port he is steering, no wind is favorable."[87]

12 • "Those who forget the lessons of history are condemned to repeat them."[88]

80. The following, adapted from ibid. p. 118, may be apposite. "A camel is a horse designed by a committee. A platypus is a bird put together by bureaucrats. An elephant is a mouse built to military specifications. A shrimp is a fish conceived in the legislative process." Coalition warfare is a course of action devised by various committees of bureaucrats and military men under the oversight of legislatures. The result defies simple description
81. Freeman, *Arts of Power*, p. 34.
82. Ralph Waldo Emerson, cited in ibid.
83. Proverb, cited in Freeman, *The Diplomat's Dictionary,* p. 313.
84. Freeman, *Arts of Power*, p. 62.
85. Attributed to Count Otto von Bismarck, cited in Freeman, *The Diplomat's Dictionary,* p. 316.
86. Roger Fisher, cited in ibid., p. 201.
87. Seneca, cited in ibid., p. 201.
88. George Santayana.

Chapter 2

Objectives and End Games in the Middle East

By early summer 1991, U.S. and other forces that had occupied southern Iraq as part of the campaign to liberate Kuwait had withdrawn. As I argued in the previous chapter, however, the failure to transform military victory into appropriate adjustments in relations with Iraq left the war with no closure. Saddam was able to parlay his survival in power into a political victory buttressed by his control of the distribution of essential resources to the Iraqi population. (As is often the case, the system of sanctions put in place by the international community inadvertently propped up its target. Only the Baghdad regime had the means to circumvent the sanctions. Meanwhile, the Oil-for-Food Program by which essential humanitarian supplies were allowed to penetrate the sanctions wall reinforced Saddam's centrality in his country's political life by increasing his patronage power. Only those who were prepared to appease him got reliable access to food and medical supplies.) Intermittent talk about removing Saddam from power was never translated into a serious U.S. policy.

Over the course of the 1990s, U.S. policy in the Gulf was essentially reactive—on autopilot, leaving the initiative to the Iraqi dictator, Saddam Hussein. When he needed to rally Iraqi nationalism or Arab sympathy to his side, he would goad the United States and United Kingdom into bombing Iraq. Meanwhile, while maintaining a public stance of defiance, he complied in practice with U.N. demands that he destroy his WMDs and end the programs by which he had developed them. His concealment of this compliance reflected his fear that it would be seen by Iraqi nationalists and other Arabs as a sign of weakness that could undermine his case for remaining in power and even lead to his overthrow. Ironically, he managed to convince the George W. Bush administration, if not Iraq's neighbors, that he and his government remained a menace. On the night of March 19 to 20, 2003, after an absence of twelve years, U.S. forces reinvaded Iraq, this time with the objective of engineering regime change in Baghdad.

This American lurch into the strategic ambush of Iraq caused me to spend a lot of time thinking about how the short victorious war of 1990 to 1991 could have failed to preclude the long, ruinous misadventure that began in 2003. (As I write, this misadventure *has yet to conclude.) I came in time to the conclusion that the botched interventions in Afghanistan and Iraq reflect a basic dysfunctionality in the American way of war that is deeply rooted in the exceptional geopolitical circumstances and historical experiences of the United States.*

Later in this book, I present a series of personal snapshots of the Afghan and Iraq Wars as they unfolded. Suffice it to say here that, by late 2004, it was getting really hard to overlook the extent to which American policies and actions were linking trends and events in Palestine with those in Afghanistan, Iraq, Iran, and the Gulf.

Excerpts from a talk at the Institute for Defense Analyses[1]

November 10, 2004

William Tecumseh Sherman once succinctly observed that "the legitimate purpose of war is a more perfect peace."[2] It is the political results of war that translate battlefield successes into victory. And it is the defeated, not the victors, who decide when the war has ended. No war ends until the vanquished accept their defeat. Therefore, as I noted in my 1994 book *The Diplomat's Dictionary*,

> the first question anyone planning to start a war or to respond with force to an act of aggression should ask is not whether his nation's force can prevail in battle, though that is indeed a vital question. He should ask what objectives, once achieved, would justify ending the war and why anyone on the other side should regard these changes in the status quo as either temporarily or permanently acceptable. How will the fighting be ended? On what terms? Negotiated by and with whom? What happens after the conflict is over? Will the seeds of future military actions be planted in the terms of the peace?[3]

As U.S. ambassador to Saudi Arabia, I repeatedly put these questions to the first Bush administration before our liberation of Kuwait from Saddam Hussein's occupation. My cables were never answered. There was no war termination strategy. Generals Schwarzkopf and Khalid bin Sultan met their Iraqi counterparts at Safwan without political instructions. Saddam was never forced to accept the political consequences of his defeat. Therefore, he remained in power. And the war never ended. It continued as low-intensity conflict until our March 20, 2003, inva-

---

1. This text also incorporates remarks made to the Rhode Island Yale Club.

2. *The Diplomat's Dictionary*, 2nd ed. (Washington, D.C.: United States Institute of Peace Press, 2010), p. 245.

3. Ibid., p. 243.

sion and subsequent conquest of Iraq. The Gulf War thus failed General Sherman's test; it did not produce a better peace. Iraq and Afghanistan do not seem likely to do better.

I've spent a lot of time trying to understand how a politico-military integration failure of this magnitude could have occurred. My first instinct was to blame the nature of coalition warfare. Coalitions harmonize objectives to the lowest common denominator; they are the enemies of clarity. But, on further reflection, I have come to the conclusion something more fundamental was at work, reflecting a basic flaw in the American way of war.

In the Asian tradition of Sunzi and the European tradition of Clausewitz, war is a means of accomplishing political objectives that cannot be achieved by less costly means. When the fighting ends, negotiations between victor and vanquished define the adjustments—in frontiers, territories, or behavior—necessary to make peace.

Long ago, for example, in our war for independence and the Mexican War Americans fought that way too. But the ending of wars through negotiation has not been our formative experience. Our views of war have been shaped in existential struggles against enemies we demonized and whose continued existence we pronounced to be morally unacceptable. In our civil war, in World War I, and in World War II, as well as in the cold war, we fought with the expectation of unconditional surrender and the subsequent reconstruction of our enemies.

Not surprisingly, it is these experiences rather than the awkward stalemate in Korea or dishonorable retreat from Indochina that inspire us when we go to war. The Spanish-American War, in which military success against enemy forces preceded any serious effort to concoct war aims, is also not a model, except perhaps in terms of encouraging us to believe that we can somehow sort out how to deal with the aftermath of war after we've destroyed the enemy's combat power.

The American idea of war termination is the annihilation of the enemy's forces and the temporary replacement of his sovereignty with our own. We seem to have no notion of how to settle for less than that. In this context, it is hardly surprising that we should have been unable to formulate a war termination strategy for the Gulf War, which was fought to repel aggression and restore a regional balance of power disturbed by the Iran-Iraq War. The failure to craft a sustainable postwar order for the Gulf and to assign Iraq an appropriate role in it meant that there was no postwar regional balance. This, in turn, left the United States to fill the power vacuum.

Many Americans were inclined to see anything less than the occupation and reconstruction of Iraq as an incomplete war, even if that had not been our original objective. The war was indeed incomplete, but this was not why. The sad fact is that Saddam's military defeat was never translated into his political humiliation. Thus, our military triumph never became a political victory over the Iraqi dictator, and humiliated and resentful Iraqi nationalists in Baghdad were not motivated to overthrow him. We showed, once again, that one can win every battle and prevail in every military contest of strength and still lose politically. To lose politically, as we should have learned in Vietnam, is to be defeated.

This brings me to the conflicts in Afghanistan, Iraq, and with terrorists throughout the world today. To gain victory in these conflicts, we must have clear and unwavering objectives. To consolidate victory in these conflicts we must think through how they should conclude. Where do we now stand? Let's start with 9/11.

In the more than three years since America was cruelly maimed by terrorist attacks on New York and Washington, the United States has disrupted the corporate headquarters of al-Qaeda, killed much of its original leadership, and driven from power those who gave it safe haven in Afghanistan. In doing so, we more or less accomplished our original objectives of apprehending the perpetrators of 9/11 and punishing their Afghan hosts so as to deter other countries from sheltering al-Qaeda or its like.

But al-Qaeda has grown new leaders, reorganized, and expanded its operations internationally. It has, in short, metastasized, not collapsed or shrunk into irrelevance. The war in Afghanistan, meanwhile, is largely forgotten here, but it is far from over. It is an expensive war in every sense: 143 U.S. soldiers have died; 423 have been seriously injured.

But, as our war with Afghan insurgents has continued, we have often seemed to forget that al-Qaeda, not Afghans associated with the Taliban, did 9/11. Unlike al-Qaeda, this should make the Taliban not an enemy to be annihilated but a politico-military problem to be managed as much by political means as by force of arms. We have slain 8,587 Afghan warriors and seriously wounded 25,761. More to the point, we have killed 3,485 Afghan civilians and seriously injured 6,273. In proportion to population, the Afghan dead are the equivalent of 85,000 dead and 250,000 gravely wounded American soldiers, and 34,000 dead American civilians, with another 62,000 seriously injured. As we have turned our attention from capturing al-Qaeda's leadership to annihilating the Taliban, Afghan tolerance of our presence, not surprisingly, has begun to wear thin.

As I speak, some 18,000 American troops remain engaged in combat with various terrorist and resistance forces in Afghanistan. No one has told us—apparently no one can now say—what might constitute victory there or when our intervention can end. Afghanistan's pro-American president needed American bodyguards to conduct his successful electoral campaign. The once-discredited Taliban seems to be regaining lost political ground.

Presumably, our central objective remains strategic denial of Afghanistan to al-Qaeda and other terrorist enemies of the United States. This now depends, apparently, on maintaining a huge American pacification force there while looking the other way as contented Afghan farmers exercise their democratic right to harvest the largest opium crop in history.

A year and a half ago, in the second major development since 9/11, we invaded Iraq. We did so for a tangle of five or six theses and reasons that no one has yet been able convincingly to untangle. I will not attempt to do so this afternoon. I will simply note that our one indisputable achievement has been the overthrow of Saddam Hussein, a very bad man whose fall from power few in Iraq and no one outside it laments.

But we invaded Iraq with a bunch of dogmas rather than a set of plans. So, as we removed the Iraqi regime, we inadvertently destroyed the Iraqi state. We replaced that state not with a new regime but with an overwhelmingly American military occupation; 137 Americans died during our invasion of Iraq. During the same period, we killed about 30,000 Iraqi troops and seriously wounded another 90,000. In terms of our population, these figures equate to about 349,000 American military dead, with 1,050,000 seriously injured. Not surprisingly, Iraqis had distinctly mixed feelings about our arrival from the outset.

Since the president declared our "mission accomplished" in May 2003, another 1,079 American military personnel have given their lives in Iraq. Our military no longer do body counts, so it is hard to know how many Iraqi guerrillas or civilians have died under our occupation. Hospital-documented deaths add up to at least 15,000, with 26,000 seriously injured, while recent estimates in the British medical journal, The Lancet, suggest as many as 100,000 died. Again, to imagine the impact on ordinary Iraqis of these figures, we must translate them into American terms. They equate to between 175,000 and 1,160,000 dead American civilians. The 600 civilian deaths documented over the past week in Fallujah alone are the equivalent of nearly 7,000 in America.

It's hard to think of any occupation anywhere that has been welcomed or accepted as legitimate for long by those occupied. But, given our inability even to repair basic infrastructure, let alone reconstruct Iraq, and the figures I have just cited, our occupation is now so universally regarded as illegitimate that it invites resistance and taints any project and any person associated with it. Our aid workers and journalists are now essentially confined to fortified enclaves, military bases, or convoys escorted by our troops. The only thing keeping Iraqis from civil war is their unity in opposing our occupation.

In this increasingly hostile environment, we are nonetheless asking our military simultaneously to create a state and an army to back it while providing security for reconstruction and the installation through elections of a government with the legitimacy we and the interim authority we appointed lack. Apparently, we then plan to hang around in the 14 permanent military bases we are building, as a guarantee of Iraqi democracy and Kurdish autonomy. This is an ambitious, not to say preposterous, tasking to give the United States Army. Support of this kind from us is very likely the kiss of death for any new Iraqi government.

Under the circumstances, perhaps the best outcome we can hope for is that the January elections in Iraq come off and produce a government that asks us to leave. Declaring democracy and withdrawing may be our best option. But is that what we plan to do? And, if not, what do we plan to do?

Our vagueness—maybe it's just honest confusion—about what we are trying to accomplish in Iraq and how and when we might leave carries a heavy cost, and not just to the American taxpayer. Increasingly, Iraqis, other Arabs, and Muslims around the globe see our presence there as part of a broad assault on the fifth of the human race that is Muslim. They connect our actions in Afghanistan and Iraq with our unconditional support, including generous subsidies, for the Israeli government and its policies in the Arab territories it occupies. They do not believe our president when he promises to resume a peacemaking role between Israelis and Palestinians. They see the United States as now so closely aligned with Israel as to be essentially indistinguishable from it in policy terms and to be disqualified as a mediator.

Identification with Israel remains a big plus in American politics. But it is no longer a plus elsewhere. Here too, it helps to consider the conflict statistics. Since Ariel Sharon's provocative visit to the Al-Aqsa Mosque on September 29, 2000, the intifada has taken the lives of 942 Israelis and seriously wounded perhaps another 4,500. Critics of Israel should take note! The ascendancy of the Israeli right wing is easier to understand when one considers that this is the equivalent of 44,715 dead and 215,000 wounded Americans. After all, 3,000 deaths on 9/11 were enough to send the United States into a sort of national nervous breakdown.

We focus on the Israeli dead and wounded. Arabs and Muslims are naturally more apt to focus on the comparable Palestinian statistics. Since September 29, 2000, 3,447 Palestinians have died, while another 40,000 or so have been seriously injured. In our terms, this would be 284,964 dead and 3.4 million wounded. As I said a moment ago, rightly or wrongly, Arabs and indeed Muslims globally see this bloodbath in the Holy Land as a direct result of U.S. policy. And they now connect it to lethal American actions against Arabs and Muslims elsewhere.

The decisive shift in foreign views of the United States is the third and most significant change in our situation since 9/11. Our allies and Islamic partners were with us in Afghanistan. Our invasion of Iraq separated most of them from us and set us against three-fourths of the member states of the United Nations. Abu Ghraib and the scofflaw behavior at Guantanamo now belatedly being set right by the federal judiciary subsequently erased much of the admiration the United States enjoyed when we stood unequivocally for a just world order based on the rule of law.

Most, though not all, of our allies and friends in Europe and Asia are now skeptical, even apprehensive, about us. The political burden of proof internationally is against any leader who proposes to follow our lead. Most notably, in Muslim countries, huge majorities have now concluded that the United States is an international predator and implacable enemy of their values. Osama bin Laden and others of like mind see this not only as a boon to recruitment but as a major opportunity to build a transnational political movement to back their terrorist struggle. This is why Osama's latest message has such a confident, even upbeat tone. He thinks he's winning his war with us. If our measure of success is whether we kill more terrorists than we create, Osama may be right. In places like Fallujah, to kill one so-called terrorist is to get five free. And Fallujah is now connected to Gaza and Kandahar in the Muslim mind.

If we continue on course, we can expect the world to become ever less hospitable and safe for Americans. And we can expect others to continue to attempt to do to us what they perceive us to be doing to them. Our homeland remains highly vulnerable to attack or, as the terrorists would describe it, counterattack. As we deal with the irregular rhythms of our mounting conflict with the Muslim world, we will be hard pressed to deal with other issues of concern, like the North Korean and Iranian nuclear programs, or our precarious international financial standing. In fact, some of these issues have already been adversely affected by the various developments I have discussed. Our invasion of Iraq, for example, caused both North Korea and Iran to accelerate their plans to acquire nuclear deterrent forces. The mounting costs of the war drive up our budget deficits and increase our dependence on purchases of our national debt by the Japanese, Chinese, Koreans, and so forth.

Which brings me back to the terrible challenges facing our president. We must hope that Kaiser Wilhelm was right when he claimed that "God watches over idiots, little children, and the United States of America." Or that Winston Churchill was prescient when he observed that "one can always count on the United States to do the right thing, after it has exhausted all the alternatives." We are getting somewhat short of alternatives, I sense. But what is the right thing to do in these circumstances?

As recently as two years ago, there was no real connection between Afghanistan, Iraq, and the Holy Land. As a result of our decisions and actions, they are now inextricably connected both to each other and to the future of al-Qaeda and other Islamic extremist movements. As we deal with each of these issues, we must therefore weigh the extent to which our actions aid or impede resolution of the others.

The place to start is probably Afghanistan, where, I would argue, we have been guilty of "mission creep"—an unwitting and somewhat witless shifting of the goal posts. What are our goals in Afghanistan now that we have al-Qaeda on the run and the Taliban out of office? Are there no alternatives to perpetual military intervention in Afghanistan and to uncontrolled production of the raw material for heroin to accomplish these goals, whatever they may be?

With a presidential election in Afghanistan behind us and parliamentary elections in sight, it is time to clarify and refocus our policy to substitute diplomacy and foreign aid for military intervention. If a fraction of the money we are spending on military operations in Afghanistan were made available to its government for army and nation-building activities, with a bit left over to fund a public school program in Pakistan to give kids in the border areas an alternative to the religiously reactionary madrasas there, much might be accomplished. What's more, I believe that such an effort could attract matching money and other help from allies, partners, and friends, not just in Europe, but in Asia and even the Arab world.

An approach like this would not represent an abandonment of Afghanistan but a recognition that, in the end, Afghans are likely to be more effective in excluding

Islamist terrorists from their territory if the terrorists cannot pose as the resistance to an American-led occupation that is killing other Afghan Muslims. The Afghan government will need to be able to count on us, with other members of the international community, in its struggle to co-opt regional warlords and end the Taliban insurgency. Our withdrawal must be orderly and phased. As we withdraw, we should do everything possible to help the Afghan government succeed, while ensuring that we retain the capacity to re-intervene in the unlikely event that a future Afghan government repeats the error of offering a home to terrorists with global reach.

Then there is Iraq. Here, too, policy clarification is urgently required. The biggest gift we could give to the Iraqi constituent assembly to be elected in January would be a clear statement that our first order of business with it will be to negotiate the terms of our orderly withdrawal from Iraq. We might add that we intend, as and after we withdraw, to channel a continuing flow of American and other international assistance to Iraqi reconstruction through the Iraqi government and Iraqi companies, not carpetbaggers from the United States. As part of our withdrawal plan, we should propose protective arrangements with Iraq's neighbors.

The fledgling Iraqi state needs assurances of non-intervention from Iran, Syria, and Turkey. It needs help rather than opposition from Saudi Arabia and Kuwait, and it requires the cooperation of Jordan. Among Iraq's neighbors, the most important in terms of capacity to intervene in Iraqi politics is Iran. As a neighbor of Afghanistan, Iran is important in that context too. If the Bush Administration can find a way to do business with Col. Qaddafi's wacky regime in Libya, where the stakes are much smaller, one may hope that it might have the political courage to deal with Iran.

This brings us to the Israeli-Palestinian dispute, which is at the core of al-Qaeda's and other extremists' hopes of uniting the Muslim world against the United States. There was, as far as I could tell, no difference at all between the presidential candidates on any issue touching on Israel and our relations with it. That is truly remarkable because Israelis themselves are deeply divided and carry on a vigorous debate about these issues. American politicians now compete for the favor of whoever is prime minister in Israel, regardless of whether that prime minister pays any attention at all to American opinions or views. All this recalls the fact that it was the Middle East that first gave hypocrisy a bad name. It leads me to the conclusion that an answer to the question of how to secure peace between Israelis and Palestinians is more likely to originate with outspoken Israelis and Palestinians than it is among brain-dead and intimidated politicians here.

But here's the rub. Well-intentioned American subsidies and pledges of unconditional support for Israel, regardless of its policies, mean not only that Israelis can act without regard to American interests and views. They also mean that Israelis don't have to make the hard choices they would have to make if they were—or feared they might end up—on their own.

Confident of subsidies from the American taxpayer, Israelis are under little, if any, pressure to reform their inefficient, socialist economy, now one of the most statist in the world. Peace is not impossible, as the Geneva Accords negotiated between former Israeli and current Palestinian officials attest. Assured of military superiority and support against the Arabs, however, Israelis do not need to end their expansion into Palestinian lands or make the diplomatic compromises necessary to define their borders with a viable and therefore stable Palestinian state. Israelis could benefit from some tough love from their American backers.

Israel is the strongest power in the Middle East by a wide margin, even if its security were not guaranteed by the United States, as it is and will continue to be. The only thing that could now call Israel's existence into question is a long-term failure on its part to make peace with its neighbors. Israel's cold war with the Arabs has now emerged as a grave threat to U.S. interests as well as to those of the Jewish state. It is time, therefore, to use American leverage to help change the political context in Israel. We should be trying to help those within Israel who advocate policies intended to achieve peace rather than continued oppression of the Palestinians and expansion into Arab lands. American support for the existence of the state of Israel is and should be unquestionable. American support for particular policies of that state should not, however, be exempt from scrutiny and debate.

Let me conclude. I do not apologize for the grave tone of my remarks. Systematically thinking through what we are trying to accomplish in Afghanistan, Iraq, and the Arab-Israeli dispute is now an imperative for our country. So is developing strategies for the successful consolidation of victory in these conflicts on terms that advance our national interests. We cannot hope to end hatred and enmity toward the United States in the hearts of all, but we can reverse current trends that are causing that hatred and enmity to deepen and spread internationally. Terrorists represent a grave threat to our liberties as well as to our wealth and power as a nation. We are not winning our struggle with them at present. But I believe that, with clear objectives and well-defined end-games, with the right policies and actions, we can.

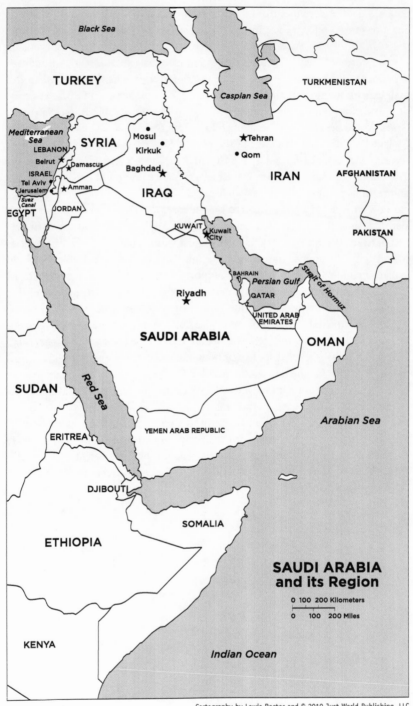

Black Sea

TURKEY

TURKMENISTAN

Caspian Sea

Mediterranean
Sea

SYRIA

• Mosul
• Kirkuk

★ Tehran

• Qom

IRAN

AFGHANISTAN

LEBANON
Beirut
ISRAEL
Tel Aviv
Jerusalem
Suez
Canal
EGYPT

★ Damascus

★ Baghdad

IRAQ

★ Amman

JORDAN

PAKISTAN

KUWAIT

★ Kuwait
City

BAHRAIN
Persian Gulf

QATAR

UNITED ARAB
EMIRATES

Strait of Hormuz

Riyadh
★

SAUDI ARABIA

OMAN

SUDAN

Red Sea

ERITREA

YEMEN ARAB REPUBLIC

Arabian Sea

DJIBOUTI

SOMALIA

ETHIOPIA

KENYA

Indian Ocean

SAUDI ARABIA
and its Region

0 100 200 Kilometers

0   100   200 Miles

Cartography by Lewis Rector and © 2010 Just World Publishing, LLC

PART II

Into the Ambush of Iraq

The following chapters record the texts of speeches I delivered to the annual policy conferences of the National Council on U.S.-Arab Relations (NCUSAR) in Washington, D.C. from 2002 through 2005. Typically, I was the final speaker at these conferences, giving my remarks as only the halt and the lame and those desperate to hang around for drinks and canapés remained in the hall. The speeches show the evolution of my thinking as events unfolded. I began by disbelieving that we could do anything as unnecessary and foolish as invading Iraq. I began to see that we had, without debate, greatly expanded our objectives in Afghanistan to the point at which they were infeasible. And I observed with horror that as we did these things, the level of mayhem in the Holy Land was constantly escalating. This led me into discussion of broader U.S. interests in the Middle East, and the impact on those interests of the policies and actions of America's long-standing Israeli protectorate.

Chapter 3
Reflections on a War with Iraq

September 9, 2002

General Tommy Franks—who, as CINCCENT, led the assault on Iraq six months later—was in the audience, doodling and idly taking notes as I spoke. I noticed that the only thing that seemed to interest him was my discussion of the logistical requirements for the conduct of war in the Persian Gulf.

I make no apology for my failure to anticipate that, contrary to everything that was then almost universally assumed, Saddam Hussein had, in fact, complied with United Nations demands that he end his research, development, and production of WMDs. A vast amount of effort by both Saddam and the Bush administration had gone into creating and sustaining conventional wisdom to the contrary. Like everyone else, I was duped. (Despite efforts at revisionism, almost no one can document a claim that he or she doubted that, in 2002, Saddam was somehow concealing WMDs; in fact, what he was concealing was his own weakness, as evidenced in his capitulation to international pressure.)

In this talk, I examined the likely consequences of our invading Iraq on the assumption that Iraq possessed WMDs. I also raised questions about most of the planning assumptions on which the neo-conservative architects of the invasion policy were insisting. I was certainly wrong to be so concerned about the WMD issue, but I got a lot of the rest of the story right.

Over the course of the day, I gather, various speakers have either discussed—or diplomatically sought to avoid discussion of—our present national obsession with precluding hypothetical threats of future carnage, even as we ignore and do nothing about ending the escalating mayhem in the Holy Land.

On Thursday, the president promises to explain our stand on these issues. I hope that his address to the United Nations will help us understand:

- How we should respond to the view of friends in the region that it is nothing short of obscene to be planning to add an American war against Arabs in the northern Gulf to existing U.S. backing for steadily escalating Israeli war with the Arabs in Palestine.

- How we should respond to the judgment of allies and friends in Europe and Asia that the notion of preemptive attack at will by the United States amounts both to a return to the pre-modern notion of 'might makes right' and to the abandonment of a century of largely successful American effort to create a rules-based international society.

The president's willingness to join a debate, as five members of his cabinet suddenly did yesterday, is welcome indeed. It may help to replace oppressive groupthink by a handful of pundits and politicians within the Washington Beltway with a wider and more reasoned discussion.

Over much of this year, in relation to regime change in Iraq, Washington has resembled nothing so much as a dog determinedly chasing a car—caught up in the joy of the chase and apparently unable or unwilling to consider what risks it runs by yapping at a speeding vehicle or what it might do if it actually caught up with it and could sink its teeth in its tires. Perhaps it's time to put the dog on a leash—or set it to chasing something else.

There are a few specific and not inconsequential questions we might usefully ponder before launching an unprovoked but preemptive attack on Iraq. In my brief time with you today, I will try to do just that.

I agree, of course, there's no reason to doubt that Iraq—like North Korea and Iran—is actively seeking nuclear weapons. But why would changing the Iraqi regime end this effort?

- Why does Iraq want chemical, biological, and nuclear weapons? Is this a strategy that springs from the evil mind of Saddam Hussein alone? Or is this a more broadly grounded strategy based on an Iraqi national interest in deterring a resumption of past assaults by Iran, Israel, Turkey and the United States?

- What, in fact, is Iraq's defense against Israeli and Iranian WMDs other than its own WMDs? The UN Charter? Is the UN Charter now an effective constraint on U.S., Israeli, or Iranian action against Iraq?

- Would regime change as such alter the geostrategic challenges facing Baghdad or in any way redefine Iraqi national interests?

- Might not a democratically elected Iraqi government be just as interested in WMD as a deterrent as the democratically elected government of Israel has been?

- If regime change is the answer, what was the question?

But, some may ask, might not Saddam attack the United States?

• If the proposed doctrine of preemptive attack is endorsed by the international community, Saddam might be justified in preemptively attacking the United States, given all the threats the United States has made against him and his regime. Why hasn't he?

• Is there any reason to doubt that Saddam does not understand the strength of the United States and our capacity to retaliate a thousand-fold for any attack on us?

• Is there any evidence that Saddam or his regime are suicidal?

• Stupid as Saddam is, why—given all our bluster—would he not by now have prepared and possibly even prepositioned retaliation against the U.S. homeland?

• Isn't the most likely, indeed almost the only conceivable circumstance leading to an Iraqi attack on the United States, a U.S. attack on Iraq that leaves Saddam nothing to lose by retaliating against us? (It is, perhaps, noteworthy in this regard that in 1991 Saddam did not attack Saudi oil refineries or wells but, when he felt he had nothing to lose, he set Kuwait's wells on fire.)

Given his behavior, why should we accept the assertion that Saddam Hussein cannot be deterred?

• He did not use WMDs in 1991.

• He is an aggressor, but a cowardly one, who attacks only the weak and unprepared (internationally isolated Iran—to U.S. applause; and regionally isolated Kuwait—to anticipated U.S. indifference).

• He has not rebuilt a capacity for military offense against his neighbors.

• With the exception of a despicable assassination attempt on former President Bush in Kuwait nearly 10 years ago, after Bush had left office—for which Iraq was duly punished with heavy bombing—Saddam has answered U.S. and British military attacks on him with political rather than military moves of his own. In other words, looking at the pattern of U.S.-Iraqi interaction over the past decade, the use of force has invariably been instigated by the stronger party, the United States, rather than by Iraq, which has clearly understood its own relative weakness. Some people might argue that Saddam's behavior is a textbook example of deterrence in action.

• Saddam's neighbors, with the possible exception of Kuwait, apparently do not consider him an active or unmanageable military threat at present. Surely, they both know him better and have more reason to worry than we do.

But might not Saddam transfer WMDs to other enemies of the United States, including al-Qaeda?

• It is true that we have the capacity to unite our enemies against us rather than dividing them as classic strategic thinking suggests we should, if we choose to do so.

• Is there, however, any evidence that this is actually happening?

• If the worry is about nuclear weapons, how likely is it that Saddam would turn over control to someone else of most or all of the tiny nuclear arsenal he may eventually acquire? (Such generosity is rare indeed in the annals of statecraft.)

• Why is this not an instance in which deterrence is possible and in which making it clear where U.S. redlines are is the best policy?

But isn't it better to be safe than sorry? How much do we have to lose? Iraq is weak and more vulnerable than North Korea or Iran. Wouldn't an invasion be a "cakewalk"?

• Iraq is, in fact, far weaker than it was at the end of eight years of war with Iran, but it is stronger than after the U.S. bombing campaign of January 17 to February 23, 1991 when we launched our ground attack on it.

• In 1991, Iraqi troops, mainly conscripts, were seeking to hold Kuwait, not defend Iraq. They knew their cause was unjust. They had been bombed at the rate of one bomb per minute for 37 days and were politically and emotionally isolated within the Arab world. Is their behavior in February 1991 a good predictor of the behavior of a more professional army defending its motherland nearly a dozen years later against foreign invasion and egged on by Arab opinion?

But, wouldn't Iraqis, like Afghans, welcome liberation by the United States?

• By all accounts, 10 years of sanctions and bombing have not endeared Americans to the Iraqi people, whatever they may think of Saddam. The United States, apparently, has many Iraqi admirers outside Iraq but few, if any, left inside it.

• Sanctions have concentrated patronage in Saddam's hands and helped him consolidate his rule of Iraq.

• Why do we accept the speculative statements of Iraqi exiles about Saddam's illegitimacy as more persuasive than the undeniable fact of his undisturbed control of Iraq? The Russian people, after all, fought for Stalin against foreign invaders, much as they had reason to loathe the Soviet dictator.

• Finally, of course, with the exception of Kurdish ethnic separatism—which is unacceptable to Iraq's neighbors—there is no civil war in Iraq, so we cannot gain a quick and relatively easy victory there by facilitating a win by one faction over another, as we did in Afghanistan.

Despite what they say, wouldn't Arab states and European allies welcome Saddam's overthrow if we succeeded in bringing it about?

• Perhaps so, after the fact, for few indeed would lament Saddam's passing. But how is this helpful in persuading them to help us up front in mounting a military campaign against Iraq?

• Why should we assume that Arabs, in particular, do not mean what they say about a U.S. attack on Iraq making further cooperation with the United States impossible?

• If, as some argue, the U.S.-led democratization of Iraq would catalyze democratic revolutions that would overthrow regimes elsewhere in the Arab world, why should such regimes support this course of action by the United States and thus help us to contrive their own demise?

• How much support, if any, can we expect from NATO allies and Japan? How much acquiescence will they give? Can we take for granted the sustained use of bases in Europe and Japan that was originally granted for purposes of common defense unrelated to unilateral U.S. actions to which they object, in places far away from them? What are the implications for our alliances of U.S. actions that depend on the infrastructure of those alliances while ignoring the objections of allies to those actions?

But doesn't the Afghan operation show we don't need allies and partners to project enough power to take down the regime in Baghdad?

• Our ability to project power to Afghanistan has rested on use of bases in friendly countries in the Persian Gulf and facilities as well as overflight rights in Afghanistan's immediate neighbors. It has entailed the conclusion of logistical support agreements with some 85 nations. The ability to refuel aircraft en route to the region and within it has been crucial to our military success.

• In the Gulf War, we based 550,000 troops in theater and stuffed 23 airbases there to the bursting point. If Iraq's neighbors deny us use of their airspace, ports and bases how do we even get there from here, still less sustain large-scale combat operations in Iraq?

• Why do we assume that an attack on Iraq that is opposed by most of the nations currently supporting or facilitating our Afghan campaign would not lead to their withdrawal of support for our increasingly unpopular operations in Afghanistan?

• If we succeed in overthrowing the regime in Baghdad, who will join us in occupying and doing the nation-building necessary to reform it, assuming that is possible at all?

How much might war with Iraq cost? Who will pay for it?

• In the Gulf War, U.S. expenditures came to $60 billion, every cent of it paid for by the Saudis, Emiratis, Kuwaitis, Japanese, Germans, Qataris, and others. Saudi Arabia alone paid $17 billion to the United States and spent an additional $50 billion on fuel, food, equipment, facilities modification, and a host of other expenses. In addition to cash transfers to the United States, much support in kind was provided by host nations and allies paid their own way. Kuwait paid for its own reconstruction. The total cost of the war was probably something like $200 billion.

• Is the United States ready on our own to fund a war with Iraq and the subsequent nation-building effort there?

• Do we have commitments in place from Saudi Arabia and other oil producers to do what they did in 1990 to 1991—to forego the opportunity for windfall profits from sharp increases in oil prices that could devastate the U.S. and the global economies?

Why are we so confident we can transform a "thugdom" into a democracy?

• What evidence is there of Iraqi traditions of democracy similar to those |in the Weimar Republic or Japan in the 1920s on which to build a new and stable democracy?

• Who is the equivalent of the Japanese emperor in terms of assuring Iraqi cooperation rather than resistance to a U.S. occupation? Are Iraqis by nature as docile as Japanese or as disciplined as Germans?

• If by democracy we mean a regime in Iraq that endorses U.S. policies and supports U.S. interests in the Middle East, including those based on U.S. solidarity with Israel, why do we assume such a regime could have any legitimacy in Iraq or regionally?

• If an Iraqi democracy decided to build weapons of mass destruction for avowedly deterrent purposes, would we respect its people's support for such a policy?

I could raise additional questions, but it's late in the day; these should be enough to help get the debate started. I hope that my brief remarks have contributed to that process.

Chapter 4

American Unilateralism at Play in the Land of the Two Rivers

Nat'l Council on US-Arab Relations

September 8, 2003

On the night of March 19 to 20, 2003, U.S. forces did indeed launch the invasion of Iraq toward which President Bush had been steering the country throughout the past year. Six months later, when I addressed the NCUSAR once again, it was becoming obvious that we had bitten off more than we could chew financially and that we were increasingly isolated internationally. The American civilian and military policy elite were, however, deep in denial. It was considered unpatriotic to question neoconservative assertions that everything was under control and improving in Iraq. It was not yet obvious to most how very bad things were going to get militarily and otherwise, and it was politically incorrect to suggest that we were in trouble. Still, if one dared to look beyond the policy mirage, one could see the outlines of an emerging insurgency in Iraq. One could also discern the effects of the increasing exploitation of Iraqi nationalist grievances by a new but growing international terrorist presence there. Al-Qaeda was exultant about its ability to feed on Iraqi resentment of the Anglo-American occupation and the anarchy it had brought to Iraq.

I must say that, in the past year, in three areas of concern to me, as someone concerned with the quality of U.S.-Arab relations and U.S. policy in the Middle East, things have not gone well.

First, there is no doubt that Saudi Arabia and Arabs generally have been successfully vilified in the eyes of the American public. The consequences of this are manifest in many ways. For those from the region who take delight in the distress of the Saudis, let me point out that the Saudis' problems drag all Arabs down.

When one looks at polls in the United States showing that a large majority of the American people believe that Iraq was complicit in the events of 9/11, one does not see considered judgments by our compatriots but rather a simple awareness that some bad Arabs did very bad things to the United States. Coupled with this, I am sorry to say, is the judgment that most Arabs are probably bad.

It has been obvious for a long time what needed to be done by both sides about this. I will not dwell on this. But it is sad that so much time has been wasted and that the trends have been so consistently negative in this area.

Second, perhaps first in importance, the Israeli-Palestinian interaction has seen the road map obliterated by zero-sum gamesmanship on both sides. The extremists run the government in Israel; they dominate the politics of Palestinians, with no hope remaining among Palestinians for resolution of their problems by peaceful means. We must now be concerned whether the violence of the Holy Land will not, once again, spread beyond its borders.

Finally there is the issue of Iraq, one we took up last year. It is sad to say, half a year after Americans neo-conned ourselves into invading Iraq, that we still don't know why we're there. And we haven't figured out what to do with it. Last night's presidential address did not answer either question.

The ouster of Saddam, the one achievement of U.S. policy that is lauded everywhere is, we have learned, not enough. It leaves too much undone in Iraq. It leaves too many disputes with allies and friends untouched and untended. And it leaves too many questions about America's proper role in the world undefined. Saddam's tyranny, a decade of international sanctions, and three weeks of highly destructive U.S. Air Force bombing have made a thorough mess of Iraq, the full dimensions of which we have only belatedly grasped. The task of reconstruction, as the president finally admitted last night, will be a lot longer and will be a great deal more expensive than we thought

Who's going to pay for this? The United States with a little help from a few friends—or the broader international community with a lot of help from the United States? This will be decided by who occupies Iraq and by what authority that occupation is there. If Iraq remains a Pentagon-operated theme park, the United States, not the international community, will be held accountable for what happens there, and Americans, almost alone, will pay for it in both blood and treasure.

We can't share the glory of the brilliant military victory that our British allies and we achieved over Saddam Hussein; however, it is in our interest to share the credit, and the burden, of success in nation building, as well as the blame if we fail to midwife a new Iraq.

American circumvention of the United Nations and the cold shoulder we gave to our allies and friends as we went into Iraq have between them created a serious problem that won't easily go away. With promises of state visits to Washington and other inducements, the administration did manage to extract statements of support from about a fourth of the world's member states. This enabled the president to assure Americans that "a broad coalition of nations" backed our actions in Iraq.

But with a few truly remarkable exceptions (I think of Japan's unprecedented offer of troops as well as aid) the countries we enlisted lack the will, the money, or the troops to work alongside the United States and Britain effectively in Iraq. Some—for example, Poland and Ukraine—are willing to risk the lives of their soldiers if we pay for them. But it turns out that when it comes to paying bills or carrying out perilous military tasks, lip service from a penniless, unarmed claque is a very poor substitute for support from the coalition of major powers at the heart of the UNSC.

In the real world, to manage and pay for real change in Iraq, we need both political cover and a lot of financial help from the three-fourths of the world's nations that six months ago openly derided our rhetoric as deceptive, our attitudes as insulting, our reasoning as amoral, and our actions as those of a scofflaw. Given these attitudes, simply asking the international community to give us the money to let the Pentagon do the job in Iraq, as we've done, is not a promising course.

Those critical of the United States, who include some of our historically closest allies in Europe and elsewhere, say that they'll help us in Iraq if they have a real say in what happens there through the United Nations. They're pretty confident we won't call their bluff by letting them have any such role. And their attitude toward our difficulties in Iraq, frankly, is pretty unattractive. It is, "You broke it, you own it. Gee, we're sorry to see you make such a mess of it."

The contempt—like the cynical Schadenfreude—is, of course, mutual. But if Iraq, which has been up to now primarily an embarrassment for the Pentagon civilian leadership, becomes a debacle for the United States, it will be a debacle with global reach, threatening not just U.S.-Arab and U.S.-Muslim relations and the regional order in the Middle East but the international order as a whole.

Conversely, if Iraq goes right, and it still could, the whole world stands to gain. Enough is at stake to justify a real hard look at ourselves and a serious effort by all parties to get past the ugly, shortsighted mood we've all been in. We need to reforge alliances and friendships and partnerships that can enlist the whole power of the international community behind the earliest possible self-determination of a reconstructed Iraq.

Tall tales about weapons of mass destruction may have helped to inveigle America into Iraq, but this doesn't alter the fact that we are there. Whatever the domestic political fallout of the war may be, whether people do or do not thank some in the Pentagon for putting the "con" back into conservative, the challenges of consequence management press urgently upon us in Iraq. How to restore basic services and rebuild a country while being shot at, in no small measure because of anger borne of the failure to restore those same basic services? How to prevent sporadic acts of resistance to occupation by Iraqi nationalists from escalating into a broader guerrilla war? How to prevent radicals throughout the Arab and Muslim world from making common cause with disgruntled Iraqis, using the American occupation forces in Iraq as target practice, and training for global jihad? How to make sure that democratization means something other than de-secularization, the empowerment of Sunni and Shiite religious extremists, and the emergence of faith-based politics in a society that was long notable for its separation of religion from political life?

These aren't easy questions. Addressing them means that we need to come to some kind of agreement about why we are in Iraq now that we are there. Rehashing old arguments about Saddam's weapons of mass destruction or connections with terrorism frankly doesn't help this process. Nor do attempts to hoist a sort of UN fig leaf over a chain of command that keeps the U.S. Secretary of Defense calling the shots and running the reconstruction in Iraq. That won't work.

President Bush used to say that the U.S. military should not be tasked with nation building. I think he was right. They are superb war fighters. They are not cut out to be politicians, gendarmes, or social workers. The U.S. military should not be left to hold the bag in Iraq.

I think just about everyone would agree that the U.S. mission in Iraq will be a success if we accomplish true regime change—not just regime removal, which is all we've done to date; and if the Iraqi people, other Arabs, and the international community conclude that we have liberated, not conquered and subjugated Iraq. Frankly, neither objective requires U.S., still less Pentagon, control to be achieved. In fact, both would be advanced by the earliest possible de-Americanization of the occupation, its true internationalization, and the development of a timetable for U.S. military disengagement from Iraq. It would be a great deal cheaper to fund an international development effort in Iraq than to try to run Iraq as a Defense Department satrapy. Internationalization seems to me to be key to the speedy return to Iraqis of full sovereignty and accountability for what happens in their country. This is the liberation we promised them.

If there is no credible timetable for this, and if the United States remains in control on the streets and in the ministries in Baghdad, then no matter how many Iraqi faces we put out front, Americans will continue to bear full responsibility and pay the full price for whatever happens in Iraq. Iraqi nationalists, some of them at least, have already begun to view the only good American as a dead American. And they have begun to seek allies among religious extremists with the proven capacity to strike at the U.S. homeland. Without a credible, internationally endorsed plan for U.S. military withdrawal backed by an effective multinational reconstruction effort with generous funding by the United States, Iraq resistance to our presence in their country will broaden and deepen. So will the demands on our military and the attacks on Americans everywhere.

By asking for $87 billion for the coming year—perhaps the first of many years—in Iraq, the President has taken an important first step. American money is essential, but American money alone will not free the United States of Iraq, or Iraq of the United States.

Let me conclude. Such are the perils of empire, I suppose some will say. Americans frankly understand these perils of empire more than most people. Our republic was born in a reaction to imperial administrators and military garrisons. In the past century we've fought two world wars and numerous skirmishes during a near-world war, the Cold War, in an attempt to liberate captive nations and to prevent their occupation, not subjugate them.

The traditions of American internationalism extol the uniqueness of our refusal to acquire the empire our power would have permitted us to create. What's happening in Iraq frankly invites us to rededicate ourselves to these important American traditions, not abandon them.

We want to see ourselves and to be seen by others as the liberators, not the imperial administrators of the Iraqi people. We want to be seen as the benefactors, not the conquerors of Iraq. But neither we nor the world will see us this way until we've shown that we are more interested in liberating Iraq than in commanding and controlling it—and more interested in accomplishing Iraqi reconstruction than in vindicating the unilateralism that took us there.

Chapter 5

Flip-Flops, Confusion, and the Asphyxiation of Political Debate

September 13, 2004

I spoke to the NCUSAR on the eve of a presidential election in which, despite the obvious failure of U.S. national security policies, there was no serious discussion of them!

Rereading what I said to this conference about this in 2001, 2002, and 2003, I am pleased but appalled to find that I got a few things right. This year, I am far less confident I can see the future.

Seven weeks before elections in this country, neither candidate is saying much, if anything, about how he would address the very serious problems he will confront at home and abroad, including in the Middle East. Instead, the parties are engaged in an embarrassingly trivial debate about whether John Kerry really earned his silver star in Vietnam and whether George Bush did or did not make himself available to bomb the Vietcong if they turned up in Alabama. This is too bad. There are a lot of serious questions before our country, our army, and our people. What we decide and do greatly affect the world.

The past four years have established what honesty compels me to describe as, without doubt, the most erratic foreign policy record in our history. The events of 9/11 showed the administration's early obsession with national missile defense and indifference to more conventional terrorist threats to have been fundamentally in error. Fortunately, the president reacted effectively on that occasion by rallying the country to fight the "terrorists with global reach" who had attacked us.

But no sooner had we successfully dispersed al-Qaeda's leaders and punished their hosts in Afghanistan than we lurched off "in search of other monsters to destroy" and invaded Iraq. Ill defined as they were, our objectives and priorities in that new battlefield shifted with kaleidoscopic ease under the ministrations of the spin doctors. WMDs, then democratization. De-Baathification, then remobilization. Improving the lot of ordinary Iraqis, then restoring their oil production and exports. Transformation of the region, then killing the jihadis and anti-occupation rebels that our presence itself spawned. Now, we're told that this hugely costly adventure was really just about getting rid of one man: Saddam Hussein. With the dictator exhumed from his manhole: "Mission accomplished!" But for some, so far unexplained reason, we nevertheless have to keep forces in Iraq for at least another four years. Or is it five, or 20, years?

The flip-flops, "ad hoc'ery," and confusion about objectives are not limited to our policies on terrorism or Iraq. Consider North Korea. The administration first declared Pyongyang's nuclear program intolerable, threatened dire consequences, and refused to talk to the North Koreans until they ended their program. When years of all-stick-no-carrot diplomacy predictably failed, the White House began to prepare us to live with a nuclear-armed North Korea. Some suspect we are seeing the same pattern with respect to Iran.

Then there's the Israeli-Palestinian issue. Disengagement, followed by half-hearted diplomacy, followed by passivity. A roadmap drawn, muttered over, revised, shelved, announced as a major initiative, and then set aside. Israeli military incursions in the occupied territories opposed, then endorsed. Israeli unilateralism condemned, then acquiesced in, and finally applauded. Negotiations by Americans with Israelis and Palestinians, then with Israelis alone, and now only among Israelis, with no American input except from the Israeli lobby here.

I have catalogued only a fraction of the numerous examples of this amazing pattern of strategic about-faces, convulsions, and abdications. It's hard to imagine how it could get worse. But if George Bush and Dick Cheney are right, and perhaps they are, John Kerry and John Edwards would be equally or even more spastic and inconstant as policymakers. Apparently, whoever wins, the United States will continue to vex and alarm the world with idiosyncratic and erratic actions abroad. This is not encouraging.

Come on, guys! There are issues of peace and war that—you know, and we all know—you will have to deal with if you are elected. Serious, real problems with major consequences for the United States and the world. Is it asking too much for you to reassure us that you are at least thinking about these issues by telling us something about how you expect to manage them?

How about explaining to us:

What are we now trying to accomplish in the war in Afghanistan beyond running down Osama bin Laden? What would victory look like? Are we into long-term nation building in Afghanistan? What's the end game, or is this the forever war?

What do we need to accomplish in Iraq to enable us to claim success for our invasion and occupation of that nation? In a region in which we kill one enemy and get five free, what needs to happen to let us stop killing Iraqis and other Arabs and being killed by them?

With Arabs concluding that Americans are indifferent to their suffering and untroubled by injustice and Americans equating Islam with terrorism, the estrangement between Americans and the Muslim fifth of the human race continues to deepen. By every measure available, the pool of potential recruits for terrorism against the United States and the long-term danger to our country from aggrieved Muslims are expanding. How do you propose to reverse these trends? If they cannot be reversed, what further measures do you propose to restore our security and domestic tranquility while preserving our civil liberties?

Given all the threats that neo-conservatives and right-wing Israelis have uttered, level with us, please. If you're elected, is the invasion of Iran a serious prospect? How about Syria? What does all the current demagoguery against the Saudi royal family portend for policy?

What do you propose to do about the mounting bloodshed in the Holy Land? Let it burn? Whatever Sharon asks you to do? Or something else? If so, what?

What are you going to do about the acknowledged "genocide" in Darfur?

What role do you foresee for a liberated Iraq in the balance of power and security in the Persian Gulf? What role for the GCC or other Arabs in defending themselves?

How do you propose to deal with the requirement of Arab states for a deterrent against nuclear attack, once Iran joins Israel in acquiring nuclear weapons?

I also wouldn't mind hearing what you intend to do about the Korean nuclear issue, which now apparently has a South as well as a North Korean dimension. Or about the Taiwan issue and China. Or about Russia. Or about rebuilding relations with allies and reestablishing a mutually productive relationship with the United Nations.

And, with some of our most senior economists telling us that there is a 75 percent chance of a dollar collapse sometime during the next five years, I think it might be helpful for you to tell us what you propose to do about the budget, trade, and balance of payments deficits that threaten both our national prosperity and the global economy.

Ladies and gentlemen, I was asked to tell you where I thought we might go from here. I apologize for not doing so. But I've given up on the possibility of either the media or Congress asking the questions that need to be asked of our presidential candidates and other politicians. As in the run-up to the Iraq invasion, both have defaulted on their responsibility to question those who lead or aspire to lead us. So I have fallen back on asking these questions myself.

If I've asked the wrong questions, please step forward and ask the right ones. Maybe, if we all ask with sufficient insistence, one or the other of the candidates will actually address an issue or two. That would be most welcome. I, for one, would like to be reassured that we're going somewhere better than where we've been.

Chapter 6

Occupations and their National Security Consequences

September 12, 2005

Almost four years after the invasion of Afghanistan and two-and-a-half years after the occupation of Iraq, events continued to demonstrate the limitations of American military power. At the same time, Islamic opposition to American policies was congealing into increasingly adamant antipathy. There was a disquieting absence of notice, let alone debate, in the United States about these developments. When I visited the region, moreover, the widening consequences for the United States of the Israeli occupation of Palestinian lands and the manner in which it was being conducted were impossible to overlook. I found it impossible honestly to assess the impact of events in the Islamic world for American interests without speaking at length on the interconnectedness of politico-military trends in the Holy Land, the broader Middle East, and South Asia.

Some things are, of course, going right in the Middle East. The Saudis are clearly winning their struggle against violent extremists. Palestinians in Gaza have been released from direct occupation by Israeli settlers and soldiers. Lebanese are exploring a new measure of autonomy, following the long-overdue Syrian withdrawal from their country. Syrians, relieved of the burden of keeping order in Lebanon, may finally attempt their own reforms. Women are being admitted to a larger role in society in some Gulf Arab countries. Annoying as the results are to many, the expanded press freedoms pioneered in Qatar continue to spread throughout the region. Experiments with elections as a means of selecting leaders continue to occur. High oil prices have produced an economic boom in many Arab countries, though not, of course, in all. But, with few exceptions, despite the propensity of the spin doctors here in Washington to claim credit for anything positive that happens in the Middle East, these developments owe little to the state of U.S.-Arab relations and have little impact one way or the other on American relations with the Islamic world.

Our relations with the Arabs and with Muslims generally are at a historic nadir. All of us, Americans or Arabs, who are present want to do something about this. But what? We must start with an honest appraisal of where we are.

My country's tragically misguided lurch into militarism after 9/11 has already cost us more on the broader international stage than anyone could have imagined. In the span of a single presidential term of office, four years, we have forfeited the international esteem that once undergirded our global influence. We have lost the admiring deference to our leadership of allies and friends alike, without gaining the respect of our enemies and adversaries. Once seen as the reliable champion of a generous and just international order based on the rule of law, the United States is now widely viewed as an inveterately selfish spoiler in international organizations and a scofflaw in international affairs. Once seen as the last, best hope of humankind, the United States is now—according to many polls—more feared than admired in a lengthening list of countries. We are much the weaker for all of this.

Nowhere is this dismaying reversal in foreign views of my country more advanced than in the Arab and Islamic worlds. The mutual estrangement of Arabs and Americans is driven by the consequences of ill-considered U.S. policies in Iraq, the Holy Land, Afghanistan, and at home. It is exacerbated by hypocrisy, irresponsible passivity, and an absence of forceful leadership on the Arab side. Adverse trends in American-Arab relations, in turn, poison American relationships with the broader world of Islam. Different policies and approaches on both sides will be needed to regain the enormous amount of common ground we have lost. More artful and articulate explanations for policies that are fundamentally mistaken will not do the trick.

The Anglo-American invasion and occupation of Iraq have cost my country its international reputation, many lives, and hundreds of billions of borrowed dollars. It is severely eroding both the structure and the professional competence of our army. It has destroyed the Iraqi state and destabilized and desecularized Iraqi politics, while expanding the regional power and influence of Iran. It has catalyzed violent struggles, verging on civil war, between Iraqi Arabs and Kurds, between Arab Sunnis and Shias, and among Shiite factions. It has generated at least three separate but loosely coordinated insurgencies in Iraq. The occupation, which seemed like the solution, has become the problem.

Our occupation in Iraq is drawing youth from throughout the Islamic world into attacks on Americans, by some estimates multiplying our enemies ten-fold. By a process of Darwinian natural selection administered by the very competent officers and men of the United States Army and Marines, we are creating an ever fitter cadre of enemies, expert in urban warfare, bomb building, and the military choreography of the ambush. We have transformed Iraq from a reliable supplier of oil to the United States and other markets into an unreliable one. The Iraq conflict and its side effects have contributed to raising energy prices to levels that are beginning to take a serious toll on our economy.

Our inability to prevail on the battlefield in Iraq has underscored the limits of our military power and emboldened our enemies. Now Hurricane Katrina has shown how little we have learned about how to deal with the consequences of large-scale traumatic events. The suffering of New Orleans has earned us the pity of the world and the scorn of our enemies. It invites renewed attempts by extremists to mount spectacularly deadly attacks on our homeland.

I suspect that many, if not most leaders in the Arab world would privately agree with the very negative assessment of American intervention in Iraq that I have just given. Some, I know, have spoken candidly to our president about Iraq, Israel, and the parlous state of American relations with the broader Islamic world. Candor, not fawning evasion and the hypocritical concealment of sincere differences of opinion, is the mark of true friendship. And it is in that spirit that I say to our Arab friends here today, if you do not express your views and advocate your own interests, do not be surprised if they are insouciantly ignored and trampled upon. No one heeds the lion that does not roar but rolls over and plays dead as others cross his territory at will. And no one respects the dog that whines but seldom growls and never bites.

It is particularly important that our Arab friends speak candidly to us about Iraq and Iran. The best outcome still possible in Iraq, it now seems, is a Shia-dominated state with a largely autonomous southern region heavily influenced by Iran and a Kurdish region independent in all but name. Such an Iraq may or may not contain U.S. garrisons and bases. The United States has not clarified its intentions. No one has demanded that it do so. Some of the same people who neo-conned the United States into invading Iraq are now arguing for an attack on Iran as a means of ensuring that it does not eventually acquire nuclear weapons. If these outcomes in Iraq and courses of action against Iran would serve the interests of the Arabs, then Arabs need only remain silent. If they would not serve Arab interests, as I believe they would not serve the interests of the United States, then Arabs must speak out to help the United States and the international community come up with alternatives to them that would better serve our interests—or suffer the consequences.

In Iraq, the problem is not now—if it ever was—WMDs, bad government, or even terrorism; it is the occupation. The occupation generates the very phenomena it was intended to cure. In that respect, the Anglo-American occupation of Iraq has come to have much in common with the Israeli occupation of Palestinian lands. In Iraq, as in Palestine, ending the occupation is the prerequisite for reversing the growth of terrorism and restoring peace.

Not long ago, many Arabs took obvious pleasure in seeing a few thousand Israeli settlers in Gaza suffer the same sense of powerlessness and dispossession that hundreds of thousands of Palestinians have experienced over the years. It is all too easy to forget that the Israeli withdrawal was unilaterally imposed by the Israeli military on Israelis and Palestinians alike. It was not agreed with the Palestinians as part of a peace process, and it has no clear implications for any other part of the occupied territories. It seems likely, in fact, that the people of Gaza have exchanged occupation by Israeli colonists and soldiers not for freedom but for a state of siege, in which their access to the outside world will continue to be controlled and perhaps severely restricted by their Israeli neighbors. Meanwhile, Mr. Sharon, having driven off on his own road, has made it clear that he has no intention of pulling Washington's 2002 Road Map out of the glove compartment and using it to navigate. He gives every evidence of a firm intention to continue to impose rather than negotiate changes in Israel's relationship with its Palestinian captives.

The fact is, of course, that Israeli occupation and settlement of Arab lands is inherently violent. Occupations are acts of violence. The dispossession of people from their land is an act of violence. Preventing people from coming to and going from their own country is an act of violence. And as long as such Israeli violence against Palestinians continues, it is utterly unrealistic to expect that Palestinians will stand down from violent resistance and retaliation against Israelis. Mr. Sharon is far from a stupid man; he understands this. So, when he sets the complete absence of Palestinian violence as a precondition for implementing the Road Map or any other negotiating process, he is deliberately setting a precondition he knows can never be met.

As long as the United States continues unconditionally to provide the subsidies and political protection that make the Israeli occupation and the high-handed and self-defeating policies it engenders possible, there is little, if any, reason to hope that anything resembling the former peace process can be resurrected. Originally intended to provide a basis for trading land for peace, the occupation has itself become the problem. As long as it continues, neither Palestinians nor Israelis will have personal security. As long as it continues, Israel will not find the acceptance by its Arab neighbors that was offered at Beirut in 2002. Moreover, the violent confrontation could at any moment, as it did in the past, spread its murder and mayhem well beyond the region. The most immediate victims of the continuing savagery and injustice in the Holy Land are, of course, Palestinians and Israelis. But their agony disturbs the peace of the world and wounds the hearts of billions beyond their borders.

The extremism and terrorism bred by the continuing injustices and crimes against humanity in the Holy Land thus continue to take their toll in places as remote from the Holy Land as Britain, Thailand, Nigeria, Indonesia, India, Pakistan, and Afghanistan. In Afghanistan, an American-led military operation to apprehend the perpetrators of 9/11 and to punish those Afghan Salafis who had given them shelter has now taken on a seemingly eternal life of its own. No one can now say when or what might allow the United States to disengage from combat against the once discredited but now-resurgent Taliban. As in Iraq and Israel, the occupation is becoming the cause of the very problems it was meant to resolve. If one recalls that the objective of al-Qaeda and its extremist ilk has been to drive the United States and the West from the Dar al Islam so that they can seize control of it, the growing antipathy to the American presence is sobering.

Finally, a couple of necessary observations about the American home front. I have recited a daunting list of policy challenges, not to say catastrophes, for the United States. We have a political system premised on the notion of competition between two parties—an adversary process in which one party criticizes and proposes alternatives to the policies of the other. This system has clearly broken down. Patriotism is confused with silent acquiescence in the policies proposed by our leaders. Policies that should be the subject of active debate are accepted without a word of protest by a gullible public. Those who know better say nothing even when they can see the country being led into disaster. The opposition party not only does not oppose, it does not propose alternatives either because it has no ideas or because lacks confidence in those it has been too timid to advance. This is not just a political problem; it is a systemic breakdown in American democracy.

What can and must be done in these circumstances? None of you would be here at this late hour of the day if you did not care deeply about the issues I have been discussing. I appeal to you. Those of you who are Arabs, lend us your ideas for how to lead ourselves out of the dilemmas we now face. Those of you who are American, speak out. Reaffirm your patriotism by restoring life to our democracy!

ISRAEL and its Region

Beirut

LEBANON

Damascus

Mediterranean Sea

SYRIA

Golan Heights

Sea of Galilee

West Bank

Jordan River

Tel Aviv

Amman

Jericho

Jerusalem

JORDAN

Gaza City

Dead Sea

Hebron

Gaza Strip

ISRAEL

Occupied by Israel
(June 1967)

EGYPT

0   15   30   45 kilometers
0   15   30   45 Miles

Cartography by Lewis Rector and © 2010 Just World Publishing, LLC

PART III
Policy Consequences

On January 25, 2006, at American insistence, Palestinian legislative elections were held, the first of their kind since 1996. The elections were universally judged to be free and fair. Hamas won a substantial majority (74 out of 120 seats) and pursued various formulas for bringing other parties and independent parliamentarians into a governing coalition as junior partners. Throughout 2006, Israel and the United States successfully blocked all those attempts. Israel—with full American backing—swiftly slapped a tight blockade on Gaza, the principal seat of the new Hamas government, and began a campaign to oust Hamas from power and replace it with its defeated rival, Fatah. (A year and a half later, in response to this campaign, Hamas ended its political cooperation with Fatah and, over violent resistance from Fatah, took direct control of all of Gaza. In response, Israel tightened the blockade yet further, describing it as a means to turn the people of Gaza against Hamas.)

In July 2006, in response to an escalating border skirmish with Lebanon's Hezbollah movement, Israel began a month-long campaign of massive air and artillery strikes that destroyed much of Lebanon's civilian infrastructure. This failed to achieve Israel's stated objectives. It did not halt Hezbollah rocket counterattacks on northern Israel. An Israeli ground campaign in southern Lebanon went poorly for Israel. Most observers were impressed by Hezbollah's performance, while the Israeli Defense Forces were judged to have lost much of their former credibility. Hezbollah's prestige was raised and it was propelled to the commanding heights of Lebanese politics.

The war killed at least 1,400 people, mostly Lebanese civilians, while displacing 1 million Lebanese and, while it continued, 300,000 to 500,000 Israelis. After the fighting ended, some parts of southern Lebanon remained uninhabitable due to unexploded ordnance from Israel's last-minute use of cluster bombs.

Meanwhile, ostracism of Iran, combined with threats to bomb it, had done nothing to halt its efforts to master the nuclear fuel cycle, a precondition for it to develop nuclear weapons.

During the summer of 2006, Iran's political influence in Lebanon was, indeed, greatly enhanced by the political and military successes of its Hezbollah allies.

These disasters were widely ignored in the United States, where the national media and public opinion were strongly supportive rather than questioning of Israeli policies and American support for them. By fall 2006, however, as midterm elections approached, the American public was beginning to recognize that the U.S. intervention in Iraq was headed for catastrophic failure. (Though all eyes were on the battle for Baghdad, the five-year-old American-led NATO pacification campaign in Afghanistan was also failing in this period.)

Chapter 7
The GCC and the Management of Policy Consequences[1]

October 31, 2006

The Gulf Cooperation Council (GCC) began in a time of crisis 25 years ago. Since then, it has passed through many stressful strategic environments. It was, after all, formed to cope with the challenges that caused Americans first to declare the Gulf a region of vital interest to the United States—the Islamic revolution in Iran, the Soviet invasion of Afghanistan, and the outbreak of the Iran-Iraq War. The GCC was also, of course, created to provide a means of dealing with the sudden rise in U.S. interest and military activity in the Gulf in the wake of these events, the oil boom, and the Camp David accords between Egypt and Israel.

The GCC functioned as a coherent alliance during the U.S.-led war to liberate Kuwait from Iraqi occupation that followed the end of the Iran-Iraq war. Its members separately provided essential staging areas and support bases for the U.S. invasion and occupation of Iraq a dozen years later. Some have since deepened their reliance on the United States, while others have hedged their previous dependency.

Now the GCC member states may be facing their greatest challenge: the changes brought about by the progressive collapse of American policies in the region, including U.S. efforts to transform Iraq, to block Iran's acquisition of nuclear weapons, and to achieve security for Israel by persuading it to respect the right of Palestinians to democratic self-determination in a secure homeland.

The U.S. military have developed the useful concept of "consequence management." The idea is to set aside for later study the questions of why and how widespread devastation followed the use of WMD or a large-scale natural disaster, and instead to acknowledge the damage while focusing on actions to mitigate it and prevent it from worsening. It is time to apply consequence management to the mounting wreckage of our policies in the Middle East.

Only true believers in the neoconservative dream can now fail to recognize that it has wrought a deepening nightmare in Iraq. The shattered Iraqi state has been succeeded (outside Kurdish areas) by near-universal resistance to the foreign occu-

---

1 Remarks to the annual conference of NCUSAR. The theme of the conference was the 25th anniversary of the establishment of the GCC.

pation that supplanted it. The aggravation of secular and ethnic divisions by ill-conceived constitutional bargaining and elections has created a new political culture in Iraq in which theocratic feudalism, militia building, and terrorist violence are the principal modes of self-expression.

The attempt to cure the resulting anarchy by building a strong army and police force for the Iraqi central government misses the point. The Baghdad government is itself a key participant in all of the pathologies of contemporary Iraq. In practice, it is more a vengeful tyranny of the majority in a temporary marriage of convenience with Kurdish separatists than a government of all the people. It is hard to disprove the thesis that it seeks a monopoly on the use of force only to consolidate either a Shiite version of Saddam's dictatorship or an Iraqi version of the Iranian theocracy. The sad fact is that, to many Iraqis, these outcomes now seem to offer the most realistic hope for renewed domestic tranquility in their country.

All but a small minority of Iraqi Arabs now reject the legitimacy of any continuing U.S. military presence on Iraqi soil. On the one hand, the occupation has become the indispensable prop of the current order in Iraq, such as it is; on the other, the prolongation of the occupation is the main reason Iraqis wage an insurgent war against that order. The occupation thus supplies its own opposition; its continuation feeds the violence that makes its eventual curtailment inevitable.

The unpopularity of the occupation continues to provide a rewarding opening for outside agitators. Al-Qaeda now openly acknowledges a major stake in the U.S. staying in Iraq for as long as possible. Our military presence is not just a potent motivator of anti-Americanism and a source of volunteers for terrorism, it has put us in the position of providing instructors to "Jihad U," the graduate school we have inadvertently created in Iraq for terrorists with global reach—an advanced curriculum, where failure is punished by death at our hands, but course completion is rewarded by a chance to take part in future terrorist operations in Europe, Asia, and North America. The costs of the occupation must be measured in much more than the hundreds of billions of dollars we continue to spend on it.

No one can predict how U.S. forces will withdraw from Iraq, but no one now doubts that their departure is only a matter of time. While some wish to soldier on, few see any prospect that the United States will leave behind an Iraq at peace with itself, a united Iraq capable of playing a constructive role in regional affairs, or a strong Iraq willing and able to balance Iran as it once did. The United States invaded Iraq against the counsel of our allies and friends, drunk with our own self-importance, convinced by our own delusions, apparently invincible in our ignorance, and utterly unprepared for the quasi-colonial mission we assumed. Contemporary Iraq is a monument to American martial prowess and civil ineptitude.

It now seems likely our withdrawal will be undertaken for domestic American political reasons, again without much attention to Iraqi and regional realities. But withdrawal risks escalating the conflict inside Iraq, infecting other parts of the region with Iraq's sectarian strife, and providing an early graduation ceremony for terrorists bent on applying elsewhere what they have learned in Iraq. Unless diplomacy has first crafted a regional context that limits the damage, a politically dictated withdrawal will crown our incompetence with disgrace and devaluation as a security partner. What kind of country is it that invades another, trashes it, sets it on fire, and then walks away to let inhabitants and neighbors alike die in the flames or perish of smoke inhalation? Who will wish to associate themselves with such a country, still less entrust their security to cooperation with it?

We did not consult the GCC countries or others in the region about the strategy or tactics of our invasion of Iraq. We would do well to seek their advice, counsel, and support—and they would do well to insist on our consulting them—as we make our next moves, whether these are within Iraq or away from it. Techniques of asymmetric warfare pioneered in Iraq now find their way within weeks to Afghanistan and elsewhere. The targeting of GCC rulers and oil and gas facilities by terrorists with connections to the mayhem in Iraq underscores our common interest in countering spillover from the jihadi intervention in that country. Similarly, the well-founded concern that areas in the Gulf with mixed Sunni and Shiite populations might suffer contagion from the religious struggles in Iraq emphasizes the imperative of containing them.

These are closely connected and clearly anticipatable problems that affect many countries in the region. They must not be left to be addressed ad hoc and at the last minute.

Then, there are the problems presented by Iranian ambitions, not just for nuclear weaponry but for preponderant influence in the Gulf. These go well beyond the issue of whether bombing Iran would not provoke it to attempt regime change in the countries from whose bases the attack had been launched, or simply confirm it and others in their judgment that the only effective protection against preemptive attack by the United States is the possession of a nuclear deterrent.

Assuming, as we must—in light of the results that similar U.S. policies toward North Korea have produced—that Iran will eventually acquire a nuclear deterrent, how do the GCC countries plan to deal with Iran as a nuclear power? Will each respond separately, or will the response be collective? Will there be piecemeal appeasement or defiant reaffirmations of sovereign independence? If a nuclear umbrella or deterrent to the nuclear threat from Iran is deemed necessary, will this be collectively managed or will each country seek its own protection? In either context, what role, if any, do the Gulf Arabs desire for the United States or other nuclear powers? Is the role they envisage for us one that Americans can or will undertake?

Then, too, having destroyed Iraq's utility in balancing Iran, we and the GCC have yet to concert a strategy for a new and sustainable balance of power. Such a balance cannot be sustained if, as was the case in Saudi Arabia, the American military presence becomes not an asset to national security but its principal liability, thanks to the provocation it offers to political extremists. How do we propose to manage the contradiction between our desire to assure the stability of the Gulf and the fact that our presence in it is inherently destabilizing? If we are to avoid a strategic debacle, we cannot leave Iraq without agreeing on answers to these questions with our Gulf Arab partners.

Iran is emerging as yet another proof that diplomacy-free foreign policy does not work. Neither do lack of planning or the refusal to talk to interested allies and adversaries. It's not hard to anticipate the questions that will arise from the probable future course of events in Iran itself and in Iran's relationships with Iraq and other countries in the region. These, too, must not be left to tactical responses, improvised on the spot in the absence of strategy and sprung with no warning upon those whose cooperation or forbearance is essential to enable them to succeed.

Finally, let me allude briefly to the issue of Israel, a country that has yet to be accepted as part of the Middle East and whose inability to find peace with the Palestinians and other Arabs is the driving factor in the region's radicalization and anti-Americanism.

The talented European settlers who formed the state of Israel endowed it with substantial intellectual and technological superiority over any other society in the Middle East. The dynamism of Israel's immigrant culture and the generous help of the Jewish Diaspora rapidly gave Israel a standard of living equivalent to that of European countries. For fifty years Israel has enjoyed military superiority in its region. Demonstrably, Israel excels at war; sadly, it has shown no talent for peace.

For almost forty years, Israel has had land beyond its previously established borders to trade for peace. It has been unable to make this exchange except when a deal was crafted for it by the United States, imposed on it by American pressure, and sustained at American taxpayer expense. For the past half-decade, Israel has enjoyed carte blanche from the United States to experiment with any policy it favored to stabilize its relations with the Palestinians and its other Arab neighbors, including most recently its efforts to bomb Lebanon into peaceful coexistence and to smother Palestinian democracy in its cradle.

The suspension of the independent exercise of American judgment about what best serves our interests as well as those of Israelis and Arabs has caused the Arabs to lose confidence in the United States as a peace partner. To their credit, they have, therefore, stepped forward with their own plan for a comprehensive peace. By sad contrast, the American decision to let Israel call the shots in the Middle East has revealed how frightened Israelis now are of their Arab neighbors and how reluctant this fear has made them to risk respectful coexistence with the other peoples of their region. The results of the experiment are in: Left to its own devices, the Israeli establishment will make decisions that harm Israelis, threaten all associated with them, and enrage those who are not.

Tragically, despite all the advantages and opportunities Israel has had over the 58 years of its existence, it has failed to achieve concord and reconciliation with anyone in its region, still less to gain their admiration or affection. Instead, with each decade, Israel's behavior has deviated farther from the humane ideals of its founders and the high ethical standards of the religion that most of its inhabitants profess. Israel and the Palestinians, in particular, are caught up in an endless cycle of reprisal and retaliation that guarantees the perpetuation of conflict in which levels of mutual atrocities continue to escalate. As a result, each generation of Israelis and Palestinians has accumulated new reasons to loathe the behavior of the other, and each generation of Arabs has detested Israel with more passion than its predecessor. This is not how peace is made. Here, too, a break with the past and a change in course are clearly in order.

The framework proposed by Saudi Arabia's King Abdullah in Beirut in 2002 offers Israel an opportunity to accomplish both. It has the support of all Arab governments. It would exchange Arab acceptance of Israel and a secure place for the Jewish state in the region for Israel's recognition of Palestinians as human beings with equal weight in the eyes of God, entitled to the same rights of democratic self-determination and domestic tranquility within secure borders that Israelis themselves wish to enjoy. The proposal proceeds from self-interest. It recognizes how much the Arabs would gain from normal relations with Israel if the necessary conditions for mutual respect and reconciliation could be created.

Despite the fact that such a peace is so obviously also in Israel's vital and moral interests, history and the Israeli response to date both strongly suggest that without some tough love from Americans, including especially Israel's American coreligionists, Israel will not risk the uncertainties of peace. Instead, it will persist in the belief, despite all the evidence to the contrary, that it can gain safety through the officially sanctioned assassination of potential opponents, the terrorization of Arab civilians, and the cluster bombing of neighbors rather than negotiation with them. These policies have not worked; they will not work. But unless they are changed, the Arab peace plan will run out of vitality and usefulness, and Arabs will revert to their previous views that Israel is an ethnomaniacal society with which it is impossible for others to coexist and that peace can be achieved by only Israel's eventual annihilation, much as the Crusader kingdoms that once occupied Palestine were eventually destroyed.

Americans need to be clear about the consequences of continuing our current counterproductive approaches to security in the Middle East. We have paid heavily and often in treasure in the past for our unflinching support and unstinting subsidies of Israel's approach to managing its relations with the Arabs. Five years ago, we began to pay with the blood of our citizens here at home. We are now paying with the lives of our soldiers, sailors, airmen, and marines on battlefields in several regions of the realm of Islam, with more such regions said by our government's neoconservative mentors to be in prospect. Our policies in Afghanistan and Iraq are adding to the threats to our security and well-being, not reducing them. They have added and are adding to our difficulties and those of allies and partners, including Israel. They are not advancing the resolution of these problems or making anyone more secure. They degrade our moral standing and diminish our value as an ally. They delight our enemies and dismay our friends.

In the interest of all, it is therefore time for a change of course. But, as Seneca remarked almost 2,000 years ago, "if a man does not know to what port he is steering, no wind is favorable." It is past time that we agreed on our destination and devised a strategy for reaching it. As events belatedly force us to come up with a workable approach to consequence management and lay a course to take us beyond it, Americans will need the advice of our partners in the GCC and others in the region.

If we pay no attention to the opinions and interests of these partners, we should not be surprised to discover that we have forfeited their friendship and coopera-tion. Without both, we cannot hope to manage and overcome the consequences of the series of policy disasters we have contrived or to devise new and effective poli-cies. And we here, like our friends in the region and elsewhere, will all pay again for this failure—and pay heavily. We must not allow that to come to pass.

Chapter 8
American Foreign Policy and the Arab World[1]

June 25, 2007

I was away from Washington in fall 2007 and did not speak, as I usually had, to the annual conference of the NCUSAR. Had I done so, I would have offered my judgment of the so-called surge in Iraq, which was the dominant news story of the year.

The surge itself was a success, not a victory. It headed off a humiliating politico-military defeat for the United States. It stabilized our occupation of Iraq but not Iraq itself. It came after a couple of years of well-financed Saudi efforts to turn Iraq's tribes (which are by and large the same as those on the Saudi side of their joint border) against al-Qaeda. Although they were unaware of the Saudi program, the U.S. Marines had long seen the opportunities represented by this so-called 'Awakening' in Iraq's Anbar Province. Coincident with the surge, the United States finally took advantage of these opportunities. This was a major defeat for al-Qaeda in Iraq.

However, the United States still had no coherent strategic approach to the management of its relations with the Arab and Islamic worlds. I thought it was time to go back to basics.

The U.S. relationship with the Arabs and Islam has grown from a minor concern 60 years ago to become, by stages leading to 9/11, a national obsession. For most of this period, most Americans didn't pay much attention to the Arabs except when the price of gas went up or the Israelis bombed them or some Arab bombed Israel back. Now, our involvement in the Arab world is direct, continuous, expensive, overwhelmingly military, traumatic, politically divisive, highly problematic, and sometimes fatal. We are stuck in what the Bush administration briefly named "the long war." This is a war with an enemy we are having trouble identifying and whom we clearly don't understand. It promises to be long indeed, both because we don't

---

1. Remarks to the Summer Institute of the Washington World Affairs Council.

know how to win it and because we will never admit that we may be losing it.

On the final day of the program, you will hear from a senior official of the Department of State, a dedicated public servant who will tell you what the U.S. government thinks it's doing— or at least what it wants you to think it's doing—to advance our interests vis–à–vis the Arabs. I spent 30 years as an advocate for our country's foreign policy as it was conducted under seven presidents. I admire the dedicated professionalism of those to whom this baton has now passed—but can hardly tell you how delighted I am to have handed it off. I will let the senior official speak for the government. I will, as usual, speak for only myself.

U.S.-Arab relations have become a tough subject to speak about in polite company. Since 9/11, the Arabs and we have worked hard to vilify each other. Each side has succeeded in blackening the reputation of the other. And, as if the resulting negative political overtones were not enough, the U.S.-Arab relationship is also an exceptionally complex one—to which it is difficult to do justice in a brief discussion.

This is not just because, while the United States is a single nation-state that acts with a single will, the Arabs are a nation of 23 politically diverse states that often compete with each other and only rarely unite. Americans and Arabs are also each part of complex larger groupings of people with similar values—in our case, the 850 million–strong community we call the West; in theirs, the 1.4 billion Muslims who make up the realm of Islam.

We need the oil and gas that the Arabs sell; they need the goods and services that we produce. We are in the main a devout and hospitable people. The Arabs are, if anything, even more so. We are roughly equal in numbers. Like us, Arabs come in all shapes, sizes, and skin and hair colors. We are each united not by our ethnicity but by the common languages and cultures that mark us as members of great nations that occupy wide swaths of the globe. Americans, like Arabs, have a predominant religion—ours, various forms of Christianity, theirs, various tendencies of Islam—but both of us harbor substantial minorities who profess other Abrahamic faiths. Just as most Americans are Christians but some are Jews or Muslims, most Arabs are Muslims, but many are Christians, and some are Jews.

With so much in common, we should be friends. For much of the brief history of our relationship, we have been. No more. Anyone who cares about and follows U.S.-Arab relations knows that they are now the worst they have ever been.

Well, so what? Does it really matter?

In foreign policy, national interest is the measure of all things. The United States has important interests in West Asia and North Africa that ensure that our relations with the Arabs can have very large consequences for us. These interests don't go away in response to events or shifting perceptions or changes of administration in Washington. Let me enumerate six things that are, and will remain, at stake in our relations with the Arabs.

First—let's face it. We are energy junkies.

Once the world's biggest oil exporter, we are now its biggest oil and gas importer.

We complain a lot about the price of oil. But, in practice, we seem willing to pay whatever price is on the pump to be able to drive to our homes and shopping malls in the suburbs rather than walk or take public transport around our cities. We depend on the global oil market for imports that meet two-thirds of our demand for petroleum products. In turn, the global oil market depends, to a great and growing extent, on Arab oil. The Arabs now supply one-fourth of the world's oil; in a decade, they will supply one-third. Switching from oil to gas is not a work-around. Arab countries already produce 35 percent of the world's traded gas. This percentage is set to double in the coming years. Arab countries hold 60 percent of the world's oil reserves. The world—including the United States—is destined to become steadily more dependent on them for its energy supplies, not less.

This gives the world an interest (as energy gluttons, we in this country have a particular interest) in expanded Arab oil production and exports to meet our energy needs as well as those of large new consumers like China and India. That, in turn, gives us an interest in peace and stability in the Arab world. Consider, for example, the effects of the anarchy we have created in Iraq. Before our invasion, Iraq was a reliable supplier to the United States and other markets, with good prospects for expanding exports over time. The fact that occupied Iraq is now an erratic supplier with very uncertain prospects is one of the reasons that the price of oil has risen to current levels.

In addition to an interest in access to expanded Arab production of oil and gas, we have an obvious stake in avoiding disruption of their sales of these vital commodities abroad. While other interests may, on occasion, outweigh concerns about the general welfare of our country, it is clearly prudent to try to reduce the dangers of war in West Asia and thereby to preclude a repeat of the sort of confrontation and resulting energy crisis that occurred during the Egyptian-Israeli war of 1973. Then, the sudden requirement to shore up Israel's war-making capacity provoked a retaliatory Arab oil embargo. That hit us hard even though our economy was then about only half as dependent on imports as it is now.

Second, we have acquired a clear national interest in achieving the peaceful integration of Israel into its region.

Israel cannot hope to enjoy peaceful coexistence with its Arab and Muslim neighbors through endless military intimidation of them or their Palestinian kin. Nor will the Arabs accept the legitimacy of a Jewish state in their midst if Israel rules its captive Arab population under the cruelties of martial law while high-handedly expanding its borders at Arab expense. Until it negotiates peace with the Palestinians, Israel will remain under siege and insecure.

After nearly sixty years of existence, the State of Israel is an established fact, but its future remains precarious. Arab leaders now publicly acknowledge Israel's existence and express willingness to accept it—providing Israel ends its oppression of the Palestinians and halts its dispossession of them from their homes. But resentment and loathing of Israel among Arab publics has never been so intense. The result is constant low-intensity conflict, punctuated by occasional outbursts of large-scale warfare in which the United States is inevitably implicated. The danger that conflict in the Holy Land will erupt into a global struggle between the supporters of Israel and its foes is also ever present.

Meanwhile, without the personal security that only peace can provide, many of Israel's most productive Jewish inhabitants have begun openly to contemplate seeking peace and security by leaving the country to find new homes abroad. It is entirely possible that, without peace, the Zionist experiment will wither away, leaving behind it only the bitter hatreds that it and the Arab reaction to it have engendered. In terms of U.S. interests, there is nothing optional about the pursuit of peaceful coexistence between Israel, the Palestinians, and Israel's other Arab neighbors; it is an imperative. The alternative is not just more violence in the short term; it is the permanent embitterment of the Arabs and the end of Israel in the long term.

Third, as differences between Israel, the West, and the Arabs have come increasingly to be defined in religious terms, we have acquired an interest in the character of the religious order in which Arabs participate.

There are 325 million Arabs—most Muslim but many Christian and some Jewish, despite Israel's in-gathering of the world's Jews. Arab Muslims make up only one–fifth of the 1.4 billion member global Muslim community, but they are a decisively influential fifth. The Islamic holy places are in Arabia and the language of Islam is Arabic.

Religion creates a sense of shared identity that can transcend ethnicity, especially in response to denigration of their faith or discrimination, humiliation, or assaults by outsiders on those who share it. Attacks on Arabs, whether Palestinian or Iraqi, are felt by other Muslims. The brutality that has attended the Israeli colonization of Palestinian lands, the many deaths in Iraq from a decade of American sanctions, followed by our invasion and occupation of Iraq, and last summer's U.S.-approved Israeli savaging of Lebanon are all cases in point. Arab rage at perceived injustice easily translates into Muslim anger toward its perceived perpetrators. Increasingly hostile relations with the Arabs are estranging Muslims everywhere from Americans.

The effects of U.S. policy toward West Asia and North Africa thus spill over to affect our relations with the rest of Asia and Africa, including non-Arab but Muslim Iran and Turkey and Central, South, and Southeast Asia as well as key countries like Nigeria. The United States has many interests in cooperative relations with these countries, not least in preventing them from becoming supporters of terrorist actions against Americans. Consider, too, the energy dimension. These nations hold yet another 20 percent of the world's oil and gas reserves.

A fourth interest arises from the fact that Arab countries and predominantly Muslim lands like Indonesia, Malaysia, and Iran straddle or abut the world's major transportation routes.

It's not just the security of oil and gas supplies that is the issue here, though the

Straits of Lombok, Macassar, Malacca, Hormuz, and the Bab al–Mandeb are vital links in the energy trade. You can't travel between Asia (which is becoming the world's economic center of gravity) and Europe without transiting these countries' air or sea space. Our status as a global power depends on the maintenance of a permissive environment for the transit of our armed forces. In military affairs, logistics are key. Our country has a big stake in sustaining cooperative military ties with the Arabs and other Muslim peoples and access to their air and sea space. Hostile relationships with these countries have the potential to cripple our capacity to project our power not just in the Middle East but beyond it. As an example, consider the difficulties the Pentagon is now having finding a North African Arab country willing to welcome the headquarters of its new Africa command.

Fifth, we have a major economic interest in encouraging the Arabs to reinvest the money they earn from energy sales in ways that benefit us.

More than 30 years ago, as increased oil prices began to flood their economies with "petrodollars," Arab oil producers made a commitment to plow this money back into the American economy. Both we and they benefited greatly from this. But today our posture toward Arab investment is decidedly unwelcoming. Arabs doubt that money they put here can be secure from politically motivated intervention by our monetary authorities or harassment by the army of tort litigators who live off the legal blackmail that our system now facilitates. The result has been Arab disinvestment from the United States, followed by the redirection of new investment elsewhere, for example to China. There is even talk about Arab abandonment of the use of the dollar as the unit of account for the oil trade, and one major Arab oil producer recently decided to end the peg that had tied its currency to the dollar. Oil-exporting countries are now accumulating annual surpluses of $600 billion or more. The consequences for our economy of a change in the role of the dollar in international energy and related commodity markets would be profound.

Sixth and last, but far from least, we have an interest in preventing and, ultimately, reducing anti-Americanism, especially anti-Americanism that takes the form of terrorist action against Americans.

It has generally been thought wise in foreign affairs to try to divide one's enemies rather than to say or do things that unite them. Frankly, as we have drifted into what is now seen among Muslims everywhere as an assault on Islam and its believers, we have steadily broadened the political base of Arab and Muslim anti-Americanism. Al-Qaeda and other enemies of the United States now think they have a chance to unite much of the Muslim world to their cause, form a broad coalition against us, and multiply their numbers manyfold.

The ignorance of most Americans, even educated Americans, about Islam and the Arab world has made a large contribution to these strategic failures with both Arabs and Muslims. Lacking understanding of those who oppose us, we have reasoned from fallacious analogies with our former foes in Nazi Germany and Soviet Russia. Instead of trying to understand and rebut al-Qaeda's case against our direct and indirect interventions in the Arab and Islamic worlds, we have ascribed to it an ideology that does not exist. "Islamofascism" is a word invented in America, redolent with politically evocative overtones of the European Holocaust, and totally disconnected from both Islam and Arab history. Rather than analyzing the objectives that al-Qaeda and its allies profess—which have to do with freeing the realm of Islam of our presence so that they and other Islamic extremists can direct its course to the future—we assign to them an objective of world conquest similar to that of our past Eurasian enemies. Our ignorance, confusion, and self-indulgence have led us to impose unfounded stereotypes on Muslims and to mistake Arab friends for Arab enemies—and, no doubt, vice versa.

The great Chinese strategist, Sunzi, once sagely observed: "Know your enemy and know yourself and you can win every war." Conversely, I would argue, if we continue to contend with imaginary demons and to invade countries to vindicate our hallucinations, we will lose every contest. The consequences of American failure against Islamic militants could be very large. The fact that al-Qaeda and its ilk do not much resemble the picture of them painted by our pundits does not make them any less dangerous—just dangerous in different ways. They must be countered by more realistic, appropriate, and effective means than those we are so counterproductively employing at present.

The only good news is that al-Qaeda has been almost equally inept. Many of its actions horrify Arabs and other Muslims as much as they do those they are designed to shock in the West, and its doctrines are too obviously deviant to have wide appeal in the Islamic world. Still, al-Qaeda has shown that it can learn from failure and adjust its tactics. In the long run, we must assume it will correct its mistakes.

Over time, therefore, Islamic extremists are likely to become more, not less, formidable as enemies of both the United States and those Arab regimes that remain aligned with us. In this regard, the deepening estrangement of Arab and other Muslim populations from the United States has very adverse consequences for us. It provides a political environment favorable to recruitment efforts, operational support, and concealment among the people by our extremist enemies. It inclines Arab leaders to shrink from public association or cooperation with us, even against terrorists who are targeting us only to deter us from continuing to support these leaders. It complicates our ability to counter the Iranian inroads our policies in Iraq, Lebanon, and the Holy Land have facilitated. It increases the incentives for the Arabs to accommodate Iran, and it deprives us of the political cover they might otherwise provide for an orderly and honorable end to our military intervention in Iraq.

The causes of Arab and Muslim alienation from the United States are not hard to discern and describe. They are policies that have demonstrably served our interests no better than theirs, or for that matter, Israel's. They include:

• Our decision to back Israeli efforts to pacify the Palestinians rather than to continue to try to mediate a Palestinian-Israeli peace. This succeeded only in discrediting us as peacemakers without gaining security for Israel, and it empowered Islamist unilateralists among the Palestinians to match the equally unilateralist Israeli government.

• Our collusion with Israel in the effort to isolate and overthrow the democratically elected Hamas government. This first left Hamas nowhere to go but further into the Iranian embrace. It then catalyzed armed conflict among Palestinians, partitioned the occupied territories, encouraged an Israeli effort to crush or starve the Gaza ghetto into submission, and made the prospect of a just and lasting peace between Israelis and Palestinians based on a two-state solution more remote than ever.

• Our witless transformation of our punitive expedition to capture al-Qaeda leaders and chastise their Taliban hosts into a long-term occupation of Afghanistan directed at excluding radical Muslims from a role in governing it. This has turned the Islamic world against our intervention there, conferred new life and undeserved nationalist resistance credentials on the Taliban, and lent unhelpful credibility to al-Qaeda's charge that we are engaged in an anti-Muslim crusade. (It has also had the perverse result of making Afghanistan so safe for poppy cultivation that it is now the source of almost all the world's heroin.)

• Our catastrophic march into the strategic ambush of Iraq, where we remain pinned down. Iraq is now a country militarily occupied by us but politically occupied by Iran. Our "transformational diplomacy" there has birthed a catastrophic mixture of anarchy and gang warfare, mounting civilian casualties and infrastructure collapse and an eruption of embittered refugees to every corner of the mostly Sunni Arab world.

• Our continual demonstrations of strategic ineptitude and politico-military incompetence. We persist in an attempt to impose military solutions on political problems in Iraq—thereby precluding political solutions to them—even as we cooperate in Shiite suppression and ethnic cleansing of Sunni Arabs and thrash about in search of a way out of the mess we've made.

• Our apparent plans to perpetuate our occupation of Iraq through the establishment of permanent military bases there from which we can dominate the Arab world. This is the one thing we've come up with that has succeeded in uniting Sunni and Shiite Iraqi Arabs—in almost universal opposition to such bases.

• Our open encouragement of Israel's sadistic mutilation of Lebanon last summer. This cemented Hezbollah's ties to Iran while transforming it into the dominant political force in Lebanon.

• Our recent efforts to block peace talks between Israel and Syria. This ensures a continued state of war along Israel's Golan front, continued proxy wars in Lebanon, continued Syrian reliance on Iran, and continued stalemate in U.S.-Syrian relations.

The policies that have produced these disasters for our interests and those of our friends could clearly do with some revision. As I noted, al-Qaeda has shown that it has the capacity to learn from its mistakes and correct them. Do we?

Chapter 9

American Interests, Policies, and Results in the Middle East:

Energy, Israel, Access, and the Containment of Muslim Rage[1]

February 11, 2008

Interests are the foundation of all successful foreign policies. As the George W. Bush administration staggered toward the finish line, I thought it might be timely to reexamine U.S. policies in the Middle East from the bottom up. What interests does the United States have? What policies would one expect, all things being equal, to see? What policies are actually in place?

The last time I was in this hall, I spoke about the uplifting subject of the return of China to wealth and power.

Tonight, I will speak about another region of the world, part of which is also accumulating wealth and power at a huge rate. The Arab Gulf now racks up about $800 billion in balance of payments surplus each year, and the amount seems set to grow. The cost of energy—the region's major export—shows every sign of remaining high, indeed, rising higher still in years to come. The flow of global liquidity to the Arabian Peninsula and adjacent areas is not a short-term phenomenon but a long-term shift in global wealth, with enormous implications for the United States and other countries.

This rise in wealth delights the region's inhabitants but, from an American perspective, the Middle East is currently a depressing place. It is a region from whose peoples we are increasingly estranged. It is a part of the world in which the introduction of a massive American military presence has paradoxically coincided with the steady diminution of U.S. political influence, loss of market share by American business, and displacement of America's former cultural preeminence.

1 Remarks to the Massachusetts Institute of Technology Security Studies Program.

A few weeks ago, President George W. Bush made his first visit to the Middle East. (This is something that presidents seem to decide is the thing to do as they prepare to leave office. An earlier example is Richard Nixon's nostalgic tour of the region just before his impeachment. Nixon evidently felt unappreciated in Washington—"mis-underestimated," as it were—and sought solace in Arab hospitality.)

Those of you who have spent time with the Arabs will understand this. I don't know what his Arab hosts thought about Nixon, but Arabs are reliably polite to guests—even guests they do not like. As a case in point, consider the cordial man-ner in which they recently received the Iranian president, Mr. Ahmadinejad, despite his having numerous characteristics that they, like others, consider obnoxious—not to mention an incorrigible character flaw in their eyes in that he, poor fellow, is Persian.

The Arabs are marvelously hospitable. Yet for the first time that anyone can recall they greeted an important American guest, the 43rd president of the United States, with a series of exceptionally blunt public comments that no American can take pleasure in reading. Their opinions of American policies in the Holy Land, in Iraq, in Afghanistan, and most pointedly toward Iran make very painful reading indeed. On his first full day in Riyadh, for example, President Bush was greeted with an editorial in the leading English language paper that analyzed his policies and concluded: "This is not diplomacy in search of peace, but madness in search of war." That sort of language would have been unthinkable only a few years ago.

Clearly, the new century has brought with it a new world. The problems for us to ponder tonight are why this new world is off to a particularly bad start in the Middle East and what we can do about this. American policies in the Middle East, more than anywhere else, account for the dramatic fall in our prestige around the globe. The new world of the 21st century is being shaped by events there and our role in them. The Middle East—except in its own estimation—has long been peripheral to global politics. It has now moved to their center.

I have come to this conclusion with some reluctance. I spent my whole career trying to avoid the Middle East. After all, it was where hypocrisy first got a bad name. It is a long time since it has been the home of a world power, so its diploma-cy is inherently parochial and aimed at manipulating external actors. And, while the United States has long seemed attracted to the Arab-Israeli conflict like a moth to a flame, I am not into self-immolation.

When the first President Bush asked me to serve as his ambassador to Saudi Arabia in 1989, he went out of his way to assure me that it was a quiet sort of place, where nothing ever happened. With that happy prospect in mind, I settled into life in Riyadh just in time to play a role in shaping Operations Desert Shield and Desert Storm. The intensity of that experience built relationships with people and leaders of the region that have kept me engaged with it ever since, despite my better judgment.

Why isn't the United States doing well in the Middle East? It seems useful to go back to basics. I will speak tonight in very general terms about this region from the perspective of American interests. What are American interests in the Middle East, and how do they relate to each other? All things being equal, what sort of policies would you expect the United States to follow, in light of those interests? What policies are we actually following? And what are their consequences? If things are not working out as we hoped they would, what might we do to remedy or mitigate this situation and turn it to our advantage?

I will address these questions briefly and, therefore, somewhat superficially. Years ago, however, a great professor of political science from Massachusetts Institute of Technology, who knew what he was talking about, told me that if something is worth doing, it is worth doing superficially. I have always taken his advice to heart.

The most obvious American interest in the Middle East does not distinguish us from others. We want reliable supplies of energy from it. About 60 percent of the world's energy reserves are to be found in and around the Persian Gulf. Sixty percent! The entire world is dependent on these reserves, both for present supplies of oil and gas and even more so for future supplies. Saudi Arabia alone has about one-fourth of global reserves. Iran and Iraq each have another one-eighth or so. More than two-thirds of future additions to global oil and gas supplies will originate in this part of the Middle East. Almost one-third of current supply comes from the Persian Gulf region.

It is, therefore, not surprising to turn on the TV news (which, of course, bears the same resemblance to analysis that pornography does to art) and to observe much gnashing of teeth about "U.S. dependence on Middle East oil." But it's wrong for our political pundits to encourage us to think about energy as a matter of bilateral trade. It is not.

Energy is sold into a global market and bought from a global market. This market functions like a pool or reservoir. Producers discharge their product into it, and consumers draw what they need from it. The level of the liquid in the pool rises or falls in response to the balance between input and output. Prices rise and fall accordingly.

It is not the United States that is dependent on energy imports from the Middle East; it is the world. It doesn't matter whether America imports energy directly from the Middle East or not—actually we are less dependent on the Middle East for energy than the Europeans, Japanese, Chinese, and Indians. If supplies to us from the region are cut off, we can and will buy elsewhere. But if Middle East oil supplies are interrupted to any customer, everyone in the world, including American consumers and the U.S. economy, suffers a price rise and takes an economic hit. The economic importance of Middle East energy lies in its indispensable contribution to the global economy, not how much of it flows to the United States as opposed to elsewhere. What is at stake is not an American interest but a global interest in which we Americans participate.

On this basis you would expect, first, that the United States would pursue policies that promoted stability in the Persian Gulf region, thereby bolstering the stability of its oil and gas production and exports, and reducing price volatility and its impact on both the U.S. and global economies. And you would expect the United States and others to be concerned about permitting a single producer, especially an unfriendly one, to dominate the region's oil and gas production and gain leverage over the global economy. To that end, you would expect the United States to be interested in sustaining a balance of power within the region rather than allowing a single nation to dominate it militarily. (Indeed, the Carter Doctrine and the Gulf War were both, in large part, efforts to preclude such dominance, in the first instance by the Soviet Union and in the second by Saddam Hussein's Iraq.) And you would expect the United States to do everything we could to avoid the destabilizing radicalization of the region's politics or the spread of conflicts that could interrupt energy exports. The last thing on earth we should want in terms of our own well-being is an escalating conflict between ourselves and the oil producers of the Middle East.

A policy emphasis on stability would, I think, have a natural corollary. Since energy exports from the Persian Gulf are a vital interest of all participants in the global economy, not just the United States, you would expect Americans to seek burden sharing, asking other consumers of energy to do something other than take a free ride on us. After all, we are only one of many beneficiaries of Persian Gulf stability. Why should the United States take sole responsibility for managing the security and assuring the exports of the peoples of that region? Why should our soldiers, sailors, airmen, and marines risk their lives to assure China's, Europe's, Japan's, and India's economic prosperity and well-being through reliable access to Persian Gulf energy? Ponder that, please!

A second very important American interest in the Middle East, given the prestige we have committed to it, is securing the state of Israel by achieving acceptance for it in the region in which it has been established. Israel cannot enjoy security if it is regarded as legitimate only by those outside its own region. It is not enough for Europeans (who initially sponsored the colonization of Palestine by European Jews and then carried out, collaborated with, or did nothing to stop the Holocaust) and Americans (who liberated European death camps at the end of World War II) to declare the establishment of Israel to have been right and proper. To assure the long-term survival of a Jewish state in the Middle East, Israel must be accepted by the other peoples of the Middle East.

Given the commitment of the United States to achieving Israel's acceptance, you would expect us to place great importance on the following:

- Brokering of mutually respectful arrangements for stable borders between Israel and the Palestinians;

- Peaceful coexistence between Israel and its neighboring states; and

- Israel's political, economic, and cultural integration into its region.

Among other things, to the extent we Americans believe that the spread of democracy bolsters stability, you would expect us to wish to see the example of Israel's democracy emulated in the region. Israel's democracy denies full rights of citizenship to one-fifth of its inhabitants and any rights at all to the millions it rules in the occupied territories, but it is still perhaps the world's most robust democracy, with a level of public discourse on policy matters that is or should be an inspiration to other countries, including our own. In short, you would expect the United States to use our influence to promote reconciliation and make peace rather than to widen conflicts or begin new wars in the region.

The erratic and often half-hearted manner in which we have pursued these goals, especially in recent years, accounts, in part, for Israel's isolation from other states in the Middle East. The sad fact is that 60 years after the State of Israel's founding, almost all Americans and many Europeans strongly back it, but it is still seen as illegitimate by the peoples of the region where it was established. The Arabs see Israel as an artifact of Western colonialism in their midst, an unappeasable power in perpetual search of Lebensraum at Arab expense, a cruelly oppressive sectarian occupier whose policies justify violent resistance, and the principal impetus for the radicalization of politics in both the region and the broader Muslim world. The region sees Israel as a hegemonic military threat, not as an appropriate partner in its politics, economics, or culture.

These perceptions, no matter how objectionable to an American audience, represent a major failure of both American policy and the Israeli policies that the United States has facilitated and underwritten. They underscore the boldness of Saudi Arabian King Abdullah's promise that, if Israel can work out a mutually acceptable deal with the Palestinians, he and his Kingdom will ensure that all Arab states normalize relations with Israel.

Our third interest is military, commercial, cultural, and religious access. We need access to the region for our military because we can't travel between Europe and Asia or vice versa without going through it or over it. The Arabian Peninsula is the size of Western Europe. Tens of thousands of aircraft cross it each year. The U.S. military could not operate in Iraq or in Afghanistan without overflight of Saudi Arabia. Nor could we use the huge airbase that has been made available to us by Qatar and from which we direct all air operations in both Iraq and Afghanistan. We could not access the headquarters of the 5th Fleet in Bahrain or our army installations in Kuwait that support our military operations in Iraq. We could not confront Iran if we decided, in accordance with our constitutional processes or even despite them, that it was in our interest to do so. In terms of its location astride strategic lines of communication, the Middle East is an area that is vitally important to our ability to act as a world power. No wonder al-Qaeda focuses on breaking the Saudi-American relationship and making cooperation between us infeasible!

But military access is not the only kind of access we need. The adherents of all three Abrahamic religions—Jews, Christians, and Muslims—want untrammeled access to their holy places in Jerusalem. For the world's Muslims, pilgrimage to Mecca (in the Hejaz on the Red Sea coast of Saudi Arabia) is a religious obligation, and a visit to the historically related sites in Medina is also important. The United States, I have been reliably informed, is still a secular country, but we have a great interest in nondiscriminatory access to holy sites by those attached to the great world religions. Denial of such access embitters and enrages. It promotes conflict, not reconciliation, and it provides the moral justification for wars of resistance.

Then, too, we want access to the Middle East for our businesses, for the benefit of our economy. Commercial access is particularly important when, as now, high oil prices lead to huge transfers of dollars to the region. Dubai is merely the best-publicized example of the mind-boggling boom that the Gulf is experiencing. This is a region that was once the preserve of American business, the only place outside North America, where cars designed in Detroit were the dominant form of transportation. (Gulf Arabs like SUVs and other gas guzzlers as much as Americans do. But the economics of gas-guzzling there are different. In Saudi Arabia, for example, they currently pay only about 17 cents a gallon at the pump.)

Our declining market share and the inability of our companies to compete effectively for the huge new projects underway in the region or its rapidly expanding markets, are a tragedy for our companies and a blow to our economy. It is especially ironic, given the extent to which we have failed to respond to higher prices by curbing our appetite for the region's major export—oil.

The United States also needs to maintain access to the region culturally. It is in our interest for the peoples there to come to our schools, universities, staff colleges, and training facilities and to carry home with them both an understanding of the United States and feelings toward us that facilitate cooperation. It is in our interest to understand them. To do this, we must meet them on their own ground. We can't do business with them if they can't visit our showrooms or train on our equipment; nor can we do so if we cannot serve them where they live.

You would, therefore, expect the United States to lay major emphasis on military partnerships in the region as well as trade promotion, cultural outreach, and the encouragement of travel between the Middle East and the United States.

Fourth, we have an interest in the containment of problems that arise in the Middle East. Some of you may remember Dean Rusk's insight that "at any time of day or night, two thirds of the world's people are awake, and some of them are up to no good." Well, the Middle East is the epicenter of that phenomenon today. Its anguish, fear, and rage are uniquely infectious, given its status as the focus of three of the world's great religions. One-and-a-half billion Muslims—a fifth of humanity—pray in the direction of Mecca five times each day. Not a few of the 34,000 sects into which the world's 2 billion–plus Christians divide themselves believe that the reestablishment of a Jewish state in the Middle East heralds the rapture of Judgment Day. Many, if not most, of the 7 million members of the Jewish Diaspora are passionately connected to Israel. The bitter divisions of the Middle East are contagious and can easily translate into global wars of religion, prejudice, persecution, and terrorist campaigns. It is not in the American interest, still less the world's, for the 21st century to be dominated, as most of the 12th to 17th centuries were, by religious strife linked to a "clash of civilizations." European history provides ample evidence of how ugly and destructive such conflicts and the hatred and discrimination they engender can be—and of how difficult it is to halt them once they begin.

Based on this, you would expect a careful American attention to dialogue between faiths and the enlistment of religious authority in the cause of reasoned compromise among the various contending parties in the Middle East. You might also expect the United States to seek allies amongst these authorities who could discredit extremism among their co-religionists.

If these are descriptions of the main interests of the United States in the Middle East and the policy approaches they might logically produce, what policies are we currently following?

With respect to stability in the Persian Gulf region, we have given up on the idea of maintaining a regional balance of power and substituted our own unilateral military presence for this. When there was a rough balance between Iraq and Iran, the United States did not have to be present in the region in force. We could remain over the horizon and practice rapid deployment so that, if the balance started tilting too much in one direction or another, we could throw our weight behind the weaker side without ourselves becoming directly involved on the battle fields of the Middle East. This is what we did during the Iran-Iraq War.

When that war exhausted Iran but left Iraq still vigorous enough to try to take advantage of the imbalance by invading Kuwait, we were prepared to intervene to liberate Kuwait and to cut Iraq back to a level that Iran could balance. We accomplished both objectives with Operation Desert Storm.

Then, out of frustration with Saddam Hussein's unexpected survival in power, we unilaterally decided that we would practice what was called "dual containment," a policy that required us to maintain a large military presence in the region to balance both Iraq and Iran. This policy, which is the father of the current one, was and remains the most expensive, the most strategically fatiguing, and the most politically irritating of all strategies we might conceivably adopt. It guarantees continuing friction with the peoples of the countries hosting our forces and raises the possibility of mounting "blowback." Now that we have flattened Iraq, however, there is no obvious alternative to it. It appears we are stuck in both Iraq and the lower Gulf.

Our invasion removed Iraq as a reliable supplier of oil to world markets. Our threats to bomb Iran have added to regional instability and uncertainty, and led to additional rises in oil and gas prices. Recent polling data shows that we are now seen by the region's peoples as the greatest threat, not the greatest contributor, to its security.

By pursuing a unilateral course, rather than organizing our allies, friends, and other nations who have a stake in the secure flow of energy to assist us in maintaining order and stability in the region, we have put ourselves in the position of being held accountable for anything and everything that may go wrong there. We have also chosen to give everyone else a free ride on our unilaterally assumed responsibility for the security of the world's energy trade. As a consumer nation, we share interests with other major oil and gas importers, including newly emerging importers like China and India.

Instead of making common cause with them, however, we have chosen to deal with oil and gas producers through uncoordinated bilateral relationships or, in the case of Iran and Sudan, non-relationships. This has compounded the incoherence of our domestic energy policy, leaving us with no policy response to rising energy prices, no strategy for future energy security, no commitment to conservation or demand management, and no answer to climate change beyond an apparently counterproductive farm subsidy program.

Meanwhile, next door in the Holy Land, it has been years since we made a serious effort to promote negotiations between Israelis and Palestinians or even exercised our own judgment about the issues that divide them. Rather, we have reflexively supported the efforts of a series of right-wing Israeli governments to undo the Oslo accords and to pacify the Palestinians rather than make peace with them. Our recent embrace of the partition of Palestine into a Jewish and a secular Arab state —the so-called two-state solution—is widely seen in the region as too late and too little: too late, because so much land has been colonized by Israel that there is not enough left for a viable Palestinian state alongside Israel; too little because what is on offer looks to Palestinians more like an Indian reservation than a country. Such status will not be accepted by the inhabitants of the occupied territories; nor will it be accepted by the 6 to 7 million–strong Palestinian Diaspora. It would inflame rather than relieve Arab resentment of Israel. It would not lead to normalization of Israel's relations with other Arab states. Far from achieving the acceptance of Israel that is essential to its long-term survival, it would assure the continuation of efforts by other states in the region to erase Israel from the map. It would risk further globalization of asymmetric warfare in the form of terrorism against Israel and its supporters overseas, including the United States.

Ironically, last November's gathering at Annapolis was, as feared, all spectacle and contained neither process nor substance. The glimpse of Israel's unilateralist vision of the Palestinian future that the run-up to it afforded has invigorated interest in a one-state, as opposed to a two-state, solution. As he left Annapolis, Israeli Prime Minister Olmert pointedly noted the danger of this trend, which promises to force his country to choose between its character as a Jewish state and a democracy that rejects the practice of apartheid. This is not a choice that the founders of the State of Israel ever envisioned. It is one from which thoughtful people must recoil. If there is a better way forward, we must help Israelis and Palestinians find it.

Let me turn now to the issue of access. In every respect other than military, our access to the region has steadily diminished. Despite the amazing level of economic activity in the Gulf catalyzed by the rise in energy demand and prices, most business is going to European and Asian rather than American companies. This is a trend that would call out for reversal, even if we weren't running a chronic trade deficit. The region's imports are increasingly priced in euros, sterling, and other currencies, while its exports are still denominated in dollars. The dollar is sinking under the impact of chronic budget, trade, and balance of payments deficits. This is fueling inflation both in the Middle East and here at home. It is creating strong domestic political pressure on oil producers to dump the dollar. Serious questions are being raised about whether the little green portraits of dead presidents we have been in the habit of exchanging for oil and other commodities might have to be converted into some other currency before they can exchanged for energy. The impact on our economy of such a development would be grave.

As our business presence in the region declines, Arab travel to the United States for business, study, or pleasure has not recovered from its post-9/11 collapse. Far from it. While visa issuance rates are up, visa applications are way down. Those few who are able to obtain a visa often encounter degrading search and interrogation practices at the point of entry to the United States as well as while traveling within it. The human ties that are essential to resilient relationships among us continue to fray and attenuate, despite far-sighted efforts by a few in the region, like Saudi Arabian King Abdullah, to sustain them.

Militarily, despite all the hoopla about our offer to sell $20 billion in weapons to the Saudis and other Gulf Arabs, it is not at all clear that they intend to pick up on the sales pitches our companies have made. Increasingly, others who are more politically acceptable—Britain, France, Russia, and South Africa—overshadow us as arms suppliers in the region, and China, India, Korea, and Pakistan are queuing up behind them to take their piece of the action in a game we no longer dominate. We continue to transit in high volume to bases we have been lent in the Gulf and to those we have built in Iraq. But this is on sufferance, not pursuant to defense treaties or agreements, still less an agreed strategy. Our talk about attacking Iran in association with Israel has further encouraged the Gulf Arabs and Egypt to seek new and less belligerent military partners in Europe and Eurasia as well as to pursue rapprochement with Tehran.

And finally, to turn to matters of religion: From Indonesia to Guyana, the United States is now perceived as conducting a Crusade against Islam, not a war on extremists who usurp the good name of Islam for their own foul purposes. The unwelcome notion of a clash of civilizations is turning out to be a case of self-fulfilling paranoia. We have no dialogue of consequence with Muslim religious authorities. Nor have we sought allies among the many Muslims who share our disgust with the perverted actions of Islamist extremists. If the first requirement for a successful campaign against terrorist insurgents is the discrediting of their cause and their ideology, we have yet even to attempt this. If the measure of success in such a campaign is, as former Secretary of Defense Rumsfeld declared, eliminating more terrorists than we create, then we are losing this war.

Overall, this is not a pretty picture. Given our substitution of talk radio for serious analysis of the sources of Muslim rage and the paralysis of our politics since 9/11, it has taken some time for our society to recognize that things have not been going well and to begin to ask what we might do to change course. The next administration is clearly going to inherit a thoroughgoing mess in the Middle East with implications that extend well beyond it. We face an unprecedentedly complex challenge to our statecraft in the continuing anarchy and mayhem in Iraq; the siege of the Gaza ghetto; the refurbishment of Taliban credentials as the defenders of Islam and the political rights of the largest ethnic group in Afghanistan; the entrenchment of Iranian political influence in Iraq, Lebanon, Palestine, and Syria; the collapse of the peace process between Israelis and Palestinians; our estrangement from Turkey; the emergence of a democratic opposition in Egypt openly committed to abrogating the Camp David arrangements; the unrebutted appearance of an American military crusade against Islam; the lack of an energy security strategy; Iran's continuing development of a nuclear industrial base that will, in time, permit it to field nuclear weapons; the impending spread of nuclear technology throughout the rest of the region; the alienation of allies and potential partners in dealing with these problems; and the absence of strategies or proposals to address any of them except through air strikes.

What is to be done?

Given the daunting number of challenges, I'm tempted to leave them to whomever we elect on November 4. But, since none of the presidential candidates has dared take them on, let me propose a number of thoughts for your consideration.

Perhaps it is time for the major consumers of oil to organize ourselves to join Arab and other producers of oil in managing the global oil market to mutual advantage. At present, there is no organized exchange of information or collective bargaining between producers and consumers of energy. Both sides could benefit from exchanging planning information and views; like unions and management, we share an interest in assuring each other's continuing economic development and prosperity and avoiding unpleasant surprises. It would also be timely and appropriate for the United States to discuss with other consumers how to share the burden of defending the seaborne oil trade and of bolstering a renewed balance of power in the Gulf. As a related matter, we might do well to put our heads together about how to develop a truly multilateral reserve currency system to replace over-reliance on the dollar and reduce the perils to our economic health that that increasingly entails.

Second, we need to develop war termination strategies for both Afghanistan and Iraq. Iraq is the more urgent of the two. It is in our interest to achieve the earliest possible restoration of Iraqi sovereignty and independence. Iraq today is not, in most respects, a sovereign country but one occupied by the United States.

Although we did not want this, we stand there in the position of a colonial power. Iraq's inhabitants look to the United States military—not to the Iraqi government we shelter in our "green zone"—for patronage, support and resolution of their problems. They also see our presence as a more pressing problem than the political presence that Iran has established in their country under cover of our occupation of it. So, for the first time in history, many Iraqis lean toward Iran. If we weren't there, most likely they would distance themselves from Iran.

3   For many years our permanent presence in the Gulf consisted of nothing but four ships. We now have hundreds of thousands of sailors, soldiers, airmen, marines, and contractors on station. The region does not want this. Most Americans do not want it. In the end, such a presence is not politically sustainable. We must find a way, once again, to rely on a regional balance of power between the Gulf Arabs, including Iraq, and Iran. Our withdrawal from Iraq should be conducted in such a way as to facilitate the phased achievement of this.

4   It is also time for the United States to develop different policies toward Israel and the Arab lands it occupies. Our objective should be a peace that would trigger the broad normalization of Israel's relationship with the Arabs that the Saudi-orchestrated Arab League proposal promises. It serves neither our interest nor Israel's (as opposed to the interests of expansionist politicians in Israel) to support Israeli policies and practices that, far from serving the objective of winning such a peace, undercut it. The blank check we currently offer Israel enables it to adopt policies that serve parochial and short-term interests at the expense of long-term interests. Principal among such long-term interests is Israel's survival as a democratic state with a Jewish identity. Our unconditional support deprives Israelis of the need to make choices they must make in their own interest, and it aids and abets the adoption of policies that are unilateralist, militarist, counterproductive, and inevitably self-defeating. Our assistance to Israel, as well as our diplomacy, must be conditioned on goals and benchmarks that produce progress toward reduction of tension and negotiated coexistence in the Holy Land. There are many in Israel who have clear ideas about how to do this and who are eager to harness our power to the ending of their conflict with the Palestinians, if only they are empowered to do so.

5   Finally, we need to start over in our relationship with the religious leaders of Islam and their secular counterparts, and to focus them on cooperation against the terrorist enemies of both Islam and the United States. We have begun to do this at the local level in Iraq and, as a result, al-Qaeda is now on the run there. Both in Iraq and elsewhere, al-Qaeda has murdered huge numbers of Muslims—many more than it has killed Christians or Jews. Yet our public diplomacy, such as it is, has concentrated on explaining away or defending Abu Ghraib, Guantanamo, and "extraordinary rendition" rather than on seeking common ground with the world's Muslims, most of whom share our horror at al-Qaeda's amoral tactics and reject its deviant vision of Islam. We have an open invitation from the religious leaders of

the Islamic world to open a dialogue to explore the possibility of a coordinated approach. It is past time for us to respond.

Part of this response must, I believe, embrace reconsideration of the garrison state we are currently constructing at home. We need to strike a much better balance between the open society that is the source of our greatness as a nation and security from those determined to punish us for the perceived iniquities of our policies. We are a nation defined by our ideals, not our territory or ethnic origins. That is the source of our appeal to the world and the font of both our domestic tranquility and our influence abroad. If we abandon our ideals in the name of defending them, we defeat ourselves. I have long felt that all the world—including its most troubled regions—would still follow America, if they could only find it. We must rediscover it for them.

Chapter 10

West Asia and the Next President: More of the Same Won't Do[1]

October 31, 2008

After eight years of neglect of peacemaking in the Holy Land, seven years of war and esca-
lating insurgency in Afghanistan, and five-and-a-half years of teetering on the brink of
failure in Iraq, Americans were deeply divided but seemed ready to try something new.

Next Tuesday, just four days from now, we Americans will select a new president
and his back-up. Exactly eleven weeks later they will take office. They will inherit a
dog's breakfast of policy catastrophes from the outgoing administration. Everyone
will look to them to clean these up. In West Asia, the Bush administration's legacy
to America and the world includes two ongoing wars, a hostile relationship with
Arabs and Muslims, and the loss of our ability to inspire others elsewhere to follow
our lead.

Here at home, we've spent ourselves into socialized banking. The incomprehen-
sibly huge operations of our government, including its military operations and
those of our vastly expanded public sector, continue to rely on foreign-financed
credit rollovers for their sustainment. We've more than doubled our national debt
over the past eight years and are driving hard for a debt level equal to our GDP.

The next president must help us survive a deep recession. At the same time, he
must restore pay-as-you-go government. He must talk Americans into paying the
taxes and foreigners into lending us the money needed to make this transition. Our
financial system and economic model have been discredited. The next administration will have to come up with a financial workout plan. We need to convince creditors that we are en route to national solvency. Those we are asking to buy our
debt—Arabs, Brazilians, Chinese, Europeans, Russians, and others—are the very
peoples who object to the self-righteousness and global dominance we have unilaterally asserted. They have seen our recent behavior as bullying. Persuading them to

---

1. Remarks to the NCUSAR annual conference.

pay for continuing military adventurism will be far from easy. It's said that sales-manship starts when the other party says no. The next president is going to have to be a wickedly good salesman.

In 1967, Britain was forced to the conclusion that it could no longer afford to police the world East of Suez. The United States is not at such a moment, but we are much too close to it for comfort. Our sticks are foreign financed; the repo man has his eye on our carrots. Long wars cannot be fought on other peoples' money, especially when those who must lend us the money suspect that we see them as eventual targets of the military campaigns and modernization we want them to finance. For the first time in living memory, resource constraints will compel the United States to choose among our priorities—domestic and overseas; civilian and military. These constraints will also force us to stop trying to do everything on our own and to seek partners to share the human and financial costs of global and regional order and energy security.

The fact that you and I haven't heard a lot from either presidential candidate about these challenges is instructive. It suggests that much of what both have been saying on the campaign trail is irrelevant. The campaign rhetoric provides no guide to what the next president will actually do in the radically changed circumstances of post-meltdown America. Very likely he doesn't know himself. So rather than try to predict what the next president will do, perhaps we should ask what he ought to try to do. One way or another, there will be major changes in how America oper-ates at home and abroad. Given the terrible mess in the Middle East in particular, thinking about new approaches there seems especially appropriate. Let me offer a few thoughts on the current situation and what may be in store for us.

I'd like to begin on a note of optimism. Miracles evidently still happen in the Middle East. After all, God just spoke, though somewhat belatedly, to Ehud Olmert. And, lo! God convinced Mr. Olmert that there can be no two-state solution in Palestine without ample land for the Palestinians and that creating a single Eretz Yisrael but dividing it into two zones—in one of which Arabs have limited rights as second-class citizens and in the other of which they have no rights at all—is a very good way to destroy the State of Israel. It promises, among other things, to set off an international campaign to isolate and punish the Jewish state for the prac-tice of apartheid and related sins. Earlier, God had spoken on the same subject to our retired president, Jimmy Carter.

Since God now seems to be into counseling retirees, perhaps he'll also speak to Calamitous George as he leaves office, to convey the insight that writing blank checks to Israel harms it by depriving Israelis of any immediate incentive to make the hard choices they must make to achieve long-term security for themselves and their state. In our own interest, we must act to create conditions that allow Israelis and Arabs to accept and coexist with each other on a mutually respectful basis. In this connection, it benefits no one for the United States to continue to underwrite the injustices, indignities, and humiliations of the occupation. These injustices have corrupted Israel's moral standing. These indignities inspire terrorism. These humiliations are so intolerable as to make peaceful coexistence with Israel impossible for Palestinians and unacceptable to other Arabs. They, therefore, preclude the broad regional embrace of Israel proposed in the Saudi peace plan of 2002.

Mr. Olmert is a bit late but far from alone among Israelis in his recognition of what must be done. The prerequisite for both peace and the survival of Israel as a Jewish state is the end of the Jewish holy war for Arab land and the withdrawal of Jewish colonists from the properties they have grabbed from Palestinian owners since 1967. There is, of course, a common retort to this observation. It is that, even if decolonization is both right and necessary to achieve acceptance for Israel's existence where it counts, it is politically impossible for Israel to do it. This amounts to saying that it is politically impossible for Israel to do either what is right or what it must do to achieve acceptance for its existence as a state in the Middle East. The long-term implications of this self-imposed moral and political incapacity are not pleasant to contemplate. Israel is a small country surrounded by much larger neighbors of growing wealth and power. It has done much to secure their enmity and nothing to win their affection.

Meanwhile, divine intervention is unlikely to be required for U.S. taxpayers to choose between alleviating the suffering of Americans made destitute by the collapsing economy here at home and subsidizing a prosperous lifestyle for some but not all inhabitants of the Holy Land. If Americans are asked to make tough choices and pay our own way—as we will be—most will not see it as either unreasonable or anti-Semitic to ask Israelis to do likewise. Given the attitudes of our creditors on the matter, it's also possible that, at some point, when Israel tries to cash an American subsidy check, it will bounce.

Whatever the next president does to encourage peace among Israelis, Palestinians, and their neighbors, the last eight years show that doing and demanding nothing can and will make things worse. But even as he repositions the United States to promote peace in the Levant, the next president must deal with the challenges of the Afghan-Pakistan region and Iraq. The seven-year-old war in Afghanistan is not going well for anyone except opium farmers, Pashtun nationalists, and al-Qaeda. More than five-and-a-half years after we invaded Iraq, changes in our campaign plan there—backed by higher troop levels and lots of money to pay off insurgents—have stabilized both our occupation of Iraq and the politics of the war here, but they have not stabilized Iraq itself. The $859 billion we have so far committed to the so-called "Global War on Terror" has yet to win us a significant victory anywhere. In Afghanistan and Iraq, too, more of the same is not an option.

This is not just because we can't sustain the current pace of military operations or their costs without breaking our army or bankrupting ourselves. It is also because much of what we are doing in these two very different countries seems to be harming rather than advancing our interests. Reconnecting our policies to those interests, tying our core objectives narrowly to them, and not allowing ourselves to be diverted from the efficient pursuit of them will be the keys to success.

Let me start with Afghanistan. I am sure I am not alone in recalling that we went there to accomplish two straightforward things: first, to avenge ourselves on the sponsors of 9/11—to kill or bring to justice the leaders of al-Qaeda; second, to punish those who had given safe haven to them. We sought to ensure that neither the Taliban nor anyone else would ever again risk the consequences of harboring terrorists who plot violence against the United States. Our enemy, we understood, was al-Qaeda. Our dislodgment of the Taliban from power was the means by which we expected to ensure that that enemy could not reconstitute itself in Afghanistan.

In broad terms, what we sought was strategic denial of Afghanistan to terrorists with global reach. We had pretty much achieved this by the time of the battle of Tora Bora, only two months after our invasion began. It is not clear that we have advanced much since then. We may in fact have slipped backward. Al-Qaeda has not been smashed. The Taliban and its fellow travelers in other Muslim lands no longer view us as too formidable to defy.

What began as a punitive raid aimed at beheading al-Qaeda and chastising its Afghan household staff has somehow morphed—with no real discussion or debate—into a prolonged effort to pacify Afghanistan and transform its society. This moving of the goal posts gratified neoconservatives and liberal interventionists alike. Our new purpose became giving Afghanistan a centrally directed state—something it had never had. We now fight to exclude reactionary Muslims from a role in governing the new Afghanistan. Our aid programs focus on making it safe for women's rights and a growing list of other noble causes, regardless of how many Afghans these programs agitate into enmity. The fact is we lost our strategic focus in Afghanistan well before we shifted our attention from it to the unrelated issue of Saddam Hussein's secular regime in Iraq.

Most observers judge our position in the Afghan-Pakistan theater to have become precarious. Pakistan's support for us and our military operations is increasingly shaky. Our intervention is fostering attitudes among Afghans conducive to terrorism (and congenial to the poppy cultivation that funds terrorist insurgents.) The Pashtun homeland that straddles the Afghan-Pakistan border has become a zone of lawlessness in which terrorists operate with reliable local support. That is the very opposite of what we hoped to achieve. While intelligence operatives and special forces do continue to hunt al-Qaeda, our overall war effort now seems mainly aimed at keeping 'our guys' in power in Kabul by suppressing uppity Pashtun warlords and a resurgent Taliban.

Almost everyone believes we need a different strategy and approach. Both presidential candidates have pledged to add many more American soldiers to the 31,000 now in Afghanistan and to escalate our military struggle there. But a strategy that continues to rely primarily on military means seems likely to deepen our confrontation with Pashtun nationalism, push the destabilization of Pakistan to a new stage, and promote the further spread of anti-American terrorism.

We need to recall the reason we went to Afghanistan in the first place. Our purpose was not to reform it or to rectify our lamentable lack of attention to it after the Soviet defeat there 20 years ago. It was to deny the use of Afghan territory to terrorists with global reach. That was and is an attainable objective. It is a limited objective that can be achieved at a reasonable cost. We must return to a ruthless focus on this objective. We cannot afford to pursue goals, however worthy, that contradict or undermine it. The reform of Afghan politics, society, and mores must wait. First things first. Our policies and programs toward that country must aim, above all, to reduce the likelihood of its involvement in terrorist attacks on the United States or Americans abroad. Bombing, strafing, seizing, and mercilessly interrogating villagers from a warrior culture do not support this objective. Nor does denigrating and seeking to erase aspects of Afghan culture we consider benighted—even if they are. A little collateral damage and disparagement can convert a lot of formerly harmless people into supporters of terrorism.

We must now ask ourselves some very basic questions, drawing on our experience in Iraq as well as in Afghanistan. In a struggle to dominate and deny human rather than physical terrain, is the large-scale use of force an effective way to achieve positive political results? Can measures that produce less collateral damage—like intelligence and law enforcement efforts, backed as required by commandos—obviate the need for conventional military operations? Does foreign military occupation of xenophobic Muslim societies inevitably evoke an allergic reaction that generates rather than inhibits terrorism? If so, can counterterrorist operations be staged without occupying the countries in which their targets are located? And how are we to avoid reprisal from those whose sovereignty we violate?

In the case of Afghanistan in particular, does our effort to prop up a largely ineffectual national government raise or lower Afghan support for terrorists who have us in their sights? Can we co-opt hostile local authorities and insurgents with respectful dialogue, cash, and programs of material assistance, as we did in Iraq? Are there allies with Islamic credentials who could do better than we at this task? If so, how do we enlist them? Arab governments are threatened by the same extremists who threaten us. Would they be willing to design, fund, and staff religious curricula in Afghanistan and adjacent areas of Pakistan that could discredit extremist ideology and delegitimize terrorism, as Saudi Arabia has finally done at home? Should we be talking to the Taliban about a deal that drives al-Qaeda from the Pakistani part of Pashtunistan as well as from all of Afghanistan? Should we be talking to Afghanistan's powerful neighbors—China and Iran as well as Pakistan—about this?

If our next president listens, he will find that these questions and others like them, absent though they are from public discussion in this country, are very much on the minds of our allies and friends. The lack of evidence that we have seriously considered them or are prepared to answer them accounts in large part for our allies' unwillingness to commit more forces to the U.S.-led global war on terrorism in Afghanistan. The Bush administration has just launched a thorough review of our strategy there. The next president will receive its recommendations. He does not have to agree with what he hears, but he does have to decide how to steer us on a new course. We cannot succeed with more of the same in Afghanistan. That is also true in Iraq.

We finally know where we are headed in Iraq. We are headed out. At the insistence of the Iraqi authorities, the U.S. military will spend the next three years redeploying. Our patrols are to leave Iraq's cities by next summer. All U.S. combat forces are to be gone from Iraq no later than the end of 2011. It will be quite a trick to accomplish this disengagement without tipping the country back into anarchy and civil war or facilitating even greater political inroads by Iran.

The purpose of the surge was to create the preconditions for political reconciliation in Iraq. Its focus on Baghdad prevented the fall of that city, stabilized the foreign occupation of Iraq, and took the war off the front pages of U.S. newspapers. In the process, our military became active participants in Iraqi politics and governance at the local level. But the only reconciliation there has been is among the U.S. armed forces and Iraq's Sunni Arab insurgents, whom we have put on our payroll. There has been no reconciliation, and there is no trust between the (Sunni) Sons of Iraq and the Shiite-dominated administration in Baghdad, still less the various Shiite militias that support or sympathize with that administration, or the Iranians on whom some of them rely.

It was the U.S. military, assisted by Iraqi troops and militias, not the Iraqi government, that impartially separated communities and combatants and kept the lid on intercommunal strife in Iraq. Iraqis still look first to their American occupiers for the just and efficient provision of community services and support. Many of them see their own government as inefficient, sectarian, and corrupt. Not a few regard it as a running dog of Tehran. In short, stability in Iraq, such as it is, has depended on foreign occupation authorities doing what the Iraqi government has been either unable or unwilling to do. The withdrawal of U.S. forces will rebalance power and patronage in Iraq with consequences that are difficult to predict.

Iraq's infrastructure has been smashed, its domestic tranquility shattered, and a fifth of Iraqis—the equivalent of sixty million Americans—are displaced from their homes, driven into exile, or dead. Iraq resembles nothing so much as many of the American veterans who have served there: It is battered, embittered, and in physical and mental pain. The fact that the Iraqi polity has somewhat stabilized in this condition is better than the alternative, but it does not provide much cause for celebration.

As Ambassador Ryan Crocker[2] has observed, "in today's Iraq, Sunni Arabs fear the future; Shiites fear the past; and Kurds fear both the past and the future." Our current attempt to hand off to the Maliki government responsibility for command, control, and cash transfers to the Sons of Iraq is a test, but only the first test, of whether that government can and will conduct itself in such a way as to gain the

2. Then American Ambassador to the Republic of Iraq.

confidence of those beyond its political base and avoid renewed communal violence. If Iraqis pass this test, as we must hope they will, there will be many more tests ahead of them.

The jihadi movement in Iraq was a by-product of our invasion and Iraqi resistance to it, on which its members gorged like jackals after a slaughter. It never consisted of very many people, but it succeeded in igniting the sectarian hatred that now casts such a shadow over the Iraqi future. In the laboratory for terror that Iraq became, the jihadi movement innovated and learned. It invented weaponry and techniques of asymmetric warfare that are now being applied not just in Afghanistan but in many other places—from Chechnya to Colombia, and from Sri Lanka to Spain.

In the end, we had the good sense not to interrupt al-Qaeda as it made the mistake of making enemies of our enemies. With our help, Sunni Arab tribal leaders and their forces have now mopped up most but not all of al-Qaeda's adherents in Iraq. But the defeats extremists have suffered in Iraq do not equate to decisive victory for us, on any level. The preconditions for intercommunal mayhem have not been eliminated. We are not yet out of Iraq. No one knows who will be king of the mountain in Mesopotamia. There may be quite a fight among Iraqis to decide this. Al-Qaeda's focus has shifted to other opportunities but a rebirth of anarchy or civil war in Iraq could quickly revive its franchise there.

By now it is a cliché that the only victor in Iraq has been Iran. For five years, Iraqis have been struggling to regain their freedom from foreign domination. Many have turned to their coreligionists in Iran for support. The result has been the emergence of something resembling an Iranian political occupation of Iraq to parallel the Anglo-American military occupation. The only effective or long-term counterbalance to Iranian dominance of Iraqi politics remains Iraqi nationalism. The withdrawal of U.S. forces upon which Iraqis now insist offers them an opportunity to take back the independence they have yielded not just to us but also to their Persian neighbors.

The United States and the countries of the Arab League and GCC have every reason to back the aspirations of Iraqi nationalists. The rebirth of Iraq as a strong regional actor independent of Iran and with close ties to its Arab and Turkish neighbors is essential to regional stability. The U.S. military presence in the Gulf must now be reduced to affordable levels. The only way to do this is to adopt a strategy of using our weight and that of our allies from over the horizon. Our purpose would be to buttress the independence of the states of the region and to help them achieve and sustain a balance of power. A less intrusive approach like this is also needed to reduce the U.S. military presence to levels that do not feed terrorist reaction in the conservative Muslim societies of the region. But for "offshore balancing" of this kind to work, the Gulf must recreate the possibility of an equilibrium that the US and others can tip toward stability. No such equilibrium is conceivable without the return of Iraq to full independence.

Offshore balancing would return primary responsibility for regional peace and stability to the states of the region. But it would not end U.S. military involvement in the Gulf. It is a burden-shifting strategy, not a cop-out. It would require the United States to retain—and occasionally to demonstrate—a credible capability to intervene rapidly and decisively in support of regional balance. A framework for accomplishing this might, in time, be supplemented by burden-sharing arrangements with major energy-consuming nations. It is not unreasonable to expect them to help defend the energy supplies and supply lines on which they, like Americans, depend.

Drawing Iraq out of the Iranian orbit is also a prerequisite for peace and stability in Iraq itself. Sunni Arab Iraqis must learn to live with Shiite domination of their country's politics but neither they nor other patriotic Iraqis will accept a government in Baghdad that they see as a pawn of Persia. Iraq's neighbors would react badly to this, too. Iran must be brought to realize that overly ambitious policies excite opposition that threatens rather than serves its national interests. But we must acknowledge that Iran has legitimate security interests and that it cannot be excluded from an appropriate role in its own region.

American ambivalence over what to do about Iran has given Iranian hard-liners everything they have wanted—a justification for building a nuclear deterrent and an excuse to develop the capacity to conduct asymmetric warfare directly and through proxies. We have continually said and done things that increase Iran's concerns about its vulnerability to attack, even as we demand its disarmament. We have professed a desire to contain Iran's influence and the threat it may pose to Israel, but we have simultaneously driven Palestinians into an unnatural dependence on Tehran, cemented Syria to it, and empowered it in Lebanon. Both presidential candidates have recognized that our Iran policy is bankrupt and that we need to engage Iran rather than ignore it. (They just differ on whether to take it on with bombers or at the negotiating table.) The next president will have to develop a coherent policy toward Iran, persuade our allies and friends that it is workable, and press forward with it. Without military power, diplomacy is toothless; however, without diplomacy, the use of force yields no political outcome.

On every issue I have mentioned today, the United States cannot succeed without Arab and Muslim allies. We need their cooperation to bolster peace in Iraq, to balance Iran, and to achieve acceptance for Israel in its region. We need them to combat extremist ideology among their compatriots and coreligionists. We need them to prevent Muslim youth from turning their anger at perceived humiliation and injustice into the vicious retaliation of terrorism. We need them to help us identify and eliminate active threats to our nation, its citizens, and our allies. These threats are also threats to Arab and Muslim leaders and their societies. So they need us too. But they want us to act in ways that limit collateral political damage. They need U.S. policies that can enlist Muslim support, that harness our military prowess to their political strength, and that reflect consideration of their long-term interests as well as our short-term ones.

There is a widespread sense among Muslims that their modern societies have wandered off the straight path. Many are attracted to the argument that, to renew these societies and themselves, Muslims must revisit the earliest days of their faith. That is perhaps right. It is not for non-Muslims to say. But it is up to Muslims to insist that the extremist vision of early Islam as a totalitarian faith with a closed mind, intolerant of other religions, systematically unkind to women, and dedicated to the imposition of joylessness on humanity is wrong. The achievements of the Bait al Hikma;[2] the flourishing of non-Muslim communities in the midst of the first Muslim societies; the participation of Jews and Christians in their governance; and the great contributions of early Islam to the world's sciences and arts, including music, all stand as a rebuke to the parody of Islam espoused by al-Qaeda and its like. Muslims who seek to renew their faith by reference to its tolerant and humane traditions should be able to look to Americans as well-wishers, as friends, and as allies. We have the same enemies.

But Muslims cannot ally with us safely or in good conscience if our policies and our statements feed fears that we are engaged in a crusade against their religion. We cannot enjoy their sympathy and support—or, for that matter, that of other foreigners—if we allow assertive ignorance and aggressive xenophobia to dominate our national discourse. By the same token, we help no one but Osama bin Laden when we accept his deviant views as an authentic description of the religion he has done so much to discredit. The next president must adjust our policies to make them more effective. But he must also help Americans to persuade the world that we are still fitting partners in the pursuit of global prosperity and tranquility. Nowhere is this task more urgent than in the realm of Islam.

In my travels in Arab and Muslim lands, I find the same nostalgia for America as it was before 9/11 that one encounters in other parts of the world. No one likes how we now behave or what we have become, but they remember when we behaved with greater humility and when we more closely resembled what we aspire to be. They admire that America. They are ready to work with it, if it can be restored. The next president must restore that America. The world is ready to meet him halfway.

---

2. Bait al-Hikma ('The House of Wisdom') was a key center for learning and translation in Abbasid-era Baghdad, coming to the height of its influence under Caliph al-Ma'mun (reigned 813 – 833, C.E.) It was destroyed during the Mongol invasion of the city in 1258.

Chapter 11

U.S.-Arab Relations: Forks in the Way Forward[1]

October 16, 2009

Barack Obama began his presidency by sending multiple signals that he considered peace between Israelis and Palestinians, reconciliation between Americans, Arabs, and other Muslims, and engagement with Iran to be his foreign policy priorities. On his second day in office, he appointed a special mediator for Middle East peace. A few days later, on January 26, he gave his first exclusive interview as president—to the Dubai-based Arabic language satellite news service, Al Arabiya. He sent greetings to the Iranian people on the occasion of the March 20 Persian new year (Now Ruz). On April 6, he spoke to the Turkish parliament in Ankara of his vision for American relations with Turkey and the Middle East. And on 4 June 2009 he delivered an eloquent address "to the Muslim world" at Al Azhar University in Cairo, promising a new beginning in American policies and relations with the Middle East.

Six months later, a Chinese folk saying came to mind: "A big noise had been heard on the stairs but nobody came down." And some had begun to wonder whether anyone ever would. Still, on October 9, 2009, the Norwegian Nobel Committee announced that it had awarded the 2009 Peace Prize to "President Barack Obama for his extraordinary efforts to strengthen international diplomacy and cooperation between peoples."

When you look back, some years can be seen as having inflected history, moving people and events along paths they would otherwise not have taken; 2001—the year of 9/11—was such a time. This year is shaping up as another, not just for the decisions that will be made but for those that most likely will not be.

1. Remarks delivered to the NCUSAR Arab-U.S. Policymakers Conference. Edited versions of this speech have appeared in both *Middle East Policy* and *The Foreign Service Journal*.

The second President Bush bequeathed his successor a set of thoroughly broken policies in the Middle East and the near-total estrangement of the United States from former allies and friends in the Arab and Muslim worlds. President Obama has responded with rhetorical "change we" —or at least five Norwegians— "can believe in." In his speech at Cairo, he clearly signaled that he recognized the imperative of solving the Israel-Palestine conflict and repairing American relations with Arabs and Muslims if the United States is to enjoy peace abroad and tranquility at home. Still, to date, in the Middle East and elsewhere his administration has made only minimal changes to long-standing American policies that are conspicuous failures. The short-term stakes in getting these policies right are large. The long-term stakes are vastly larger.

When U.S. interrogators asked Khalid Sheikh Mohammed, the confessed mastermind of the 9/11 atrocities, why al-Qaeda had done the terrible things it did that day, he gave a straightforward answer. He said that the purpose was to focus "the American people . . . on the atrocities that America is committing by supporting Israel against the Palestinian people and America's self-serving foreign policy that corrupts Arab governments and leads to further exploitation of the Arab Muslim people." In Osama bin Laden's annual "address to the American people" this September 11, he reiterated: "We have demonstrated and stated many times, for more than two-and-a-half-decades, that the cause of our disagreement with you is your support to your Israeli allies who occupy our land of Palestine."

 There is nothing at all ambiguous or unclear about these explanations of 9/11 by its planners and perpetrators. Few abroad dispute their essential validity. Yet here in America, they remain completely unreported outside the Internet. Any public reference to U.S. backing for Israel as a grievance that motivated the atrocities in New York and Washington eight years ago is vigorously disputed and suppressed as politically incorrect. This has created a large national blind spot to the seriousness of Arab Muslim reaction to a core American policy. It has left our country unable to analyze effectively the very real threat to our domestic tranquility that intermittent terrorist attacks represent. By leaving terrorist attacks on the United States and Americans abroad unexplained and disconnecting them from the trends and events in the Middle East that helped inspire them, this self-imposed mental block has distorted our threat perceptions and greatly hampered the development of a realistic national security strategy.

So it is necessary to begin by recapitulating the obvious. The 9/11 assault on the United States was carried out by Muslim extremists motivated in large measure by their resentment of U.S. support for Israel and its actions. The need to avenge 9/11 and deter a repetition of it led directly to the American invasion of Afghanistan. The so-called global war on terrorism that this invasion inaugurated provided a spurious but politically sufficient justification for the occupation of Iraq in 2003. Our labeling of Hamas as a "terrorist organization" inspired the joint U.S.-Israeli effort to reject and overturn the results of the 2006 elections in the occupied territories, even though these elections were universally judged to be free and fair. A similar view of Hezbollah caused the U.S. to encourage Israel in its savage mauling of Lebanon and to protect it from the huge international backlash against its more recent assault on Arab civilians in Gaza. Determination to avoid another 9/11 remains the strategic rationale for the ongoing war in Afghanistan and adjacent areas of Pakistan. Meanwhile, the insolent cruelties of the West Bank occupation and the siege of Gaza continue to inflame Arab and Muslim opinion.

Taken together, these developments have caused a growing number of Arabs and Muslims to posit a broad American crusade to humiliate them and their religion. Their estrangement from the United States and other non-Islamic societies has deepened. Al-Qaeda has discredited itself through its excesses, but Islamic extremism has continued to metastasize. In Gaza, for example, political forces far more fanatical than Hamas are beginning to emerge from massive suffering. What began as a conflict among Jewish colonists and indigenous Arabs has become a worldwide struggle between Jews, Muslims, and their respective allies. As Israel's sole protector, the United States has become the target of sustained asymmetric warfare by terrorists who espouse extremist Muslim agendas. Governments allied with the United States or dependent on it—especially governments in Arab and Muslim countries—are targets too. The threat we Americans now face derives less from al-Qaeda than it does from widening Muslim rage at continuing humiliation and injustice.

A just and durable peace in the Holy Land that secures the State of Israel should be an end in itself for the United States. But the fact that the conflict there enfevers and radicalizes the Islamic body politic worldwide should make the achievement of such a peace an inescapable, central task of United States strategy. This is why it was right for President Obama to take time this June to deliver a message of reconciliation to Arabs and Muslims in Cairo. Despite all the other urgent tasks before him, he has focused on resolving the Israeli-Palestinian conflict. He has repeatedly expressed determination to stabilize Israel's relations with its Arab neighbors through a "two-state" solution. The Obama administration's initial efforts have, however, met with contemptuous rejection from Israel, feckless dithering from the Palestinians, and skepticism from other Arabs. This should not surprise us. It does not augur well.

The current government of Israel rejects trading land for peace. It sees itself as on the verge of achieving a level of colonization of Palestinian Arab land that will make anything resembling a Palestinian state physically impossible. In the exclusively Jewish state of Israel that its leading figures envisage, only Jews will be full citizens. Some Arabs will have limited rights, but most will live in an archipelago of checkpoint-ringed ghettos. They will be free, should they wish, to call these ghettos a "state" but once they leave Palestine, Israel will not allow them to return. Given this Israeli vision, the American attempt to arrange a settlement freeze so that negotiations can create a Palestinian state is, from the Israeli government point of view, at best an unwelcome distraction and at worst a hostile act. Mr. Netanyahu does not fear pressure from the United States to change course. He is confident that his American lobby will arrange for Congress to punish the president if the president tries to punish Israel for its intransigence.

An Israeli cabinet-directed assassination campaign has long focused on ensuring that "there is no one to talk to" on the Palestinian side. With a little help from their Israeli conquerors and us Americans, surviving Palestinian politicians remain hopelessly divided. Israel has not presented a proposal for peace to the Palestinians. Sadly, if it now did so, there would be no one with the authority to accept on behalf of the Palestinian people. The United States, meanwhile, is seeking to ease Palestinian suffering in ways that improve the political standing of collaborators with the Israeli occupation authorities. Will Palestinian leaders emerge who are willing to take whatever they can get from Israel and who are able somehow to call off the resistance to it? That seems to be the hope, if not the plan. It is not, of course, the trend.

The Obama administration is unwilling, at least for now, to put pressure on Israel. Instead, it has fallen back on the use of diplomacy as psychotherapy for Israel's political pathologies. It is trying to induce better Israeli behavior by arranging Arab gestures that appease Israeli apprehensions and signal Arab acceptance of the Jewish state in their midst even before its borders are fixed or the status of both its captive Arab population and those who fled to the refugee camps in neighboring countries is resolved. American diplomats see these gestures as down payments on the normalization of relations with Israel that the Arab League proposed at Beirut in 2002 in the so-called Arab Peace Initiative. But the Arabs premised their willingness to accept Israel on Israel's reaching an acceptable agreement with the Palestinians. With Israel now neither doing nor promising anything that might lead to an acceptable status for the Palestinians, the Arabs see no reason to appease it. Nor do they any longer feel obliged by friendship to accommodate what they judge to be ill-considered American requests.

Adding poignancy to the impasse are two dreadful ironies. The State of Israel was established to provide the world's Jews with a homeland in which they might safely enjoy the pursuit of happiness free from continuing persecution by Gentiles. But the Jewish state has become the most dangerous place on the planet for Jews to live. And, with anti-Semitism now universally rejected in its traditional Christian heartland, Israel's actions and policies have become the only significant stimulus to anti-Jewish animus there and elsewhere. Meanwhile, the replacement of Zionist idealism, humanism, and secularism with the cynicism, racism, and religiosity of contemporary Israeli politics has precipitated a mounting moral crisis and loss of confidence among many committed to the Jewish state.

Although some settlers continue to arrive, one-fifth of Israelis now reside abroad. Jewish emigration is accelerating. Meanwhile, the Arab population of Israel and the occupied territories continues to grow, as does the size of the Palestinian

Diaspora. By 2015, barring mass deportation, half the people in Israel and the occupied territories will be Arabs. Thereafter, Jews will be a declining minority. The international community, including I daresay most of the Jewish Diaspora, does not accept the settler propositions that Jews can and should—by divine right—entrench their rule over the Arabs of the Holy Land or define them as morally inconvenient and deport them. An anti-apartheid-style campaign of ostracism, boycott, and disinvestment against this version of a Jewish state has already begun.

In combination, current trends portend the perpetuation of violent struggle by the Palestinians against their Israeli overlords, even as the Jewish state is isolated from without and corrodes from within. These trends lead to escalating antagonism between the United States and the Arab and Muslim worlds. Given the self-identification of many Jews with the State of Israel, these trends also risk a rebirth of anti-Semitism and a spillover of violence to the Jewish Diaspora.

So where does this leave the Obama administration's peace project? In Israel's own estimation and that of the region, the Jewish state is at a turning point. Time is running out on the prospects for peaceful engagement among Israel, the Palestinians, other Arabs, and non-Arab Muslims. No peace is conceivable without the full use of American moral and economic leverage to bring Israel to the negotiating table. A decision by the Obama administration to compel Israel to make the choices necessary to achieve mutually respectful coexistence with the Palestinians and other Arabs would, however, lead to immediate political crises in both Israel and the United States. The administration speaks with determination but is it really prepared to risk this? It is too early to say.

Peace with the Palestinians would enable Israel, for the first time, to be accepted by 340 million Arabs and 1.2 billion non-Arab Muslims as a legitimate part of the Middle East. It would end the conflict in the Holy Land. It is the key to de-radicalization of the Arab and Muslim worlds and to ending their violent backlash against the West. It is the prerequisite for the restoration of peace within the realm of Islam.

The alternative is the current Israeli government's effort to impose a Jewish-dominated state dotted with little Arab ghettos. This is a "success" that Israelis would almost certainly come to regret bitterly. Would a Jewish state seen by the world as embodying racism and religious bigotry retain the support of the Jewish Diaspora? Would the United States continue indefinitely to guarantee its security? The safety of such an Israel and its citizens would depend on the so-far undemonstrated ability of intimidation, ruthlessly sustained, to grind Arab resistance into acquiescence. Cairo and Amman would have to be kept within a Camp David framework that Egyptians and Jordanians, if allowed to vote, would even now overwhelmingly repudiate. Israel's right to exist as a state in the Middle East would almost certainly be reviewed in intermittent tests of arms, conducted—as in the case of the Crusader kingdoms in Palestine—over decades, if not centuries. Israel would have to sustain military hegemony in perpetuity over larger, ever more populous and ever more modernized Arab and Muslim neighbors. If these conditions were not met, as they almost certainly could not be, this unilaterally imposed outcome would be an invitation to protracted Arab and Muslim struggle against Israel and its supporters abroad.

It is hard to see this as a formula that leads to anything but eventual disaster for Israel and its foreign backers, now essentially limited to the United States. Israel's nuclear doctrine—based as it is on an amalgam of Armageddon with the heroic suicide at Masada—seems to recognize this. On the whole, for sensible people in Israel and for Americans, the peaceful emergence of a viable Palestinian state in the occupied territories and Gaza looks like a much better bet than self-isolation.

In the meantime, the region presents other challenges—even if none of them has the transformative potential of a peace or continued warfare in the Holy Land. Let me now turn briefly to these.

It is good that the end of the American misadventure in Iraq is in sight. But its termination is not likely to repair the injury it did to the standing of the United States in either the international or Muslim communities. The surge averted disaster; the withdrawal may yet deliver it. The post-occupation order in Iraq is unlikely to emerge smoothly or without further stressing regional stability. In the land between the two rivers, the United States will leave behind a battleground of grievances. The Kurdish and Sunni Arab minorities, among others, must likely undergo still more suffering before things settle down. There will be no harvest of goodwill from the carnage in Iraq.

The same seems likely to be true of our eight-year intervention in Afghanistan. We began it with simple and straightforward goals—the apprehension of al-Qaeda and the chastisement of its Afghan hosts. But these goals have been buried in a barrage of competing ideological and special interest objectives. The result is combat in a political vacuum—a war whose only apparent theme is now Western hostility to militant Islam. This has destabilized Pakistan and nurtured a particularly virulent form of terrorism there and in the Pakistani Diaspora. It has spurred a recent surge in financial contributions to the Taliban as an apparently heroic resistance to infidel trespasses on Islam.

What then to do about Afghanistan, where everyone admits the most likely outcome is now failure? If you ask a religious scholar or ideologue, you will hear a sermon. From an economist, expect a development scheme. Ask a nongovernmental organization, and prepare to receive a program proposal. People come up with the solutions they know how to put together. Ask a general what must be done, and you will get a crisp salute and the best campaign plan military science can devise.

The Obama administration is now pondering yet another military-proposed campaign plan. This one features a pacification effort extending over as much as another decade. But al-Qaeda has relocated to Pakistan from Afghanistan.

Neither the Taliban leadership nor anyone else in Afghanistan seems to want it back. The proposed pacification campaign is called a "strategy" but it is not. It strains to find a military way to transform Afghanistan, even though its authors—who are very smart soldiers—recognize there is none. Our civilian leadership finally shows signs of taking charge of policy rather than, in a strange evasion of civilian control of the military, delegating its formulation to the generals. What we need is a strategy backed by force, not the use of force as a substitute for strategy.

This brings me, at last, to Iran. Tehran had nothing to do with the assault on America on 9/11, but no nation has benefited more from the American reaction to it than the Islamic Republic. Its revolution seemed to be flickering out when 9/11 happened. In short order, its greatest enemy, the United States, then eliminated its other enemies in both Kabul and Baghdad and embarked on a military rampage through the Islamic world that estranged Americans from our traditional allies there. But, wait! It gets even better from the Iranian point of view.

In Afghanistan, the Iranians have been able to sit on the sidelines and watch us exhaust ourselves in inconclusive warfare. In Iraq, Iran is the dominant foreign influence in Iraq's newly sectarian politics. (Of course, no one can say whether Baghdad will continue its de facto alliance with Tehran after the United States withdraws.) Israel and the United States brushed aside efforts by Damascus to dilute its long-standing dependence on Tehran, thus cementing rather than eroding Iran's influence in Syria. The 2006 Israeli savaging of Lebanon drove Iran's client movement, Hezbollah, onto the commanding heights of Lebanese politics. This reduced Tehran's need to go through Damascus to affect events in Lebanon or to reach northern Israel. Israeli and American efforts to ostracize and overthrow the elected Hamas government in Palestine meanwhile left it nowhere to go but into the arms of Iran. Assertively, Shiite Iran has, for the first time, acquired the Sunni Arab following it had long sought. Current American policy seems clueless about how to reverse these Iranian gains.

Meanwhile, Tehran seems on track to acquire the ability to field its own deterrent to the threats of nuclear attack Iranians have serially heard from Saddam's Iraq, successive Israeli governments, and George Bush's America. David Ben Gurion wrote the book on how to build a clandestine nuclear weapons capability. He skillfully appeased President Kennedy's passion for non-proliferation even as his government subverted and circumvented it. The ayatollahs have read and absorbed the Israeli playbook, minus—one hopes—the bit about Masada. Israelis, better than anyone, know how this script ends. It does not end in a war that secures Israel's nuclear monopoly in its region. It is time to start thinking about how to mitigate the undeniable dangers of an Iranian as well as an Israeli nuclear arsenal.

I must not close without a brief mention of the long-standing Arab friends of the United States and the West in the Gulf and Red Sea regions. Despite welcome new activism on the part of Saudi Arabia, Egypt and the countries of the GCC have, to a great extent, been bystanders as a strange combination of American diplomatic default and military activism has dismantled the regional order that once protected them. Iraq no longer balances Iran. The United States no longer constrains Israel, which has never behaved more belligerently. Iran has acquired unprecedented prestige and influence among Arabs and Muslims. The next stage of nuclear proliferation is upon the region. For the first time ever, Shiism dominates the politics of Arab states traditionally ruled by Sunnis. Islamist terrorism menaces Egyptian and Gulf Arab domestic tranquility as well as that of the West. The United States, once attentive to Arab security and other concerns, is now obsessed with our own issues and objectives in the region.

The Gulf Arabs have the financial resources but neither the institutions nor the will to mount the unified effort needed to cope with these challenges. They are adrift; not sailing to a new strategic strong point. The drift is taking them away from their traditional reliance on America and toward new partners. These are mainly the countries of Brazil, Russia, India, and China, plus South Africa. But Egypt and the Gulf Arab states seem destined to remain on the strategic sidelines, not in the game. They will not step forward to take the lead in addressing the disputes of which I have been speaking. Hence, the need for continuing American leadership.

So what is to be done? In the case of Israel-Palestine, a failure to decide is in fact a fateful decision. The avoidance of choice risks future tragedy for America as well as Israel and the Arabs.

The best thing the United States could do for Iraq now is to engage its neighbors. All should share our interest in supporting non-violent Iraqi solutions to Iraqi problems. We need to work with Turkey and Arab allies to enlist Syria, Iran, and others in this task and hold them to it.

In the region as a whole, the American effort to build a coalition of opposition to Iran has failed. We must now join our allies and friends in offering those who have come to depend on Tehran alternatives to doing so. Iran is a proud country that will not surrender to threats. Iranians remain obsessed with the affront they believe we pose to their national identity, independence, and honor among nations. Without a parallel normalization of U.S.-Iranian relations, there is no hope of resolving the nuclear issue in a way that mitigates its menace. President Obama's several messages to the Iranian people have opened a path to respectful Iranian-American dialogue that might lead to this. We must persist in inviting Tehran to walk this path with us.

Finally, in Afghanistan, we need a comprehensive strategy, not another campaign plan. We must leverage religious and tribal realities rather than seek to overturn them. Our objective should be to consolidate the exclusion of al-Qaeda from Afghan territory. To do this, we must work with Pakistan and in partnership with friendly Arab and Muslim countries, not at cross-purposes with them, and we must support, not undercut, the Pashtun tribes. This, not a Western military presence on Afghan soil, is how we helped Afghans expel the Soviets from their homeland. This, ratified by a reconvened Loya Jirga ('Grand Assembly') and supported with generous economic assistance, is how we can keep al-Qaeda out of Afghanistan while we work to expel it from Pakistan.

President Obama's message to the world's Muslims at Cairo last June illuminated a different way forward than the road we appear to be on. We can yet take that way forward. It is time to do so.

PART IV

In Defense of Diplomacy and Intelligence

The American policies in the Middle East that followed 9/11 took a major toll on the international prestige of the United States. That is not without consequence. As Dean Acheson once remarked, "Prestige is a shadow cast by power, which is of great deterrent importance."[1] Prestige is also an ingredient of leadership. In many respects, the American lurch toward a garrison state after 9/11, our abandonment of diplomacy in favor of the use of force, and scofflaw behavior by the U.S. military and intelligence agencies made the United States unattractive. And that cost Americans their international followership.

In the speeches that follow, I explored these trends as they unfolded. This part of the book concludes with some thoughts about intelligence analysis that I delivered shortly after I withdrew my acceptance of the chairmanship of the Obama administration's National Intelligence Council.

---

1. Cited in *The Diplomat's Dictionary* (Washington, D.C.: United States Institute of Peace Press, 2010), p. 181.

Chapter 12

Why Not Let Them Hate Us, As Long as They Fear Us?[1]

October 4, 2006

We are gathered together to reflect upon our country's adoption of Caligula's motto for effective foreign policy—Oderint dum metuant—"Let them hate us, as long as they fear us." As we do so, let us observe a brief moment of silence for the United States Information Agency (USIA) and also for our republic, both of which long stood for a different approach.

Most of you devoted your many years of public service to USIA. I served with the agency twice, once abroad and once at home. I am proud to have been able to join you in making the case for America. I wish to honor and thank you for your service to our country in a time of great peril. Although most of my career was associated with the Department of State, I confess to sadness when USIA was subjected to euthanasia in 1999.

Americans began our independence with an act of public diplomacy, an appeal for international support, based upon a "a decent respect to the opinions of humankind." But 243 years later, we convinced ourselves that—inasmuch as we had won decisive victories over totalitarianism and tyranny, and democracy and the rule of law faced no serious counter arguments anywhere—our history had been fulfilled, and the requirement to explain ourselves to others had ended.

The notion that there was a lessened need for public diplomacy wasn't as foolish as you and other veteran public servants judged at the time. Nor was it as obvious as many others now agree it was.

No country was then more widely admired or emulated than ours. The superior features of our society—our insistence on individual liberty under law; the equality of opportunity we had finally extended to all; the egalitarianism of our prosperity; our openness to ideas, change, and visitors; our generous attention to the development of other nations; our sacrifices to defend small states against larger predators both in the Cold War and, most recently, in the war to liberate Kuwait;

---

1. Remarks to the USIA Alumni Association.

our championship of international order and the institutions we had created to maintain it after World War II; the vigor of our democracy and our dedication to untrammeled debate—were recognized throughout the world. Critics of our past misadventures, as in Vietnam, had been silenced by the spectacle of our demonstrable success. This, our political betters judged, made the effort to explain ourselves, our purposes, and our policies through public diplomacy an unnecessary anachronism. The spread of global media and the Internet, many believed, made official information and cultural programs irrelevant.

Our values were everywhere accepted and advancing, albeit with some lingering resistance in a few out-of-the-way places. Our policies would speak for themselves through the White House and State Department spokesmen. Why not save the money, while simplifying the organization chart?

That was, of course, before we suffered the trauma of 9/11 and underwent the equivalent of a national nervous breakdown. It was before we panicked and decided to construct a national-security state that would protect us from the risks posed by foreign visitors or evil-minded Americans armed with toenail clippers or liquid cosmetics. It was before we decided that policy debate is unpatriotic and realized that the only thing foreigners understand is the use of force. It was before we replaced the dispassionate judgments of our intelligence community with the faith-based analyses of our political leaders. It was before we embraced the spin-driven strategies that have stranded our armed forces in Afghanistan, marched them off to die in the terrorist ambush of Iraq, and multiplied and united our Muslim enemies rather than diminishing and dividing them. It was before we began to throw our values overboard in order to stay on course while evading attack. It was before, in a mere five years, we transformed ourselves from 9/11's object of almost universal sympathy and support into the planet's most despised nation, with its most hateful policies.

You can verify this deplorable reality with polling data, or you can experience it firsthand by traveling abroad. Neither is anything a thoughtful patriot can enjoy. In most Arab and Muslim lands (which include many non-Arab countries in Africa and Asia) the percentage of those who now wish us ill is statistically indistinguishable from unanimity. In many formerly friendly countries in Europe and Latin America, those with a favorable opinion of us are in the low double digits. Polls show that China is almost everywhere more admired than the United States. We used to attract 9 percent of tourists internationally; now we're down to 6 percent. The best and the brightest from around the world came to our universities; now, very often, they go elsewhere. We are steadily losing market share in the global economy.

I will not go on. It is too depressing to do so. Suffice it to say that the atmosphere is such that men like Hugo Chávez Frías and Mahmoud Ahmedinejad felt confident of a warm response to their unprecedentedly anti-American diatribes at the United Nations. And that's what they received. Clearly, we are now more than "misunderestimated," to employ a useful word coined by our president; we are poorly misevaluated and misunderstood abroad.

Here, in our country, there seem to be three reactions to the collapse of our international reputation and the rise in global antipathy to the United States.

Some, many of whom seem to inhabit the bubble universe created by our media as an alternative to the real world, agree with Caligula and the cult of his followers in the administration and on the Hill. They think it's just fine for foreigners to hate us as long as we've got the drop on them and are in a position to string 'em up. They're surprised that "shock and awe" has so far proven to be an inadequate substitute for strategy, but they're eager to try it again and again on the theory that, if force doesn't work the first time, the answer is to apply more force.

Others seem to be in denial. That's the only way I can explain the notion of "transformational diplomacy" coming up at this time. Look, I'm all for the missionary position. But let's face it; it's hard to get it on with foreigners when you've lost your sex appeal. A democracy that stifles debate at home, that picks and chooses which laws it will ignore or respect, and whose opposition party whines but does not oppose, is—I'm sorry to say—not one with much standing to promote democracy abroad. A government that responds to unwelcome election results by supporting efforts to correct them with political assassinations and cluster bombs has even less credibility in this regard. (If democracies don't fight democracies, by the way, what are Gaza and Lebanon all about? But that's another discussion.)

The third reaction is to call for a return to public diplomacy, this time on steroids. This sounds like a good idea, but there are at least a couple of difficulties with it.

The first is that, if there is no private diplomacy, there can be no public diplomacy. And as we all know, Americans no longer do diplomacy ourselves. We are very concerned that, by talking to foreigners with whom we disagree, we might inadvertently suggest that we respect them and are prepared to work with them rather than preparing to bomb them into peaceful coexistence. Both at home and abroad, we respond to critics by stigmatizing and ostracizing them. To avoid sending a signal of reasonableness or willingness to engage in dialogue, we do threats, not diplomacy. That's something we outsource to whomever we can find to take on the morally reprehensible task of conducting it.

Usually, this means entrusting our interests to people we manifestly distrust. Thus, I note, we've outsourced Korea to Beijing even as we arm ourselves against the Chinese; we've outsourced Iran to the French and other fuddy-duddies in the officially cowardly and passé "Old Europe"; and we've outsourced the United Nations to that outspoken international scofflaw, John Bolton, who, despite representing us in Turtle Bay, remains unconfirmable—as well as indescribable in polite company. We can't find anyone dumb enough to take on the Sisyphean task of rolling the Israeli rock up the hill of peace or to step in for us in Iraq so we try to pretend, with respect to both, that the absence of a peace process equates to the absence of a problem. Everything is under control and going just fine.

This brings me to the second difficulty. As our founding fathers understood so well, for public diplomacy to persuade foreigners even to give us and our policies the benefit of the doubt, let alone to support us, we must put on at least the appearance of a decent respect for their opinion. Persuasiveness begins with a reputation for wisdom, probity, and effectiveness but succeeds by showing empathy and concern for the interests of others. Finally, it's easier to make the case for judgments that have some grounding in reality—and for policies that have a plausible prospect of mutually beneficial results—than for those that don't.

I will not dwell on how poorly our current approaches measure up to these standards. Americans are now famous internationally for our ignorance and indifference to the world beyond our borders. We are becoming infamous for our disregard for the fate of foreigners who perish at our hands or from our munitions. Some of our military officers sincerely mourn the civilian Arab deaths caused by their operations and those of the forces with whom we have allied ourselves; there is no evidence that many other Americans are the least bit disturbed by them.

Not content just to let foreigners—Arabs and Muslims, in particular—hate us, we often seem to go out of our way to speak and act in such a way as to compel them to do so. Consider Abu Ghraib, Guantanamo, the practice of kidnapping and "rendition," our public defense of torture, or the spectacle a month or so ago of American officials fending off peace while urging the further maiming of Lebanon and its people. Catastrophically mistaken policies based on intelligence cooked to fit the policy recipe have combined with the debacle of Iraq reconstruction and the bungled response to Hurricane Katrina to discredit American competence with foreign governments and publics alike. It's hard to find anybody out there who believes we know what we're doing or that we have a sound grasp of our own interests, let alone any understanding or concern for theirs. We have given the terrorists what they cannot have dared dream we would—policies and practices that recruit new terrorists but that leave no space for our friends and former admirers to make their case for us or for our values or policies.

This is not, I judge, a propitious atmosphere for public diplomacy. The atmosphere will not improve until the policies do. And what is the prospect of that?

Normally, of course, one would look to elections and the natural alternation of power in a two-party system to produce a change of course. Republicans should be held accountable for what they have done and failed to do, of course. But there is no evidence that bringing the Democrats to power would cure the post-9/11 loss of contact with reality and dysfunctional behavior that account for the fix we are in.

Judging by its record, the so-called opposition party has suffered from the same hallucinations that made us so sure that there were WMDs in Iraq and that there was an urgent need to eliminate them; the same delusional beliefs that foreign occupation—because it was conducted by Americans—would be seen as liberation, that regime removal in Afghanistan and Iraq would result in democratization, and that inside every Arab there is an American struggling to come out; the same disorganized thinking that equates elections to democracy; and the same ruthless impulse to reject and punish the results of democracy when—as in the case of the Palestinian elections this past January—Americans find these results uncongenial.

Neither party is in the least introspective. Both are happy to attribute all our problems to the irrationality of foreigners and to reject consideration of whether our attitudes, concepts, and policies might not have contributed to them. Both are xenophobic, Islamophobic, Arabophobic, and anti-immigrant. The two parties vie to see which can be more sycophantic toward whoever's in charge in Israel and to be most supportive of whatever Israel and its American lobby wish us to do. Neither has a responsible or credible solution to the mess we have created in Iraq, a plan for war termination in Afghanistan, an answer for how to deal with Korean issues, a vision for relations with China or other rising powers, or a promising approach to Iran or the challenge of post-Fidel Cuba, among other issues. (I'll spare you my observations on the default of both parties on addressing the challenges of our budget and balance of payments deficits, decaying pension systems, collapsing health insurance and delivery systems, overcompensation of corporate executives at the expense of both their shareholders and the public interest, and other relevant issues that bear on our national well-being.) Neither party displays any willingness to learn from the successes and errors of foreigners, and both are unjustifiably complacent about our international competitiveness.

Both Republicans and Democrats seem to consider that statecraft boils down to two options: appeasement or sanctions followed by military assault. Both behave as though national security and grand strategy require no more than a military component and as though feeding the military-industrial complex is the only way to secure our nation. Both praise our armed forces, ignore their cavils about excessive reliance on the use of force, count on them to attempt forlorn tasks, lament their sacrifices, and blithely propose still more feckless tasks and ill-considered deployments for them. Together, our two parties are well along in destroying the finest military the world has ever seen.

I fear that, by mincing words as I have, I may have failed to make my high regard for our political parties and their leaders clear. So I will conclude with two brief observations.

The first is that the threat the United States now faces is vastly less grave but much more ill-defined than that we faced during the Cold War. That era, which most here lived through, was one in which decisions by our president and his Soviet counterpart could result in the death, within hours, of more than 100 million Americans and a comparable number of Soviet citizens. That threat was existential. The threat we now face is not. Muslim extremists seek to drive us from their lands by hurting us. They seek neither to destroy us, nor to convert or conquer us. They can in fact do none of these things. The threat we now face does not in any way justify the sacrifice of the civil liberties and related values we earlier defended, against the far greater threats posed by fascism or Soviet communism. Terrorists win if they terrorize; to defeat them, we must reject inordinate fear and the self-destructive things it may make us do.

The second observation is that the answer to the question of whether we can defend ourselves and persuade others to support us as we do so lies first and foremost in our own thoughts and deeds. Muslim extremists cannot destroy us and what we have stood for, but we can surely forfeit our moral convictions and so discredit our values that we destroy ourselves. We have lost international support not because foreigners hate our values but because they believe we are repudiating them and behaving contrary to them. To prevail, we must remember who we are and for what we stand. If we can rediscover and reaffirm the identity and values that made our republic so great, we will find much support abroad, including among those in the Muslim world we now wrongly dismiss as enemies rather than friends.

To rediscover public diplomacy and to practice it successfully, in other words, we must repudiate Caligula's maxim and replace it with our traditional respect for the opinion of mankind. I do not think it is beyond us to do so. We are a far better and more courageous people than we currently appear. But when we do restore ourselves to mental balance, we will, I fear, find that decades are required—it will take decades—to rebuild the appeal and influence our post-9/11 psychoses took a mere five years to destroy. In the process of reaffirming our traditions, as I am confident we shall, Americans may well find a renewed role for an independent agency that can facilitate the projection of our democracy and its values abroad.

Save your Charlie Wick wristwatches.[2] USIA or a reasonable facsimile of it will rise again!

And, in the interim before it does, I look forward to an active debate—not just here but ultimately in the country at large—about how we can more effectively relate to the world beyond our borders. Let the discussion begin!

2. Charles Z. Wick was the director of the USIA throughout the Reagan administration. He had been a pal of the president's in Hollywood, where his most famous film production was *Snow White and the Three Stooges*. An infamous piece of graffiti on the wall of the men's room down the corridor from his office suite proclaimed that "Mickey Mouse wears a Charlie Wick wristwatch."

Chapter 13

National Security in the Age of Terrorism[1]

January 6, 2007

This is not a happy time for national security policy. There is the strategic ambush of Iraq to manage before it explodes into a wider war. North Korea is back to trying to get our attention, and this time it's got missiles and the bomb with which to do so. Iran is well along in replacing us as the dominant influence in the Middle East and is widely believed to be working on a nuclear deterrent to the air raids on it by Israel or us that leaders there and here are threatening. Hamas, which has never run an operation against Americans, and Hezbollah, which hasn't done so for decades, seem to be psyching themselves up to respond in kind to our violent efforts to crush them. The Taliban are making a comeback in Afghanistan, which just brought in the largest poppy harvest in history. The Venezuelans are replacing the Cubans as our adversaries in this hemisphere, and, unlike the Cubans, they've got oil and money to buy allies for their endeavor. China is rising, and the dollar is declining. We have never been so politically estranged from, or so much in debt to, foreigners. Our only committed ally in Europe, Tony Blair, is about to leave office. And this is just a partial list of the problems threatening the general welfare, domestic tranquility, and liberties of Americans.

There's nothing new, of course, about the world being a troublesome place. What is new—as 9/11 showed—is that there is no longer anything much to stop our enemies from coming after us in our homeland. Foreign policy is, therefore, no longer some nasty thing that Americans do to foreigners; it is also something that they can do back to us, sometimes with fatal results.

It's not just that foreign policy has become more important to our national well-being and personal peace of mind. It's that what we do at home also has a much bigger bearing than before, not only on our domestic tranquility, but also on the support we can expect from the rest of the world. What we do at home is now

---

1. Remarks to the Congressional Research Service Seminar for New Members. The audience was 50 newly elected members of Congress and their spouses.

a major factor in determining who's with us and who's against us beyond our borders. Increasingly, as all the polls show, people abroad are against us. Many of our former friends believe we have repudiated the values for which we once stood. Our country has a lot fewer admirers overseas than it used to. But we do, manifestly, have a growing number of enemies. That's not the sort of trade-off we should welcome. And the post—Cold War world in which it is taking place is a great deal less ordered and predictable than the bipolar order that preceded it.

It's not that the dangers we face are greater. They are not. In the Cold War, the turn of a key in Moscow could have brought death to 60 million Americans within minutes or hours and to another 80 million or so within days or weeks. Horrible as a repetition of 9/11—or even a weapon of mass destruction in an American city —would be, we no longer face a threat to our national existence comparable with the one we endured from 1939 to 1989. It will, on reflection, strike any veteran of the Cold War as ironic that, with so much less to be frightened about, we seem so much more fearful than before. But no one can deny that the threats we now face are real. And no politician I've met dares to put them in perspective.

In the earlier and simpler era of the Cold War, the Soviet Union was truly determined both to do us in and to conquer the world, but its leaders tried very hard to prevent its client states and captive political movements from attacking us. They didn't want to be dragged into a nuclear exchange in which all but a few Russians and most Americans would die. But the USSR is gone; no overlord has taken Moscow's place as the leader of those with a reason to hate us. The foreign enemies we make no longer have a patron; they're on their own. So, if we kill foreigners in their homelands, there's no one they care about with a stake in stopping them from trying to kill us in ours. We must do this thankless task ourselves. We must do it by dissolving their motivation to assault us, draining them of their resolve, dissuading them from the path of violence, deterring those who cannot be dissuaded, and killing those who cannot be deterred.

This is the formula the British applied to their long struggle with the various elements of the Irish Republican Army. It is the approach that Saudi Arabia has more recently applied with equal success to the suppression of terrorist opposition to the Saudi monarchy. It requires a sophisticated strategy that supports conservative values against radical assault by discrediting extremist ideology. It demands effective diplomatic and political outreach backed by sound economic and social policies. It asks of us that we understand our enemies and act to divide rather than unite them. It depends on sophisticated intelligence collection, analysis, and law enforcement, backed as needed by the military in ways that do not make more enemies than they eliminate. And it rests on the recognition that we cannot preserve or defend our values and freedoms effectively by setting them aside or curtailing them and becoming more like our enemies than our former selves. We must remain Athens, not Sparta.

The problems we confront in Iraq and on other less central fronts in our confrontation with anti-American terrorists are primarily political, not military. What we lack is not military might but political acumen. Our failings are not those of muscle but of the mind. Our principal policy coordination mechanisms were created in 1947, when Congress overrode President Truman's objections and mandated the formation of a National Security Council (NSC). The NSC system worked fine in the Cold War, which is what it was set up to deal with. But judging purely by results, it has not been able to coordinate responses to the more complex politico-military problems we now confront.

Our current policy coordination system failed to produce a war-termination strategy during its first post–Cold War challenge, when we liberated Kuwait from Saddam's occupation; that war never really ended. Our national command authority failed to set achievable goals and stick to them in Somalia. It was for long ineffectual in coping with Bosnia. It fumbled our response to the open emergence of a nuclear arms race between India and Pakistan. It did not focus our leadership on the challenge of terrorists with global reach until they had actually attacked us. It has defaulted on the search for peace between Israelis, Palestinians, and other Arabs. It has proven unable to set clear objectives or produce a strategy for achieving them in Afghanistan. It has yet to produce anything resembling a coherent strategy for dealing with North Korea or Iran or, for that matter, China, Russia, the European Union, or the United Nations. It has not even tried to address our growing reliance on imports of foreign energy and money to sustain our lifestyle or the effects on our country of the mounting crisis in the global environment. Clearly, with the State and Defense Departments much of the time not even on speaking terms, it bungled the policy coordination role in Iraq and continues to do so. There seems to be a pattern emerging. It is not reducible to convenient partisan dimensions.

This pattern of incompetence has cost us our international followership. To lead a team, you must know how to be a team player. To inspire people or nations to follow you, you must have a reputation for moral uprightness, wisdom, and veracity. To retain authority, you must demonstrate the capacity to reward as well as to punish, and you have to rack up a record of success. To sustain the loyalty of your followers, you must be loyal to them and considerate of their views and interests as well as your own. To hold other people or nations to rules, you must show that you are prepared to follow them too. We all know these things. Why don't we act accordingly?

Part of the reason you were elected is that Americans perceive that we are no longer seen as exemplifying the characteristics of leadership I have just cited as we traditionally did. Most citizens believe that the way we now deal with national security issues has made the United States—as well as the rest of the world—less, rather than more, safe. Nearly eight in ten respondents in one recent survey thought the world saw the United States as "arrogant," and nearly 90 percent said such negative perceptions threaten national security. They're right to be concerned.

The reaction to the next major terrorist attack on the United States will not resemble the outpouring of sympathy and support that followed 9/11. Our recovery from our strategic debacle in the Middle East will not be as rapid or sure as our recovery from defeat in Vietnam. There's no common enemy, no Soviet Union, to compel our allies and friends to stick with us.

It would be comforting but wrong to blame most of these problems on the executive branch; but Congress bears considerable responsibility as well. Not only has it largely defaulted on its foreign policy oversight role in recent years, but its resistance to the reorganization of committee jurisdictions has made it impossible for Congress even to study how to reorganize the executive branch, let alone to do it. It would, I think, make sense for Congress and the executive branch to begin this year jointly to consider how to enable the government to develop the more sophisticated policy coordination that today's more complex problems demand.

The way we put things together now does not always make sense. Given the topic you've asked me to address, let me cite the example of our spending on military and related functions. We put much more effort into national defense and security than most people realize. In fiscal 2006, our defense budget was $441.5 billion. This was a good bit more than the combined military spending of the world's other 192 countries. It amounted to 3.6 percent or so of our economy—which is, by a wide margin, still the largest on the planet.

But—huge as it is—the defense budget is only part of what we spend on past, present, and future wars. When we estimate military expenditures in countries like China, we quite appropriately include a lot of defense-related expenditures that are outside the official defense budget. If we were to apply the same standard to figuring out our own military spending, we would have to add to our defense budget the supplementals to pay for the wars in Afghanistan and Iraq, the nuclear weapons and naval propulsion systems in the Department of Energy budget, veterans programs in the Veterans Administration budget, military pensions funded by the Treasury, homeland security programs, various intelligence activities, and so forth. And we would find that, even without including interest on the money we borrow to fund it, our total national defense effort comes in at around $720 billion, or about 5.7 percent of GDP. You might want to see if the Congressional Research Service can come up with a precise figure for how much we actually put into military and military-related programs and activities. No one else has been able to do this. It's worth asking, too, whether scattering national security-related expenditures all over the federal budget in such a way that no one can tell you how much we spend on them is the best way to avoid redundancy and get the biggest bang for the buck.

At any rate, all this spending has given us what are, without doubt, the most competent and lethal armed forces in history, and that's a very commendable result. But, as President Eisenhower foretold, we have also built a truly enormous and very influential military-industrial complex. You already know—or will shortly find out—how effectively defense contractors interact with Congress. I don't intend to go farther into a subject on which many here are or will shortly become far more expert than I, but I can't help bringing to your attention the newest, highly instructive example of how national security policy is made.

In summer 2003, the newly established Department of Homeland Security drew up a list of 160 sites in our country that terrorists might see as targets. Intense efforts by your constituents and others to gain access to this new source of federal funding immediately led to the widening of the definition of potential targets. Within a few months, there were 1,849 targets. By the end of 2004, there were 28,360. Today, bearded terrorists in the remote caves of Waziristan are officially feared to be planning attacks on about 300,000 targets all over our country, including—I was truly shocked and awed to learn—the Indiana Apple and Pork Festival. (I'm sure they lose a lot of sleep in Waziristan over that one.)

Evidently, our system is extraordinarily good at funding military and related functions as well as at finding ways to spread money around, but one is left to wonder whether it is optimally designed to cope with the challenges to our security and domestic tranquility in the 21st century. Clearly, too, our political culture is good at enacting sanctions and launching wars when sanctions fail, as they inevitably do, but is it competent at dealing with the challenges we now face? These aren't trivial questions.

You are politicians and, therefore, experts in both the arts of persuasion and the aggregation of political power to produce results. I want to ask you all, as experts in these things, a serious question. Why do we Americans think we should suspend common sense when we deal with foreigners? Why do we imagine that our differences with foreign miscreants require techniques of influence that we would never apply to people here? What is it in our experience that causes us to suppose that trying to put them out of business, pulling a gun on them, beating them up, or blowing up part of their property will cause them to repent and be saved, to mend their evil ways, and to embrace truth, justice, and the American way? Do we really think that public insults and a refusal to meet or talk with people with whom we disagree are the best way to persuade them to embrace our viewpoint? Do we truly believe that politely explaining to foreign leaders that what they are doing is both wrong and not in their interest is a sign of weakness? Would we reason the same way about Americans with whom we disagree? Do we judge that ostracism and beatings are the best way to teach even dogs and children to behave, let alone hostile adults? If not, why do we allow those who appear to believe these absurd things bully those who don't into silence?

Al Capone, who was as American as the Colt revolver, once remarked that: "you will get more with a kind word and a gun than with a kind word alone." True enough, but why omit the kind word? And do we want to be seen as the heirs of Al Capone in our approach to the world?

Of course, talking is better than not talking only if you know what you're trying to accomplish and what you're going to say. And there's a reason that the use of force is generally regarded as a last resort; if you use it up front and it fails, diplomacy can't do much to rectify the facts you've created on the ground. So we're back to the need to formulate strategies, set objectives, and stick to them. We're going to need that capacity more than ever over the years to come. Here are a few items that pretty clearly need tending. The first three are so obvious that I'm almost embarrassed to mention them in this well-informed company.

The Middle East. As the Baker-Hamilton Iraq Study Group pointed out, there's more to the Middle East than just Iraq and the region needs to be addressed as a whole. In Iraq, the options are all bad and not improving. They seem to boil down to "talk and walk," as recommended by the Study Group; "cut and run," as many here tonight might prefer; or "surge and scourge," as the neoconservatives are trying to persuade the Decider2 to decide, despite much military advice to the contrary. Who knows whether anything at all can work at this point? What's clear is that our occupation is in deepening difficulty. The conflict in Iraq is in real danger of triggering a wider war even as it continues to spawn a new generation of anti-American terrorists. There is mounting reason for concern about an assault on the "green zone" modeled, perhaps, on the Tet Offensive in Vietnam.

Meanwhile, Iran continues to gain regional influence and to work at bomb-building; there's still no peace process; Israel is back at settlement-building and trying to bomb Palestinians into peaceful coexistence with it; no Arab leader wants a photo op with us; Lebanon has been ravaged and destabilized; the Turks and Kurds are eying each other with mounting belligerence; there are all sorts of rumors of covert action programs directed at regime change in Syria and plans to bomb whatever nuclear-related targets we can find in Iran; and the Saudis and other Gulf Arabs are for the first time openly denouncing U.S. policy. If that's not an explosive mixture, I don't know what is. It is certainly the stuff of which terrorism is born.

Afghanistan. We have made the country safe for the poppy cultivators and warlords but not for democracy. A well-focused effort to capture the perpetrators of 9/11, punish their hosts, and deter others from hosting them has deteriorated into an aimless effort at pacification. This has endowed the Taliban with nationalist credentials they do not deserve. Meanwhile, in the broader Islamic world, Afghanistan is now seen as evidence of a broad American-led assault by the West on all Muslims. No one can say what victory in Afghanistan would look like for us. This is an unfolding tragedy that needs a rethink.

North Korea. Anyone who's had a kid that went through the "terrible twos" will have no difficulty recognizing Kim Jong-Il's effort to gain attention for what it is. Outsourcing diplomacy to China isn't an effective response to this. We are now in the lull before the next tantrum, which will likely be pretty provocative—even unnerving—and involve missiles, shooting incidents, or further nuclear blasts.

2. President George W. Bush, who was known for coining neologisms, had famously referred to himself as "the Decider."

And now, rather than attempt a comprehensive list of the challenges we face, let me briefly mention three other issues of concern, each of which illustrates the interconnectedness of domestic and foreign affairs.

The Dollar. Every day, we must persuade foreigners to lend us more than $2 billion so that we can keep our government in business, our interest rates low, and our employment rate high. So far we've been able to talk them into this. But, as someone famously once said, if something can't go on forever, sooner or later it will end. Foreign willingness to lend money to us at advantageous interest rates could end at any time.

If we let things get to the point where foreign lenders pull the plug on us, we will face interest charges at levels not seen since the 1970s. The housing and stock markets will implode, the price of everything from oil to laptops will skyrocket, and there will be a sharp rise in unemployment. In addition to screwing up our domestic economy and politics, a dollar collapse would displace us from the center of the global economy and catalyze a major, highly unfavorable shift in the balance of power. It's the sort of national security development that is worth trying hard to prevent. To do so, we need to get our act back together at home.

U.S. Complacency. Americans are used to embodying superlatives; being the biggest and the best at almost everything. But it's hard to be proud that we are recognized abroad as the world's largest debtor, its biggest market for illegal narcotics, its most prolific producer of pornography, and its most profligate consumer of imported energy. Concerned foreigners also know that we have the world's highest divorce rate, the biggest proportion of our adult population in prison, and the most elevated rate of infant mortality in the developed world. And they see that we're not necessarily the best any more in every field. The World Health Organization ranks our health care system 37th in the world in overall quality, on a par with Cuba's. Graduates of our high schools believe they are in the 90th percentile internationally but are actually in the 10th. I could cite other examples but that would be too depressing. So I'll just reiterate the obvious. We have a lot of issues to deal with at home as well as abroad.

As a result of the growing gap between our smug self-image and the way people overseas perceive us, we're neither as attractive to the rest of the world nor as sought after as we once were. This shows up clearly in polling data but an additional measure of it is that, despite the fall in the dollar, fewer highly educated and wealthy foreigners want to come here. There is a diminished foreign student presence here even as the foreign student population in Europe, Japan, China, Australia, New Zealand, and Canada is growing dramatically. There's a lot of anecdotal evidence to suggest that we are no longer attracting the very best. Meanwhile, our share of the global tourism market has fallen from nine percent at the turn of the century to less than six percent today.

Complacency is the enemy of excellence. We appear to have a bad case of it. We need to recover from it.

American Competitiveness. Only 15 percent of our college students graduate in science and technology. In China, the figure is 50 percent. Traditionally, we've made up our shortage of brains by importing them. The geek may yet inherit the Earth, but post–9/11 they won't do it from here because they can't get visas to do it. As a result, our graduate schools are now short of teaching assistants and our labs are short of engineers. Our companies are responding by moving their research and development and other high-technology operations to China and India. In part for this reason, New York has fallen to number three, behind Hong Kong and London, in the number of initial public offerings (IPOs) by new companies.

These are microcosms of a much larger issue. Our exceptional openness to ideas and to people was what enabled us to lead the global advance of science and technology and to build an unprecedentedly innovative society. Now we are much less welcoming. If we don't do something about this trend, we are in danger of losing our economic leadership as well as our political leadership of the world. That need not be; we must not let it come to pass.

Let me conclude.

We all grew up in an America that acknowledged its flaws but that was justly admired and respected internationally. Our country then led with the force of its example rather than by the power of its armed forces. I lament the unnecessary passing of that appealingly introspective America. I suppose that brands me too as passé; I admit to being a geezer. But I remain hopeful that I will once again be part of a nation made attractive by its principles, wise by its experience, shrewd by its realism, and prudent by its modesty. Such an America, proficient at arms and the arts of persuasion alike, would again have the world's support, not its animosity. Such an America could hope successfully to manage the challenges of national security in the age of terrorism.

You, who have just taken office, can help America be born again. I congratulate you even as I envy you that opportunity. And I am grateful to have had the opportunity to speak with you. Thank you for your attention.

Chapter 14

Empire without Diplomacy[1]

February 9, 2007

In 1941, as the United States sat out the wars then raging in both the Atlantic and Pacific, Henry Luce penned a famous attack on isolationism in LIFE magazine. "We Americans are unhappy," he began. "We are not happy about America. We are not happy about ourselves in relation to America. We are nervous—or gloomy—or apathetic." Luce argued that the destiny of the United States demanded that "the most powerful and vital nation in the world" step up to the international stage and assume the position of global leader. "The 20th century must be to a significant degree an American century," he declared.

And so it proved to be, as the United States led the world to victory over fascism, created a new world order mimicking the rule of law and parliamentary institutions internationally, altered the human condition with a dazzling array of new technologies, fostered global opening and reform, contained and outlasted communism, and saw the apparent triumph of democratic ideals over their alternatives. But that 20th century came to an end in 1989, with the fall of the Berlin Wall, the end of the Cold War, and the emergence of the United States as a great power without a peer. There followed a dozen intercalary years of narcissistic confusion. Americans celebrated our unrivaled military power and proclaimed ourselves "the indispensable nation" but failed to define a coherent vision of a post–Cold War order or an inspiring role for the United States within it. These essential tasks were deferred to the 21st century, which finally began in late 2001, with the shock and awe of 9/11. Then, in the panic and rage of that moment, we made the choices about our world role we had earlier declined to make.

Since 9/11 Americans have chosen to stake our domestic tranquility and the preservation of our liberties on our ability—under our commander-in-chief—to rule the world by force of arms rather than to lead, as we had in the past, by the force of our example or our arguments. And we appear to have decided that it is necessary to destroy our constitutional practices and civil liberties in order to save them. This is a trade-off we had resolutely refused to make during our far more perilous half-

1. Remarks to Diplomats and Consular Officers, Retired.

century confrontation with Nazi Germany, Imperial Japan, and the Soviet Union.

There is unfortunate historical precedent for this, as the author Robert Harris reminded us last year. In the autumn of 68 B.C., a vicious league of pirates set Rome's port at Ostia on fire, destroyed the consular war fleet, and kidnapped two prominent senators, together with their bodyguards and staff. Rome panicked. Mr. Harris comments that: "What Rome was facing was a threat very different from that posed by a conventional enemy. These pirates were a new type of ruthless foe, with no government to represent them and no treaties to bind them. Their bases were not confined to a single state. They had no unified system of command. They were a worldwide pestilence, a parasite which needed to be stamped out, otherwise Rome—despite her overwhelming military superiority—would never again know security or peace." In response to these imagined menaces, Pompey (self-styled "the Great") persuaded a compliant Senate to set aside nearly 700 years of Roman constitutional law, abridge the ancient rights and liberties of Roman citizens, and appoint him supreme commander of the armed forces. With due allowance for a bit of pointed reinterpretation, if not revisionism by Mr. Harris, most historians regard this incident and its aftermath as the beginning of the end of the Roman republic.

The ultimate effects on our republic of our own slide away from long-standing constitutional norms remain a matter of speculation. But, clearly, our departure from our previous dedication to the principles of comity and the rule of law has made us, once again, unhappy about ourselves in relation to America and the world. It has also cost us the esteem that once led foreigners to look up to us and to wish to emulate and follow us. Our ability to recover from the damage we have done to ourselves and our leadership is further impeded by the extent to which we now cower behind barricades at home and in our embassies abroad. The current wave of anti-foreign and anti-Islamic sentiment in the United States further compounds the problem. A recent poll of foreign travelers showed that two-thirds considered the United States the most disagreeably unwelcoming country to visit. There is surely no security to be found in surly discourtesy.

To fail to welcome the world's peoples to our shores is not simply to lose the economic benefits of their presence here but greatly to diminish both the vigor of our universities and the extent of our influence abroad. To lose the favor of a generation of students is to forfeit the goodwill of their children and grandchildren as well. And to fail to show respect to allies and friends is not simply to diminish our influence but to predispose growing numbers abroad to disapprove or even oppose anything we advocate. By all this, we give aid and comfort to our enemies and undercut the efficacy in dispute resolution and problem solving of measures short of war.

There has been little room for such measures—for diplomacy—in the coercive and militaristic approach we have recently applied to our foreign relations. Much of the world now sees us as its greatest bully, not its greatest hope. Self-righteous lawlessness by the world's most powerful nation inspires illegality and amorality on the part of the less powerful as well. The result of aggressive unilateralism has been to separate us from our allies, to alienate us from our friends, to embolden our detractors, to create irresistible opportunities for our adversaries and competitors, to inflate the ranks of our enemies, and to resurrect the notion—at the expense of international law and order—that might makes right. Thus, the neglect of both common courtesy and diplomacy fosters violent opposition to our global preeminence in the form of terrorism, nuclear proliferation, and war.

With the numbers of our enemies mounting, it is fortunate that our military power remains without match. The U.S. armed forces are the most competent and lethal in history. And so they are likely to remain for decades to come. Our humbling on the battlegrounds of the Middle East does not reflect military inadequacy; it is, rather, the result of the absence of strategy and its political handmaiden, diplomacy. We are learning the hard way that old allies will not aid us and new allies will not stick with us if we ignore their interests, deride their advice, impugn their motives, and denigrate their capabilities. Friends will not walk with us into either danger or opportunity if we injure their interests and brush aside their objections to our doing so. Those with whom we have professed friendship in the past cannot sustain their receptivity to our counsel if we demand that they adopt secular norms of the European Enlightenment that we no longer exemplify, while loudly disparaging their religious beliefs and traditions. Diplomacy-free foreign policy does not work any better than strategy-free warfare.

When war is not the extension of policy but the entrenchment of policy failure by other means, it easily degenerates into mindless belligerence and death without meaning. Appealing as explosions and the havoc of war may be to those who have experienced them only vicariously rather than in person, military success is not measured in battle damage but in political results. These must be secured by diplomacy.

The common view in our country that diplomacy halts when war begins is thus worse than wrong; it is catastrophically misguided. Diplomacy and war are not alternatives; they are essential partners. Diplomacy unbacked by force can be ineffectual, but force unassisted by diplomacy is almost invariably unproductive. There is a reason that diplomacy precedes war and that the use of force is a last resort. If diplomacy fails to produce results, war can sometimes lay a basis for diplomats to achieve them. When force fails to attain its intended results, diplomacy and other measures short of war can seldom accomplish them.

We properly demand that our soldiers prepare for the worst. As they do so, our leaders should work to ensure that the worst does not happen. They must build and sustain international relationships and approaches that can solve problems without loss of life and pave the way for a better future. If we must go to war, the brave men and women who engage in combat on our behalf have the right to expect that their leaders will direct diplomats to consolidate the victories they achieve, mitigate the defeats they suffer, and contrive a better peace to follow their fighting. Our military personnel deserve, in short, to be treated as something more than the disposable instruments of unilateral belligerence. And our diplomats deserve to be treated as something more than the clean-up squad in fancy dress.

Every death or crippling of an American on the battlefields of the Middle East is a poignant reminder that, in the absence of diplomacy, the sacrifices of our soldiers, sailors, airmen, and marines, however heroic, can neither yield victory nor sustain hegemony for the United States. A diplomatic strategy is needed to give our military operations persuasive political purposes, to aggregate the power of allies to our cause, to transform our battlefield successes into peace, and to reconcile the defeated to their humiliation. Sadly, our neglect of these tasks, as in Iraq and Afghanistan, has served to demonstrate the limits of our military power, not its deterrent value. This is, however, far from the greatest irony of our current predicaments.

In the competition with other nations for influence, America's comparative advantages have been, and remain, our unmatched military capabilities, our economy, and our leading role in scientific and technological innovation. We spend much, much more on our military—about 5.7 percent of our economy or $720 billion at present—than the rest of the world's other 192 nations combined. With less than a twentieth of the world's population, we account for more than a fourth of its economic activity. Almost two-thirds of central bank reserves worldwide are held in our currency, the dollar—which, much to our advantage, has dominated international financial markets for 60 years. The openness of our society to new people and ideas has made our country the greatest crucible of global technological innovation.

The moral argument put forward by both left- and right-wing proponents of aggressive American unilateralism is that, as a nation with these unexampled elements of power and uniquely admired virtues, the United States has the duty both to lead the world and to remake it in our image. But our recent confusion of command and control with leadership and conflation of autocratic dictation with consultation have stimulated ever greater resistance internationally. Thus, the aggressive unilateralism by which we have sought to consolidate our domination of world affairs has very effectively undermined both our dominion over them and our capacity to lead.

The most obvious example of this has been our inability, despite the absolute military superiority we enjoy, to impose our will on terrorists with global reach, on the several battlegrounds of the Middle East, or on Iran or North Korea. But, in many respects, these illustrations of the impotence of military power are far from the most worrisome examples of policy backfire. After all, despite all the lurid domestic rhetoric about it and the real pain it can inflict, terrorism poses no existential threat to our country—except, of course, to the extent we betray American values in the name of preserving them. The more worrisome examples are the mounting effects of unrelentingly coercive foreign policies on our political credibility, economic standing, and competitiveness.

As distaste has succeeded esteem for us in the international community, we have become ever more isolated. Our ability to rally others behind our causes has withered. We have responded by abandoning the effort to lead. We are now known internationally more for our recalcitrance than our vision. We have sought to exempt ourselves from the jurisdiction of international law. We have suspended our efforts to lead the world to further liberalization of trade and investment through the Doha Round. We no longer participate in the UN body charged with the global promotion of human rights. We decline to discuss global climate change, nuclear disarmament, or the avoidance of arms races in outer space. If we have proposals for a world more congenial to the values we espouse, we no longer articulate them. The world is a much less promising place for our silence and absence.

Our recent record in the Middle East alone includes the six-year suspension of efforts to broker peace between Israelis and Palestinians and a seeming shift from the pursuit of al-Qaeda to the suppression of Islamism in Afghanistan. Although we seem belatedly to be improving, we have become notorious for delusory or self-serving assertions masquerading as intelligence assessments. Our disregard for treaties abroad and the rule of law at home is leading to the indictment of our operatives abroad by our closest allies. Our scofflaw behavior thus undercuts transnational cooperation against terrorists. The bloody consequences of our occupation of Iraq for its inhabitants are too well known to require mention. We continue to provide military support and political cover for Israeli operations entailing intermittent massacres of civilian populations in Lebanon and Gaza. We sit on our hands while wringing them over parallel outrages in Darfur. We are indifferent to the views of our friends and refuse to speak with our enemies.

Taken together, these acts of omission and commission have devastated American standing and influence, not just in the Middle East but more widely. There are examples of such policy backfires to be found in every region; I will not cite them to this audience. You've read the polls. You've heard the speeches at the United Nations and the applause with which they were received. You know how difficult it now is for us to obtain support from the international community and how often we need to exercise our veto in the UN Security Council. The point is this: every leader needs followers; with rare exceptions, we have lost or are losing ours. And even a superpower needs political partners.

This is true for the economic arena as well. Our ability to do business with others in our own currency has been a unique aspect of our global economic power. But our budget, trade, and balance of payments deficits have grown to levels at which some foreigners now have more dollars than they know what to do with. The value of our currency has come to depend on central bankers continuing to play a reverse game of chicken, in which they nervously hang onto dollars while watching each other to make sure that no one can bail out without the others' noticing and dumping the dollar too. No central bank wants to be the first to devalue its own and everyone else's dollar-denominated reserves. So every day, Arab, Chinese, Japanese, Korean, and Russian officials as well as assorted gnomes in the "Old Europe" lend our Treasury the $2.5 billion it needs to keep employment here up, interest rates down, and the economy growing.

Unlike central bankers, however, businesses and private investors are notorious-ly bad at "coordination games." They are not willing to wait for the dollar to approach collapse before getting out of it and into other currencies and places. As a result, there are now many more euros in circulation than dollars. The euro has displaced the dollar as the preeminent currency in international bond markets. In a few years, the Chinese yuan will clearly join it in this role. Hong Kong and London have overtaken New York in IPOs. The regulatory environment in our country, including the expensive annoyances of Sarbanes-Oxley and class-action suits, does indeed, as New York Senator Charles Schumer has claimed, have some-thing to do with this. But an equally important factor is our increasingly frequent resort to unilateral sanctions and asset freezes based on assertions of extraterrito-rial jurisdiction over the dollar.

Over the past decade, we have adopted unilateral sanctions against some 95 countries and territories. Most recently, we have worked hard to shut down banking in the occupied territories of Palestine, severely curtail it in Iran, and prevent the use of the dollar in Sudan's oil trade. The nobility of our motives in each case is not the issue. But, if we assert the right to confiscate dollar-denominated wealth and to do without due process or legal recourse and remedy, it should not surprise us that people begin looking for ways to avoid the use of our currency. There is now an active search on the part of a growing number of foreign financial institutions for ways to avoid the dollar, bank-clearance procedures that touch New York, or trans-actions with U.S.-based financial institutions. Adding oil traders to the list of the dollar-averse increases the incentives for them to find alternatives to our currency.

Our ill-considered abuse of our financial power may thus have put us on the path to losing it. The dollar accounts for much of our weight in global affairs. American investors are now increasingly hedging the dollar and going heavily into non–dollar-denominated foreign equities and debt.

You would think that growing disquiet about American financial overextension would impel our government to make a major effort to boost our exports to rapid-ly growing markets like China. Our exports are in fact growing. But our govern-ment's present policy focus, judging from its hiring patterns, is not export promo-tion but an attempt to block exports of scientific knowledge and technology to China and other potential rivals. Export controllers want to require export licenses for foreign graduate students and researchers in our universities and to compel U.S. companies to conduct detailed due diligence on prospective foreign purchasers of their goods and services. These initiatives reflect the mood of national paranoia and the concomitant growth of a secrecy-obsessed garrison state that have made Osama bin Laden the greatest creator of federal employment since Franklin Delano Roosevelt. They encourage would-be customers to buy un-American.

Along with unwelcoming visa and immigration policies, such export-suppressive measures are a small part of a much broader assault on the openness of our society. The increasing restriction of American intercourse with foreigners encourages the outsourcing not just of jobs but of innovation in science and technology, research and development, engineering and design services, and industrial production. Xenophobic policies and practices have begun to erode the long-standing American scientific and technological superiority they were intended to protect. Like economic protectionism, intellectual protectionism, it turns out, weakens—not strengthens—a nation and makes it less rather than more competitive in the global marketplace.

The last half of the 20th century was, as Henry Luce had hoped, in many ways an American century. We became the preeminent society on the planet not by force of arms but by the power of our principles and the attraction of our example. The effort to replace that preeminence with military dominion is failing badly. There will be no American imperium. The effort to bully the world into accepting one has instead set in motion trends that threaten both the core values of our republic and the prospects for a world order based on something other than the law of the jungle. Militarism is not an effective substitute for diplomacy in persuading other peoples to do things one's way. Coercive measures are off-putting, not the basis for productive relationships with foreign nations. Other peoples' money can provide an excuse for continued self-indulgence; it is not a sound foundation for economic leadership. Obsessive secrecy is incompatible with innovation. Fear of foreigners and rule by cover-your-ass securocrats is a combination that breeds weakness, not strength.

More than anything now, we need to get a grip on ourselves. 9/11 was almost five and a half years ago. There has been no follow-up attack on our homeland. We are far from Waziristan and al-Qaeda's leaders are obsessed with matching, if not exceeding, their previous standard of iconic success, something even much more talented terrorists than they would find it hard to do. Perhaps, in time, they will succeed but our nation will endure. Meanwhile, al-Qaeda's associates elsewhere have felt no such operational constraints, especially in Europe. Yet, despite all the bombings there by homegrown and al-Qaeda-affiliated terrorists, government offices in Europe are still accessible to the public, security measures at transportation nodes are respectfully efficient, the rule of law continues to prevail, and the rights of citizens remain intact.

The contrast with the situation here underscores the extent to which al-Qaeda has achieved its central objectives. It has unhinged America and alienated us from the world. We are apparently willing to sacrifice everything, including the blessings of liberty for ourselves and our posterity, to achieve absolute security from risks that others rightly consider nasty but manageable. Quite aside from the fact that absolute security is absolutely impossible, this is not who we were. It is not who most of us want to be.

America defines itself by its values, not its territory or ethnicity. The supreme purpose of our foreign policy must be to defend our values and to do so by means that do not corrode them. By these measures, what we are doing now is directly counterproductive. It must be changed. Let me very briefly propose a few principles to guide such change.

First, an America driven by dread and delusion into the construction of a garrison state, ruled by a presidency claiming inherent powers rather than by our constitution and our laws, is an America that can be counted upon to respect neither the freedoms of its own people nor those of others. The key to the defense of both the United States and the freedom that defines us as a great nation is to retain our rights and cultivate our liberties, not to yield them to our government, and to honor and defend, not to invade, the sovereignty of other nations and individuals.

Second, it is time to recognize that freedom spreads by example and a helping hand to those who seek it. It cannot be imposed on others by coercive means, no matter how much shock and awe these elicit. Neither can it be installed by diatribe and denunciation, or proclaimed from the false security of fortified buildings. We must come home to our traditions, restore the openness of our society, and resume our role as "the well-wisher to the freedom and independence of all ... [but] the champion and vindicator only of our own," to paraphrase John Quincy Adams.

Third, credibility is not enhanced by persistence in counterproductive policies, no matter how much one has already invested in them. The reinforcement of failure is a poor substitute for its correction. Doing more of the same does not make bad strategy sound or snatch successful outcomes from wars of attrition. All it does is convince onlookers that one is so stubbornly foolish that one is not afraid to die. Admitting that mistakes have been made and taking remedial action generally does more for credibility than soldiering blindly on. The United States needs big course corrections on quite a range of foreign and domestic policies at present.

Fourth, we must recover the habit of listening and curb our propensity to harangue. We might, in fact, consider a war on arrogance to complement our war on terror. And to demonstrate my own humility as well as my respect for the limited attention span of any audience after lunch, even one as polite and attentive as you have been, I shall now conclude.

Guantanamo, Abu Ghraib, the thuggish kidnappings of "extraordinary rendition," the Jersey barrier, and an exceptional aptitude for electronic eavesdropping cannot be allowed permanently to displace the Statue of Liberty and a reputation for aspiration to higher standards as the symbols of America to the world. To regain both our self-respect and our power to persuade rather than coerce the world, we must restore our aspiration to distinguish our country not by the might of its armed forces but by its civility and devotion to liberty. The best way to assure the power to cope with emergencies is to refrain from the abuse of power in ordinary times.

All the world would still follow America, if they could find it. We must rediscover it to them. That, not bullying behavior or a futile effort at imperial dominion, is the surest path to security for Americans.

Chapter 15

Can American Leadership Be Restored?[1]

May 24, 2007

The audience was retired diplomats and intelligence officials. Eighteen months later, in late 2008, the onset of the Great Recession would cause some of the problems of world order I discussed back in May 2007 to become hard to continue to ignore. Other problems that I mentioned then also seem now, in mid-2010, to be on their way to wider recognition.

When our descendants look back on the end of the 20th century and the beginning of this one, they will be puzzled. The end of the Cold War relieved Americans of almost all international anxieties. It left us free to use our unparalleled economic power, military might, and cultural appeal to craft a world to our liking. We did not rise to the occasion. Still, almost the whole world stood with us after 9/11.

There is still no rival to our power, but almost no one abroad now wants to follow our lead and our ability to shape events has been greatly—perhaps irreparably—enfeebled. In less than a decade, we have discredited our capacity to enlist others in defending our interests and forfeited our moral authority as the natural leader of the global community. There is no need for me to outline to this expert audience the many respects in which our prestige and influence are now diminished. Historians will surely wonder: How did this happen?

How our global leadership collapsed is, of course, a question our politicians now evade as politically incorrect. It's also a very good question and really deserves an answer. I don't plan to try to give you one. Why deprive our posterity of all the fun of puzzling one out?

We are engaged in a war, a global war on terrorism—a long war, we are told. It is somehow more dangerous than the Cold War was, we are warned. So, to preserve

1. Remarks to the Washington Institute of Foreign Affairs.

our democracy, we must now refrain from exercising it. And, to keep our ancient liberties, we must now curtail them. These propositions may strike some here as slightly illogical, but I beg you not to say so—especially if you have a security clearance and want to keep it or are interested in a job in this or a future administration. To many now in power in Washington and in much of the country, it remains perilously unpatriotic to ask why we were struck on 9/11, or who we're fighting, or whether attempting forcibly to pacify various parts of the realm of Islam will reduce the number of our enemies or increase them.

So we're in a war whose origins it is taboo to examine, as the only presidential candidate of either party to attempt to do so, Ron Paul, so was reminded in a debate with his fellow Republicans just last week. And this is a war whose proponents assert that it must—and will—continue without end. If we accept their premises, they are right. How can a war with no defined ends beyond the avoidance of retreat ever reach a convenient stopping point? How can we win a war with an enemy so ill understood that we must invent a nonexistent ideology of "Islamofascism" for it? How can we mobilize our people to conduct a long-term struggle with a violent movement once they realize that its objective is not to conquer us but to persuade us to stay home, leaving its part of the world to decide on its own what religious doctrine should govern its societies? And how can a war with no clear objectives ever accomplish its mission and end?

The answer is that no matter how many Afghans and Arabs we kill or lock up in Guantanamo it can't and it won't. The sooner we admit this and get on with the task of reducing the war to manageable proportions, the less we will compound the damage to ourselves, our allies, our friends, and the prospects for our peaceful coexistence with the fifth of the human race that practices Islam. The sooner we decide and explain what this war is about, the fewer our enemies and the more numerous our allies will be. The sooner we define achievable objectives, the greater our hope of achieving them. The sooner we stop rummaging blindly in the hornets' nests of the Middle East, the less likely we'll be stung worse than we have been.

The pain of admitting failure will be all the greater because this disaster was completely bipartisan. Both parties colluded in catastrophically misguided policies of militarism and jingoistic xenophobia. We succumbed to panic and unreasoning dread. We got carried away with our military prowess. Our press embedded itself with the troops and jumped into bed with our government. We invaded countries that existed only in our imaginations and then were shocked by their failure to conform to our preconceptions. We asked our military to do things soldiers can do only poorly, if at all. Our representatives pawned our essential freedoms to our commander-in-chief in exchange for implied promises that he would reduce the risks to our security by means that he later declined to disclose or explain.

Not many among us voiced public objections. Those who did found the press too busy demonstrating its patriotism to publicize dissenting views. The issues were, as always, too complex for television. As a wise commentator recently pointed out, television has the same relationship to news that bumper stickers do to philosophy.

Perhaps that's why we decided to try out a made-for-TV approach to international negotiation in which our leaders demonstrate their resolve by refusing to allow our diplomats to talk to bad guys until they come out with their hands up. When that approach produces the predictable impasse, we fall back on the "shoot first, let God worry about what happens next" neo-con school of war planning. In the mess that ensues, our primary concern is rightly to support our troops. But supporting the troops is a domestic political imperative, not a strategy, and it doesn't tell our military what it is being asked to achieve. As force protection becomes our major preoccupation, we find we must pacify the countries we occupy so that we can continue to station troops in them to fight the terrorists our occupation is creating.

Rather than consider the possibility that the witless application to foreign societies of military pressure, no matter how immense and irresistible it may be, is more likely to generate resistance than to make states of them, we prefer to blame the inhabitants of these societies for their ingratitude and internal divisions. So we threaten to withdraw our political and economic support from them, while piling on more American troops. Asked when our soldiers may be able to declare their mission accomplished and to leave Iraq and Afghanistan, our commander-in-chief replies that this is a policy question that the generals in the field should decide, and that he's not going to decide for them. Think about that for a minute. Since when are generals responsible for making policy decisions? They are conditioned to focus on implementing policy and to avoid making it. Whatever happened to civilian control of the military or "the buck stops here?" Why should our military be left to hold the bag in this way?

How we got into this mess is, however, far less important than figuring out how we can get out of it. Much more has been destroyed than just the social and political orders in Iraq and Afghanistan. The term "collateral damage" was invented to denote the undesirable side effects of actions on the battlefield. But it certainly applies to the consequences of our confused and counterproductive conduct and the misdirection of our armed forces since 9/11. We have greatly devalued our political and moral standing with our allies and friends and foolishly degraded the deterrent value of our military power. The world now fears our savagery but has lost confidence in our fairmindedness, judgment, and competence. What are the consequences of this, and how can we overcome them?

A common concern about the belligerent unilateralism of the world's greatest military power is driving lesser powers to look for political and economic support from countries who are distant, unthreatening, or unlikely to back American agendas. So, for example, Venezuela, Brazil, Saudi Arabia, and key African states are courting China; Europe is flirting with Asia; and all are seeking the affections of the oil and gas producers of the Middle East as well as of Russia and India. In most countries, politicians now see public spats with the United States as the easiest way to rally their people and enhance their prestige. The result is the progressive displacement of our previously indispensable influence and leadership in more and more areas of the world.

Sagging demand for our leadership may be a good thing to the extent it relieves us of the burdens of our much-proclaimed status as the sole remaining superpower. But we're clearly bothered by being seen as less relevant. Our answer to this seems to be to build an even more powerful military. Some of you will recall newspaper reports that our defense spending is only about 3.6 percent of GDP, reflecting a defense budget of only—I emphasize—"only" $499.4 billion. But a lot of defense-related spending is outside the Defense Department's budget. This fiscal year, we will actually spend at least $934.9 billion (or about 6.8 percent of our GDP) on our military. Outside the Department of Defense, the Department of Energy will spend $16.6 billion on nuclear weapons. The State Department will disburse $25.3 billion in foreign military assistance. We will spend $69.1 billion on defense-related homeland security programs and $69.8 billion for treatment of wounded veterans. The Treasury will spend $38.5 billion on unfunded military retirements. We will pay $206.7 billion in interest on war debt. Other bits and pieces, including satellite launches, will add another $8.5 billion. Altogether, I repeat, that's about $935 billion. But there's no sign that all this military spending—though it is vastly more than the rest of the world combined—and the power projection capabilities it buys are regaining international leadership for us.

In Latin America, Brazil is assuming the mantle of regional leader, even as Hugo Chávez Frías and other defiant nationalists seek to build influence at our expense.

In Europe, transcontinental integration is proceeding without reference to us or our views about the roles of strategically important countries like Turkey and Ukraine. New relationships are being forged with Russia. European policies toward such problem states as Iran, Iraq, and Israel increasingly diverge from our own.

Asia is returning to its premodern status as the center of gravity of the world economy. Events there are being driven not by us, but by the restored wealth and power of China and India, a once again assertive Japan, strategic repositioning by both parts of Korea, growing partnerships between Muslim nations in Southeast Asia and the Arabs and Persians, the de-facto reintegration of Taiwan with the rest of China, and a bloom of pan-Asian political and economic arrangements from which we are absent.

In the Middle East, Iran has been empowered by our blunders in Iraq, Palestine, and Lebanon. Saudi Arabia has awakened from its traditional risk-averse passivity to fill the diplomatic vacuums we have created. Israel is even more despised and isolated than we are, and together with the Israelis, we are rapidly multiplying the ranks of terrorists with regional and global reach. And so it goes.

The world before us is both unfamiliar and unanticipated. Our military-industrial complex, securocrats, and pundits keep arguing for more carriers, submarines, and fighter bombers. This is good for the defense industrial base but, in terms of stopping terrorists, I am afraid it is an American equivalent of the Maginot Line: the building of an impregnable deterrent to the threat of the past, not the future. Like the French generals, our defense planners are preparing for the return of a familiar enemy—some new version of our sadly vanished Soviet adversary that will rise to compete with us for global hegemony and that we can hold to account for failing to constrain attacks on us by lesser enemies. But that is not what is happening, and it must now be doubted that it ever will.

In the world of the early 21st century, the major ideological contest is between those who share our past faith in the rule of law and the new American contempt for the notion that we should, like others, respect the UN Charter, the Geneva Conventions, and other elements of international law. In some senses, we have met the enemy, and he is who we used to be. We can count on no common threat to rally the world behind us. In the new era, there are no blocs and no clear battle lines. Those who are our allies for some purposes may be our adversaries with respect to others, and vice versa. For all of our military strength, the demands on our diplomatic skills will be the greatest in our history. The stakes are high and the margins for error of our foreign policies are steadily narrowing. We are, however, training our diplomats for the transformative tasks of imperial administration. Like our military planners, our diplomatic leadership has it wrong. Our empire was stillborn. We just didn't notice.

Our post–Cold War global hegemony is being undermined not by a peer competitor but by a combination of our own neoconservative-induced ineptitude and the emergence of countries with substantial power and influence in their own regions. These regional powers distrust our purposes, fear our militarism, and reject our leadership. Distrust drives them to reaffirm the principles of international law we have now abandoned. Fear drives them to pursue the development or acquisition of weapons with which to deter the policies of preemptive attack and forcible regime change we now espouse. (If the weak think the powerful consider themselves above the law, the only protection for the vulnerable is to arm themselves. So scofflaw behavior in the name of halting or reversing the proliferation of WMD actually promotes it.)

All this is creating a world of regional balances in which we play a lessened role, with some of these regional balances—as in South Asia today and the Middle East of the future—involving dangerous nuclear standoffs between two or more middle-ranking powers.

As new centers of economic and political power emerge around the world, global institutions designed to include countries whose participation is essential to problem solving are no longer in alignment with the actual distribution of either the world's power or its problems. These institutions reflect past rather than present international pecking orders. Since they exclude key players, they can't contrive workable solutions, or buy-in to them by those who must either support them or refrain from wrecking them if they are to succeed. The problem is most obvious in organizations devoted to economic matters.

Take the G-7, a self-constituted Euro-American-Japanese club of democracies plus Russia. The G-7 once played a central role in managing the global economy. It still discusses global trade and investment imbalances. But, without Chinese participation, this amounts to little more than ineffectual whining.

Or consider energy and the environment, other issues of broad concern. With the fastest-growing new energy consumers like China, India, and Brazil outside the Organization for Economic Cooperation and Development and its affiliated International Energy Agency, there is no way to coordinate an effective international response to energy shortages or crises. And when the United States absents ourselves, as we have from the Kyoto regime and from some parts of the UN system, even less can be accomplished.

The same pattern of growing misalignment between power and institutions exists throughout the international system. The membership and voting arrangements of the UN Security Council, for example, reflect both the colonial era and the outcome of World War II far better than they mirror current realities. A body charged with the management of global security and other vitally important issues is obviously handicapped in its ability to make, legitimize, and enforce its decisions if it overweights Europe, inflexibly slights India and Japan, and includes no Muslim nation or group of nations among its permanent members. The UN's difficulties are compounded by the contemptuous treatment it now receives from Washington, and by the effects on its image here and abroad of our using it primarily to fend off international condemnation of outrageous behavior by Israel. We can and must do better than this.

To regain both credibility and international respect, we Americans must, of course, restore the vigor of our constitutional democracy and its respect for civil liberties. But that in itself will be far from enough. The willingness of others to follow us in the past did not derive from our ability to intimidate or coerce them. Instead, we inspired the world with our vision and our example. Now, we know what we're against. But what are we for? Whatever happened to American optimism and idealism? To be able to lead the world again, we must once again exemplify aspirations for a higher standard of freedom and justice at home and abroad. We cannot compel— but must persuade—others to work with us. And to lead a team, we must rediscover how to be a team player.

When President Roosevelt first proposed what became the United Nations, he envisaged a concert of powers that could foster a harmonious and largely peaceful world order, increasingly free of both want and fear, and respectful of individual and collective rights as well as of the cultural diversity of humankind. That vision remains both relevant and compelling. The bipolar struggles of the cold war strangled it at birth. But the Cold War is over, and the world that is emerging, though it contains multiple strategic geometries, needs a common architecture that can flexibly address its problems and sustain its peace and development. As currently constituted, the United Nations does not serve these fundamental purposes well. It is time to admit that it has lost the confidence of many of its members. We need to update it, as we must reform other institutions—like the G-7, the World Bank, and the International Monetary Fund—to be able to manage the challenges before us. And if we cannot bring these organizations into alignment with emerging realities, we should not shrink from starting over by creating alternatives to them.

Like our own country, the United Nations was founded on the belief that liberty, tranquility, and the general welfare are best secured by the rule of law—universal adherence to rules that provide predictable order and protect the weak against the strong. That concept, like parliamentary democracy, is a unique contribution of Western culture to global civilization. It has been embraced, though not yet implemented, almost everywhere. Achieving its implementation and embedding it firmly in the structure of the emerging world order should be at the very top of our foreign policy agenda. It must be at the center of any reaffirmation of the UN's purposes through its reform or replacement.

But, if America and Europe—which originated and sponsored the idea of a tolerant, rule-bound international order as an alternative to the law of the jungle—are no longer united in support of the rule of law it is unlikely to survive, still less to prevail as the international system evolves. And as European arrest warrants for American agents engaged in officially sanctioned kidnappings and torture attest, the Atlantic community is now seriously divided. If we Americans renew our adherence to the rule of law at home, as I believe we must, we would find the European Union ready to work closely with us in promoting it abroad. Nowhere has the utility of consultative processes been more convincingly demonstrated than in Europe, where a democratic common political culture respectful of human rights has spread across a continent. A club of democracies like the G-7 may now be unable to manage the world's economy, but regular meetings at the summit of such a grouping could have a major impact on the world's political evolution if they focused on harmonizing and promoting global standards for the rule of law and parliamentary democracy. The groundwork for such an effort is already in place.

Finding common ground with Europe and Japan will also be key to curing our default on leadership with respect to the climate. China is about to overtake the United States as the world's largest emitter of greenhouse gases. The prerequisite for persuading China to behave responsibly is to join the other industrial democracies in behaving responsibly ourselves. Only then can we insist that China and other newly industrializing nations do likewise.

Let me conclude. I have been talking about how to reassert our leadership on the global level. But in the end, we face the paradox that the world, though globalized to an unprecedented degree, is made up of a series of regions in which regional powers increasingly call the shots. And all diplomacy, like all politics, is local. We face perplexing choices in every region of the world. But the policies that have brought discredit upon us center on one region—the Middle East. To restore our reputation, we must correct these policies. And the problem of terrorism that now bedevils us has its origins in one region—the Middle East. To end this terrorism, we must address the issues in the region that give rise to it.

Principal among these is the brutal oppression of the Palestinians by an Israeli occupation that is about to mark its fortieth anniversary and shows no sign of ending. Arab identification with Palestinian suffering, once variable in its intensity, is now total. American identification with Israeli policy has also become total. Those in the region and beyond it who detest Israeli behavior, which is to say almost everyone, now naturally extend their loathing to Americans. This has had the effect of universalizing anti-Americanism, legitimizing radical Islamism, and gaining Iran a foothold among Sunni as well as Shiite Arabs. For its part, Israel no longer even pretends to seek peace with the Palestinians; it strives instead to pacify them. Palestinian retaliation against this policy is as likely to be directed against Israel's American backers as against Israel itself. Under the circumstances, such retaliation—whatever form it takes—will have the support or at least the sympathy of most people in the region and many outside it. This makes the long-term escalation of terrorism against the United States a certainty, not a matter of conjecture.

The Palestine problem cannot be solved by the use of force; it requires much more than the diplomacy-free foreign policy we have practiced since 9/11. Israel is not only not managing this problem; it is severely aggravating it. Denial born of political correctness will not cure this fact. Israel has shown—not surprisingly—that, if we offer nothing but unquestioning support and political protection for whatever it does, it will feel no incentive to pay attention to either our interests or our advice. Hamas is showing that if we offer it nothing but unreasoning hostility and condemnation, it will only stiffen its position and seek allies among our enemies. In both cases, we forfeit our influence for no gain.

There will be no negotiation among Israelis and Palestinians, no peace, and no reconciliation among them—and there will be no reduction in anti-American terrorism—until we have the courage to act on our interests. These are not the same as those of any party in the region, including Israel; and we must talk with all parties, whatever we think of them or their means of struggle. Refusal to reason with those whose actions threaten injury to oneself, one's friends, and one's interests is foolish, feckless, and self-defeating. That is why it is past time for an active and honest discussion with both Israel and the government Palestinians have elected, which—in an irony that escapes few abroad—is the only democratically elected government in the Arab world.

But to restore our reputation in the region and the world, given all that has happened, and to eliminate terrorism against Americans, it is no longer enough just to go through the motions of trying to make peace between Israelis and Arabs. We must succeed in actually doing so. Nothing should be a more urgent task for American diplomacy.

Chapter 16

Diplomacy in the Age of Terror[1]

October 4, 2007

Nine years ago this August, President Clinton declared war on al-Qaeda, a terrorist movement that sees continued American friendship and cooperation with the world's 1.4 billion Muslims as the principal obstacle to the religious tyranny it hopes to impose on them. Three years later, on September 11, 2001, al-Qaeda cruelly struck our homeland.

The United States is the richest and most powerful nation in history. The terrorists who threaten us are a loose network of crazed fanatics inspired and sometimes directed by unkempt men living in caves in Waziristan. Remarkably, the cavemen think they're winning. Even more remarkably, they may be right. For the United States and the American people, the world is now an increasingly dangerous place.

A good part of the reason for this is that our enemies have a strategy and we do not. Their objective is to expel us from the Middle East so that they can overthrow Arab regimes they believe depend on us and end what they regard as the corruption of Islam by the ideas of the Western Enlightenment we have traditionally exemplified. Our objective remains unclear. And the means by which we have answered our terrorist foes—with a diplomacy-free foreign policy that relies almost exclusively on military means—is demonstrably not working. Worldwide, the production of anti-American fanatics is up.

Al-Qaeda's leaders understand that this is a war of wits, not brawn. They will not be maneuvered onto a conventional battlefield; they are determined to select the ground on which they engage us. They are fighting for the minds of the Muslim faithful, whose attraction to Western ideas they condemn and wish to suffocate in their reactionary vision. Our armed forces are without question the world's most competent and lethal. No other military can defeat them. But they are not engaged in battle with another military. In these circumstances, our soldiers, sailors, airmen, and marines are not the appropriate instruments of statecraft to lead our response to the mounting threat we face from Arab and other Muslim extremists. Armed

---

1. Remarks to the Pacific Council on International Policy and the American Academy of Diplomacy.

forces specialize in killing and capturing the enemy. But killing, incarcerating, or otherwise humiliating Arabs and other Muslims who sympathize with al-Qaeda does not defeat the enemy; it aids him. Every instance of perceived injustice and humiliation creates a dozen new enemies, determined to kill Americans.

When he was asked in Australia a little while ago how we were doing in his administration's so-called global war on terrorism, President Bush reportedly replied, with evident satisfaction, that "we are kicking ass." But, cathartic as this may be, it is not a strategy. Today, we know a lot about what we are not attempting to achieve in Iraq. Our continuing occupation of the place is not about eliminating WMD, installing a secular democracy, or creating a model society to inspire revolutions in conservative Islamic nations hostile to Israel. Judging by results, it is also not about increasing the world's oil supply and lowering gasoline prices at the pump. But our president and our Congress have yet to discuss—let alone agree on—what our continuing military presence and operations in Iraq are intended to accomplish.

The plan seems to be for the occupation to soldier on until peace spontaneously breaks out among Iraqis. That is not a strategy. Our men and women in uniform and their equipment are being ground up in the strategic ambush of Iraq. No one can explain to us what they are there to do beyond avoiding making a terrible situation even worse and saving our leaders from having to admit they got things badly wrong.

In Afghanistan, we rapidly accomplished our objectives: first, bringing most, though unfortunately not all, of the masterminds of 9/11 to justice by capturing or killing them; and second, punishing those who had given these evil men safe haven so that others who might be tempted to do so in future would be deterred. We did this with a very cleverly conducted, limited intervention that tilted the balance in a civil war among Afghans and allied us with the victorious faction. Then, we succumbed to the elation of victory and moved on to Iraq, cutting the resources we devote to Afghanistan while inflating our mission there.

Neither the Taliban nor the conservative Pashtuns from whom it draws its support participated in planning or executing the atrocities of 9/11. Our original objective was to punish them, not to ban them from a role in Afghan politics. Our subsequent designation and pursuit of the Taliban as our enemy has restored to it the international legitimacy as an Islamic and nationalist resistance movement that it had earlier forfeited by its pre-9/11 association with terrorists. Our military intervention, assisted by NATO, has yet to create a state or an effective government for Afghanistan. It has, however, made the country safe for poppy cultivation. Afghanistan is now the ultimate source of 93.5 percent of the world's heroin. This provides the Taliban (and, presumably, al-Qaeda) with annual revenues greater than the subsidies that underwrote the mujahedeen during their long and ultimately successful conflict with the Soviet Union. Surely, this is not what we intended. But no one has yet articulated a clear mission or a feasible end game for our military operations in Afghanistan.

In retrospect, al-Qaeda has played us with the finesse of a matador exhausting a great bull by guiding it into unproductive lunges at the void behind his cape. By invading Iraq, we transformed an intervention in Afghanistan that most Muslims had supported into what looks to them like a wider war against Islam. We destroyed the Iraqi state and catalyzed anarchy, sectarian violence, terrorism, and civil war in that country.

Meanwhile, we embraced Israel's enemies as our own; they responded by equating Americans with Israelis as their enemies. We abandoned the role of Middle East peacemaker to back Israel's efforts to pacify its captive and increasingly ghettoized Arab populations. We either wring our hands or sit on them as the Jewish state continues to seize ever more Arab land for its colonists. This has convinced most Palestinians that Israel cannot be appeased and is persuading increasing numbers of them that a two-state solution is infeasible. It threatens Israelis with an unwelcome choice between a democratic society and a Jewish identity for their state. Now, the United States has brought the Palestinian experience—of humiliation, dislocation, and death—to millions more in Afghanistan and Iraq. Israel and the United States each have our reasons for what we are doing, but no amount of public diplomacy can persuade the victims of our policies that their suffering is justified, or spin away their anger, or assuage their desire for reprisal and revenge.

It has generally been thought wise in both politics and foreign affairs to try to divide one's enemies, not to unite them. But our actions and rhetoric have served to persuade a very large majority of Muslims that we are engaged in a global assault on them and their faith. American relations with the Islamic world, especially the fifth of it that is Arab, have never been as hostile or mutually disrespectful. Our television and radio talk shows, aimed at domestic audiences, are heard abroad. In discussion among ourselves, we routinely equate Islam with terrorism. This has made it even harder for Muslim friends of the United States to cooperate openly with us in opposing the extremists who are our common enemies.

As a result, al-Qaeda has largely succeeded in its objective of estranging us from formerly friendly Arab states and their peoples. We have made it easy for violent takfiri (that is, intolerant and absolutist) heretics to claim that they are defending Islam and all its adherents against a global "Crusade" spearheaded by American troops. Their portrayal of their vicious attacks on American, Australian, and European citizens as justified acts of reprisal against aggression has achieved a disturbing degree of resonance. In the broader realm of Islam, not just in the Arab world, rising percentages see such attacks on us as justified. This greatly increases the risk of terrorist violence against any government or people that dares to be our partner. It makes attacks on Americans and our homeland a matter of certainty rather than speculation.

The purpose of terrorists is to spread fear for political effect. The cavemen in Waziristan have not had to work hard at fear mongering. Our leaders have done it for them, putting in place the rudiments of a garrison state that is obsessed by claims of national security. The new order rests on the previously discredited doctrine that extraordinary conditions can create extraordinary constitutional powers for the executive branch. In the name of state security, it overrides more than two centuries of American devotion to the concept of a limited government of laws, not men. In our fear, we are also abandoning the openness that has been central to our economic, scientific, and cultural success. Increasingly, our borders are closed to both people and ideas. In the years of struggle among us, al-Qaeda has not been brought to question its core values or change them. Demonstrably, we have.

There is now a strong American preference for solving problems by militaristic, unilateralist, and scofflaw behavior rather than diplomacy, cooperation with other nations, or the promotion of legal norms. We condemn terrorism as criminal but reserve the right to respond to it with actions that we ourselves previously considered criminal. This has dismayed our allies and friends in the industrial democracies and divided them from us even as it has greatly reduced the numbers of those in the Muslim world and elsewhere who view us as worthy of emulation. We are increasingly isolated and friendless. The restoration of faith in the United States and our commitment to international law and comity is among the most urgent tasks before us. As it is, when we are next struck (as we surely will be), we must be prepared for the likelihood that, this time, there will be more Schadenfreude overseas than solidarity with our distress.

To regain both spiritual strength and allied support, we must restore our country's reputation as the speaker for the world's conscience, not its most powerful abuser. To protect our interests in the widening range of regional contexts in which they are under rising challenge—from the Western Pacific, to Eurasia, to Latin America, Africa, and the broader Middle East—we must regain our ability to lead. And to restore our military capacity to defend our interests beyond Iraq, we must liberate our army and marine corps from occupation duty there and reconstitute them from the wear and tear both have endured. It is by now all too clear that these are tasks that will be left to the next administration. Or maybe, judging by what the current candidates are saying, to its successor.

The most urgent task of all before a successor administration, whatever its political complexion, will be to devise a coherent strategy to deal with the very real dangers posed by terrorists with global reach and their ideological base among the world's Muslims. The United States needs a strategy that integrates intelligence, diplomacy, economic measures, and information policy with law enforcement and military power. We need a grand strategy that unites us with the enemies of our enemies and regains the collaboration and support of now-alienated allies and friends. There is no such strategy at present. Without one, we cannot hope to prevail.

The prerequisites for such a strategy are not hard to describe.

First, we must make a serious effort to understand our enemies rather than simply caricature and malign them. Instead of examining them and their doctrine, we have reasoned from politically convenient analogies with our former foes in Nazi

Germany and Soviet Russia. Instead of addressing al-Qaeda's case against our direct and indirect interventions in the Arab and Islamic worlds, we have ascribed to it an ideology that does not exist. "Islamofascism" is a word invented in America, redolent with politically evocative overtones of the European Holocaust, and totally disconnected from both Islam and Arab history. Rather than analyzing the aims that al-Qaeda and its allies profess—which have to do with freeing the realm of Islam of our presence so that they and other Islamic radicals can direct its course to the future—we ascribe to them an objective of world conquest similar to that of our past Eurasian enemies. Ignorance, confusion, and self-indulgence have led us to impose unfounded stereotypes on Muslims and to mistake Arab friends for Arab enemies—and, no doubt, vice versa.

Second, absent compelling reasons to the contrary, we must alter policies and cease to carry out actions that inadvertently strengthen our enemies by giving them credibility in the wider world of Islam. This will be a politically painful process, requiring us to take an entirely fresh look at many American assumptions and policies with deep political roots and much emotional investment. The obvious need to change our approaches to both Iraq and Afghanistan is a case in point as is our contempt for the constraints of international law. These have become major force multipliers for our extremist enemies and inhibitions on cooperation from allies. They need radical adjustment. We must also subject our reflexive support of Israel's policies to critical examination. The default on the independent exercise of American judgment on this and other issues has not worked to the advantage of either the United States or Israel. The Holy Land is not advancing toward peace but sinking into an ever more bitter struggle for land and identity. Israel is not more secure or accepted in its region but less. Options for a peaceful resolution of the Arab-Israeli conflict are narrowing, not widening. Once a menace only to Israel and its immediate Arab neighbors, the blowback from the Arab-Israeli conflict has emerged as a major threat to our security and that of our allies. It is the principal factor radicalizing the Islamic world.

We have much in common with Israel and many human ties to it, but Israel is not an extension of the United States or our values and does not see itself as such. Israel is a foreign country, inhabited by foreigners, with many interests that are foreign to our own. Contemporary Israeli values increasingly diverge both from ours and, in the opinion of many, from the humane ethics of the religion the Jewish state was established to safeguard. In our own interest, as well as in the interest of securing Israel's long-term existence from the brilliantly shortsighted policies its governments sometimes follow, we must recover the ability to exercise our own judgment. We must be able to discuss Israel's policies and our relationship to them in the robust democratic manner with which these matters are debated in Israel itself. Serious strategic questions that are vigorously disputed among Israelis do not become instances of anti-Semitism when Americans also seek to debate them. It is particularly anomalous that Jewish Americans who feel free to speak out when in Israel are intimidated from doing so in their own country by self-appointed thought police.

Watchdog politics and media censorship imposed by political action groups through the moral blackmail of promiscuous charges of anti-Semitism or lack of patriotism on the part of those who raise controversial matters for public discussion should have no place in our democracy. Such defamatory agitprop has become a blight on our civil society. Calumny is not an acceptable response to issues that are central to protecting the domestic tranquility, managing the common defense, and securing the general welfare of all Americans. Our inability to carry out an honest and objective discussion of issues of great moment endangers us. We can no longer afford the narrow intolerance of political correctness. The thought control it attempts to impose imperils the very interests it purports to defend.

Al-Qaeda draws its strength and its recruits from the grievances of Arabs and other Muslims. Whether or not these grievances are justified, denial will not cure them. It is in our interest both to analyze them and to reduce them to the lowest possible level. This cannot be done without honest examination of how our actions appear to those they affect, unimpeded by prejudice, stereotypes, or the enforcement of political taboos. We need to understand what we are up against as it is, not as it is politically expedient to explain it. Only then can we hope to develop policies that reduce tensions and end the conflicts in the Holy Land, Iraq, and Afghanistan, not aggravate or perpetuate them.

Third, we must stop inadvertently undermining the efforts of mainstream Muslims to oppose our common enemies and to expose these enemies as the deranged and immoral fanatics they are. Our ignorant and blundering equation of terrorism with Islam has overshadowed and impeded those Muslims' efforts to regain control of their own moral space. To help them do so, we must restore respectful relationships with Muslim scholars and the governments they advise. Only then can we work with them to discredit al-Qaeda's aberrant doctrines.

In our natural preoccupation with American suffering on 9/11 or on the battlefields of Iraq and Afghanistan, we often forget that al-Qaeda's aim is the overthrow of what it calls "the near enemy"—the Saudi monarchy and the Egyptian government—and that its attacks on us—"the far enemy"—are merely a means to that end. The successful vilification of Saudi Arabia and newly disparaging attitudes toward Egypt as well as the rise of "Islamophobia" in our politics represent major victories for al-Qaeda. They are defeats for our natural allies against the novel and perverted interpretations of Islam that al-Qaeda purveys. They are, therefore, setbacks for us. We need to rebuild key alliances in the Arab and Muslim worlds that the diplomatic reductionism of "either with us or against us" has destroyed.

Fourth, we need to work with these allies to intercept and rehabilitate those tempted onto the road to terrorism and to help them to return to the straight path of Islam. Saudi Arabia has created a very successful program to do this; it is now helping the United Kingdom apply its program of religious rectification in British prisons. Enabling the misguided to reject the perverted and immoral religious interpretations they have mistakenly accepted is the key to preventing would-be recruits to terrorism from actually engaging in it. Islam is not the problem. In this context, it is the answer.

Finally, we must succeed in hunting down and killing those who have criminally attacked us, whoever and wherever they are. The cavemen in Waziristan must at last be brought to justice, if only as an example to the rest. While this is primarily the task of our intelligence and law enforcement agencies and their foreign counterparts and partners, such civilian agencies will need backing from our armed forces to accomplish this. But, with rare exceptions, the proper role of our military will be to support, not lead the effort.

The tranquility of our homeland is now inextricably linked with that of the homelands of the world's Muslims. The task of persuading our allies and friends to join us in a grand strategy aimed at restoring peace and security to all of us will be a huge challenge that places heavy demands on our diplomacy. For the sake of our posterity and their liberties, we must rise to this challenge. Yet it is nowhere ordained that we will.

Diplomacy is the most difficult of the political arts. It requires empathy, which is especially hard for democracies, given their natural fixation on the views of their own citizen-voters and their concomitant disdain for the views of foreigners who, after all, can't and don't vote. The diplomatic record of American democracy is decidedly mixed. It combined unilateralism with pacifism and sanctimony in a uniquely American brand of fecklessness in the years before World War II, then surprised the world with its creative brilliance after the war. Since winning the cold war, we have again surprised the world—by reverting to ineffectual unilateralism, this time compounding it with militarism, swagger, self-righteousness, and complacent ignorance.

Many Americans now equate diplomacy with appeasement and insist that we can talk to our enemies only when they come out with their hands up. It's been a while since we attempted the persuasive arts of diplomacy. We are more than a little out of practice at them. And, frankly, our foreign service, staffed as it is with very intelligent men and women, remains decidedly smug and amateurish in comparison with the self-critical professionalism of our armed forces.

There are many reasons for this, including lack of training, professional standards and mentoring, funding, and ésprit as well as dysfunctional policies that have forced our diplomats to cower behind the fortifications of Crusader castles, as they do in Baghdad's "Green Zone." In part, however, it is because we persist in a spoils system that led the *New York Herald Tribune* to remark in 1857 that "Diplomacy is the sewer through which flows the scum and refuse of the political puddle. A man not fit to stay at home is just the man to send abroad." As Abba Eban, one of the great diplomats of the past century, sadly pointed out:

The word 'ambassador' would normally have a professional connotation but for the American tradition of political appointees. The bizarre notion that any citizen, especially if he is rich, is fit for the representation of his country abroad has taken some hard blows through empirical evidence. But it has not been discarded.

The abandonment in the nineteenth century of the practice of appointing politicians as generals or judges was the key to the emergence of the military and legal professions. As long as its most senior positions are reserved for wealthy dilettantes, our foreign service will not attain the professionalism necessary for it to be able to match, and collaborate effectively with, our highly professional military. The wide margin of error we traditionally enjoyed in foreign policy has narrowed. We can no longer afford amateurism in diplomacy, appointing our most senior representatives abroad for the good of the party rather than the nation, and leaving them to be educated by events. Skilled work requires skilled workmen. Americans are now without peer in the military arts; to prevail against our current enemies, we must attain equal excellence in diplomacy.

Rediscovering diplomacy, professionalizing it, developing doctrine to coordinate the other instruments of statecraft with it, and training to get better at it are essential components of the grand strategy for combating Islamic terrorism that we require. There is no doubt that we can do this. The only question is whether we will.

Chapter 17

Why Not Try Diplomacy?[1]

March 28, 2008

I want to address the issue of diplomacy as an element of statecraft. By now most Americans recognize that we are in a bit of trouble both at home and abroad. What is to be done? Is diplomacy a better answer than the use of force?

The late Arthur Goldberg, who was both a justice of our Supreme Court and ambassador to the United Nations, observed that "diplomats approach every issue with an open ... mouth." A colleague and friend of mine, who served as Ambassador to China, once told me that "a diplomat is someone who thinks twice—before saying nothing." They set a high bar for a public speaker on diplomacy as an alternative to militarism, but I am willing to attempt it.

Americans believe in military power, and the United States has never spent so much on it. Internationally, given our diminished political standing and the collapse of the dollar, military prowess may be our only remaining comparative advantage. We certainly behave as though we think it is.

In current dollars, we are spending about 28 percent more on our military each year than we did during the Korean and Vietnam Wars and more than one-third more than at the height of the Reagan defense build-up against the late, unlamented Soviet Union. We are spending considerably more on military power than the rest of the world put together—three-and-a-half times as much as the highest estimate for China, Russia, Cuba, Iran, and North Korea combined; and at least 12,000 times as much as al-Qaeda and all other terrorist groups with global reach. It is not clear what enemies justify all this money. Whoever they are, if military expenditures are the key to national security, we've got them where we want them.

In the first ten years of this century, US defense outlays will total about $5.25 trillion. Military-related outlays in other parts of the federal budget—like homeland security, veterans affairs, and interest payments on war debt—will add another $2 trillion or so to this, for a cumulative total of something well over $7 trillion in military and military-related spending. Our defense budget, including supple-

1. Remarks to the University Continuing Education Association.

mentals to pay for offensive operations in Afghanistan and Iraq, is now about 5 percent of our GDP. Counting military-related outlays in other budgets, the percentage of our economy devoted to defense is around 7 percent. We have a huge economy and, in absolute terms, that is a lot of military spending.

We need a strong military even though we're not really worried about an invasion from Jamaica or Canada or Mexico or even Cuba or Iran. Unlike other nations' armed forces, what ours do is mostly not defense against foreign invasion or attacks on the homeland. Our military is configured for offensive deployment in support of foreign policy. It does deterrence, punishment, and conquest of real and potential foreign enemies. That is why our soldiers, sailors, airmen, and marines are in Korea, Afghanistan and Iraq as well as in Bosnia and dozens of other places around the world that have neither the intent nor the capability to attack us. It took 9/11 and its demonstration that we had no military means of preventing foreign attack on U.S. civilians to get us to worry about the possibility that such attacks might occur. We now have a separate department of government focused on that.

Somehow, however, despite all the money we've spent, the debt we've accumulated, and the sacrifices patriotic Americans have made in distant foreign lands, our leaders tell us that we have never been so threatened. Given all the enemies we have been making recently, they may be right. There is, of course, a time-tested political axiom in Washington that if something isn't working the answer is to add money and do more of it. So our president and the three major candidates vying to succeed him join in promising further increases in defense spending— without providing any indication of how these increases would buy us greater security. It's enough to make one wonder whether President Eisenhower wasn't onto something when he warned Americans against the danger of nurturing a "military-industrial complex" that would give us a vested interest in military spending, regardless of the nature and level of the threat to our nation.

Massive military spending has, in fact, become an indispensable part of our political economy. In addition to buying remarkably capable and costly weapons systems, it feeds hordes of consultants and contractors and houses legions of academic specialists. These are very bright people who labor to develop theories of how military coercion might control foreign behavior. They produce threat analyses to justify continuing U.S. military build-up. They consider how best to apply our military might abroad, and they work out the force packages and weapons system specifications to do it. The intellectual energy that massive spending has focused on these topics—as opposed to means of influence that do not rely on the threat or use of force—has revolutionized the American approach to foreign policy. One should never underestimate the impact of either federal spending or the resulting focus of the academy!

And one should never underestimate the ability of politicians to ignore millennia of human experience and to aspire to expediency if the academy gives them an opening to do so. Most of our leaders, in both major political parties, now espouse a reversal of the long-standing American view that coercion, especially through military means, is a last resort to be brought into play only when diplomacy—in the form of persuasion, diplomatic bargaining, alliance building, and other measures short of war—has failed. In both Afghanistan and Iraq, the sequence approved on both sides of the aisle was to shoot first, then send in the diplomats to mop up. Since this hasn't worked out too well, there is now a lot of talk about how to recruit more diplomats and buy more mops. That's probably a good idea, but it might be more effective and cheaper to involve the diplomats at the outset and avoid creating such a mess in the first place.

It used to be thought that the purpose of war was to secure a more perfect peace. That is an objective that invokes diplomacy to translate military triumph into new arrangements acceptable to both victor and vanquished. It implies war planning focused on the question: "and then what?" and the conduct of war in accordance with a strategy that unites political, economic, informational, and intelligence measures with military actions and a well-crafted plan for war termination. In Iraq, a brilliant general has belatedly come up with a credible campaign plan but his plan is still unconnected to a strategy. Our plan to end the fighting is apparently to hang around until the Iraqis decide to make peace with each other. That might take a while. In the strategy-free zone that is contemporary Washington, no one wants to second-guess a celebrity general, but any reading of David Petraeus's manual on counterinsurgency must lead to the conclusion that, in Iraq, "victory" remains undefined and missing in action.

Sadly, theories of coercion and plans to use military means to impose our will on other nations have for some time squeezed out serious consideration of diplomacy as an alternative to the use of force. Diplomacy is more than saying "nice doggie," till you can find a rock. Weapons are tools to change men's minds, but they are far from the only means of doing so. As we are learning from our misadventures in the Middle East, they are also seldom the most reliable or least expensive. The weapons of diplomats are words, and their power is their persuasiveness. Talk is cheaper than firepower and does less collateral damage, so it makes sense to try it before blazing away at the adversary.

There is another reason to regard force as a last resort. It creates ruins that cannot easily be rebuilt and resentments that cannot be easily be overcome. War is a form of demolition; its results are messy and its effects on those it touches are uncertain. In the age of globalization, moreover, military invasion is as likely to incubate terrorists with global reach as it is to overthrow governments and seize terrain. It makes sense to exhaust diplomatic remedies first, not to follow a script of "Ready! Fire! Diplomacy!"

Diplomacy is the art of pursuing the internationally possible. Its main drawback is that it involves the unpleasant task of interacting persuasively with usually disagreeable adversaries and sometimes tedious friends. Despite the example of useful, wide-ranging dialogue with our Soviet enemies (conducted on the sound theory that one should never lose contact with the enemy diplomatically or militarily), a generation of American leaders seems to have concluded that we shouldn't talk to people who disagree with us till they come out with their hands up. But not talking to those with whom one disagrees is the diplomatic equivalent of unilateral disarmament.

Figuring out why others are doing things and explaining to them why Americans disagree with this and why they should, in their own interest, do things our way is the opposite of appeasement. And it is more likely to achieve results than ducking such encounters while loudly proclaiming that those we disdain to speak with already know what they need to do to appease us, so we don't need to reason with them. Substituting reliance on the intuition of our adversaries for diplomatic communication with them leaves few options. We can live with a surging mess, or we can slap on some sanctions. When these fail, as they inevitably do, we can send in the B-2s and Abrams tanks. These are not good choices. The approach they impose creates more problems than it solves.

Our next president will inherit a daunting list of challenges: apparently interminable wars in Afghanistan and Iraq; withering alliances; diminished international prestige and deference to our leadership; deepening estrangement between the United States and the Islamic world; a mounting threat to our homeland from the growing ranks of anti-American jihadis; a war-fatigued, equipment-depleted, disenchanted, and still untransformed U.S. military; an increasingly lawless world order; and the emergence of a widening range of regional challenges to US influence and interests from the likes of Mahmoud Ahmadinejad, Hugo Chávez Frías, and Vladimir Putin.

He or she will have to deal with all these issues while wrestling with a budget and economy in chronic deficit; mounting national debt amid a credit crisis; recession; inflation; insolvent pension systems; decaying infrastructure—complete with collapsing bridges, pot-holes, and gridlock; a medical system that extracts rapidly inflating payments from middle-class Americans without caring for the poor, sick, and destitute among us; and other developments that, collectively, undermine America as a model that other nations wish to emulate. It is tempting to conclude that anyone who wants to be president under these circumstances is prima facie mentally defective and unfit for the office. Still, some poor soul will be inaugurated next January 20 and will have to deal with all these issues and then some.

The new president might start by shaking off the constipated notion that diplomacy is, like military posturing, just a way of conveying menace or containing or deterring threats. These things are, of course, part of diplomacy. Diplomacy is largely about adding the strength of others to one's own, but its greater mission is to take the political offensive by transcending the conventional wisdom and identifying or creating opportunities, and seizing them to the national advantage. That is what Truman did with the Marshall Plan and the formation of NATO. It is what Nixon did with his opening to China. It is what Carter did at Camp David. It is what Reagan did with Gorbachev at Reykjavik. The next president should look into how to restore our atrophied diplomatic capabilities so as to lift us from the mire into which we have sunk.

Resorting to diplomacy will not be as easy as it may sound. Secretary of Defense Gates has recently begun to speak to the lopsided priorities apparent in our budget, which underfunds diplomacy and forces the U.S. military to do all sorts of things that would be more appropriately and better done by civilian foreign affairs personnel. Gates points out that there are fewer professional diplomats in our Foreign Service than there are personnel in military bands or a single carrier battle group in the U.S. Navy. What our country spends on a year's diplomatic and consular operations worldwide is less than what we spend in six days of military operations in Iraq.

You get what you pay for. In this case, that's a superbly professional and supremely lethal military and an anemically staffed and undertrained diplomatic service led by inexperienced political appointees on sabbatical from high incomes. As one of the last century's greatest diplomats, Israel's Abba Eban, said of this peculiarly American practice:

> The bizarre notion that any citizen, especially if he is rich, is fit for the representation of his country abroad has taken some hard blows through empirical evidence. But it has not been discarded.

It has been 196 years since an amateur general—Andrew Jackson—last commanded U.S. troops in battle not far from here.[2] But to lead our diplomatic work abroad, especially in countries where the standard of living is high and the danger of anti-American violence is low, we still depend on amateurs who must learn on the job, hoping that their experienced subordinates will help them overcome their ignorance of the local language, paper over embarrassing gaffes, and avoid catastrophic mistakes. And in Washington, where Iraq has just reminded us how dangerous it can be to allow civilian armchair generals to substitute their military judgments for those of military professionals, we now staff our foreign policy apparatus almost entirely with people with no diplomatic experience. No other country in the world so values ideological reliability and party loyalty over professional knowledge and expertise. Only in America....

I am reminded of the story of a former U.S. ambassador to the Soviet Union, Mac Toon, a crusty career diplomat who went aboard an aircraft carrier in the Mediterranean for a meeting with the admiral who commanded its battle group. At the end of their discussion, the admiral leaned over to ask, "What's it like being an ambassador? I've always thought that after I retire I might want to try it." Ambassador Toon replied, "That's funny. I've always thought that, when I retire, I might try my hand at running a carrier battle group." The admiral said, "That's

---

2. These remarks were made in New Orleans.

ridiculous. A naval command requires years of training and experience." But so do the management of foreign policy and diplomacy, if the ship of state is not to be sailed onto the rocks or beached in the desert.

It is a truism that skilled work requires skilled workmen. Americans are now without peer in the military arts. To prevail against our current enemies, we must attain equal excellence in diplomacy. We do not have the margin for error we once did. But even if we devote the equivalent of a whole week's worth of the Pentagon budget to the arts of peace—rather than the three days or so we now do—fixing our Foreign Service will take time. As our military know better than anyone, it takes decades to train, exercise, and professionalize personnel. After years of overemphasis on military means of conducting our foreign relations, getting up to diplomatic snuff will require a serious investment in intellectual infrastructure comparable with that we have devoted to the military arts.

If we build a diplomatic capability to match our military prowess, we will gain a key building block of national strategy. But a bigger, better Foreign Service will not in itself create such a strategy. Nor will it solve the underlying problem of national strategic illiteracy. We suffer from what one of our most sophisticated foreign policy practitioners, Chester Crocker, has called a "statecraft deficit." It is inspiring to observe the professionalism of our military, which is the most competent in history. It is painful to observe the extent to which military requests for direction from the civilians whose control they are taught to revere go unanswered. The fact is that we—and those we elect and appoint to lead us—are remarkably poorly prepared for the preeminent role in world affairs we now play.

Our educational system bears major responsibility for this. Most Americans can't find Louisiana, let alone Iraq or Afghanistan, on the map. Many are unversed in history, still less diplomatic history. Few have been exposed to any instruction in how to reason about foreign affairs or statecraft and its diplomatic, intelligence, and military tools. Almost none has been tutored in strategy. This is understandable. It is largely a reflection of two factors, both of which have changed.

First, until recently, the American homeland was apparently invulnerable, and the United States was the leader in most fields of human endeavor. Foreign policy was therefore something we inflicted on others without fear of reprisal, not something they did unto us. And we didn't think we had much to learn from foreigners. Foreign affairs and national security didn't seem like anything the average American citizen had to worry about. But 9/11 changed that forever.

And, second, the formative influences of the Cold War, during which the United States led half the world against Soviet communism, are still with us. Then, the capacity of the Soviet Union to annihilate us imperiled our very existence. Its predatory ideology menaced our values; its imperial ambitions threatened our interests and those of many other nations. The threats to both values and interests became so thoroughly merged that we forgot how to distinguish the two, though they are very different in their functions and import.

Attempts at historical revisionism by the proponents of militarism notwithstanding, the fact is that we won the Cold War by patient adherence to a strategy of containment, not by butting heads on a battlefield. Containment relied on diplomacy—on measures short of war—to build and sustain alliances backed by the deterrent power of great military strength. Some may profess to regret that we did not join in battle with the Soviet Union to roll back its empire. I am glad we substituted patience for belligerence. Our strategy did not vary over 40 years. It formed the foreign policy outlook of three generations. We did not have to think about strategy. In many ways, we appear to have forgotten how to do so.

We now face a world in which our personal security and that of our communities is threatened, but our national existence is not. As a people and as a nation, we are challenged from many directions and in many ways, not by a single "evil empire" that we can count upon to rot away from within. To secure our domestic tranquility against foreign assault and to lead the 21st century as we did the last one will demand of us a higher level of strategic conceptual ability and civic literacy than we have had to demonstrate for decades. And it will require instruments of statecraft adequate to the task—diplomatic, informational, and intelligence capabilities of the first order, backed by military power without peer and a prosperous, attractive, and open society.

Two millennia ago, the Roman philosopher Seneca advised the Emperor Nero of the vital importance of setting objectives. "If a man does not know to what port he steers, no wind is favorable," he pointed out. It was good advice, even if Nero didn't take it. It is worth pondering in our current circumstances. Our debate about the challenges before us is almost entirely tactical not strategic, cast in terms of our politics rather than external realities, and focused on preventing change rather than turning it to our advantage.

Yet, for example, we risk reaping the whirlwind if we simply leave Iraq. We cannot do so safely and responsibly without defining realistic objectives and using our withdrawal to advance toward them. If we continue to aid and abet counterproductive behavior by all sides in the Middle East, we should not be surprised when they turn on us. If we do not define a feasible end-game in Afghanistan, we will just incubate more anti-American terrorists while expanding the world's heroin supply.

If we cannot decide what sort of international monetary reserve system should replace the currently collapsing one and persuade other stakeholders to act with us to fix it, we will drift into increasing economic misery. We must develop a plan to reunite the Atlantic region behind the rule of law and other Western values or see these eclipsed by ideas from other regions of the world that are rising to new prominence. Without a vision of mutually beneficial coexistence in our hemisphere, events and the anti-American dreams of others will bring needless trouble right up to our borders. If we are not positioned to help as Cuba, North Korea, Burma, and other troubled nations enter periods of transition, we must expect that they will change in ways that create new problems for us and their neighbors. If we have no positive agenda for enlisting Chinese and Indian power in common causes, they may well apply their power in ways that undercut ours, annoy us, or even injure us.

It has been a long time since Americans had a positive vision or clear objectives for these and other pressing issues. I could go on, but the afternoon advances, and the city beckons. Let me close with the obvious point that we cannot hope to appeal to the conscience of humankind if we do not continue to embody its aspirations. If we do not restore our country's good name, others will not follow when we lead or share the burdens we take up. To regain the cooperation of allies and friends, we must rediscover how to listen, how to persuade, how to be a team player, and how to follow the rules we demand that others follow.

We must do this because we Americans cannot successfully address the problems we confront on our own. Our need for foreign partners has never been greater. Fortunately, the world's desire for partnership with America has not really gone away. Beneath the layers of resentment and animosity laid down by our recent behavior, there is still much goodwill toward the United States. This "fossil friendship" will not last forever. For now, however, it is a resource that American diplomacy can mine to rebuild the respect of allies and friends for our leadership and to unite them behind an American vision of a better world. A return to diplomacy, not threats and the use of force, is the surest path to the reassertion of American leadership. It is time to rediscover and explore that path.

Chapter 18

America in the World: Magoo at the Helm[1]

June 23, 2008

In the last days of the last century, then–Secretary of State Madeleine Albright described the United States as "the indispensable nation." "We stand tall," she claimed, "and we see further than other countries into the future." She did not seek the views of any foreigners on either point. It is not recorded that many, if indeed any, agreed with her. What she said was, of course, music to American ears. But what we and non-Americans thought at the time of her smugly bumptious articulation of our self-regard is now moot. The policies the United States adopted in the first decade of this century have thoroughly refuted her theses.

A great many governments abroad now fear that Washington will behave like the ever-self-congratulatory Mr. Magoo—wandering destructively through a reality he misperceives and wreaking havoc he determinedly misinterprets as success. Few believe that our country can still combine realism with statesmanship. More tellingly, a lot have concluded that, far from involving the United States, dispensing with a role for Washington is the only way to solve problems.

Take the Middle East, for example. This is the region that, in one way or another, has been the principal focus of American foreign policy in recent years. It is also the region in which the United States has most consistently shown a preference for bluster, boycotts, and bombs and a concomitant disdain for diplomacy. I am not speaking here simply of Iraq or Iran. We have refused dialogue and attempted to dissuade Israel from negotiating with Syria. We have done the same even more adamantly with Hezbollah (which, as a consequence of the U.S.-sponsored Israeli bombing campaign of 2006, emerged as the leading force in Lebanese politics.) Meanwhile, in the name of bolstering Lebanese independence from political interference by Syrian and Iranian outsiders, we have vigorously interfered in Lebanon

---

1. Remarks to the Washington World Affairs Council Summer Institute on International Affairs. Another version of this talk was published in the *Foreign Service Journal*.

ourselves. We have repeatedly proclaimed that it would be a sin to talk with Hamas (which, thanks to elections we insisted take place, is now the democratically empowered governing authority in all areas of Palestine not directly occupied by Israel). We have tried hard to congeal Sunni Arab antagonism to Shiite Persians into an Arab bloc we hope will join us in ostracizing and punishing Iran, which the Israelis and we repeatedly threaten to assault from the air. Our domestic politics are venomously anti-Muslim; our government has made no effort to form alliances with Islamic authorities who might articulate a credible rebuttal to Muslim extremists.

These U.S. policies have not gone over well. Recent developments strongly suggest that they have resulted in decisions by all concerned in the Middle East to work around the United States rather than with us or through us. Consider Israel's resort to Turkey (rather than U.S. "shuttle diplomacy") to manage proximity talks with Syria. Or Lebanon's turn to Qatar to broker the peaceful realignment of its politics, notwithstanding our investment in them. Or Israel's reliance on Egypt to mediate a cease-fire agreement with Hamas. Or the Palestinian president's decision to enlist Arab conciliators to work out Fatah's differences with Hamas, rather than concentrating on an American-proclaimed "peace process" that most in the region have come to view as a cruel fraud. Or Israel's recourse to Germany to reach understandings with Hezbollah. Or Saudi Arabia's effort to reach a modus vivendi with Iran, to align the Muslim mainstream against extremism, and to broker renewed peace between Sunnis and Shiites in preparation for interfaith dialog with Jews and Christians. All these political openings touch on interests that Washington sees as vital. All of them are taking place notwithstanding long-standing American objections to them, and all of them are unfolding in our diplomatic absence.

This is not just because Mr. Magoo has seemingly succeeded Uncle Sam at the helm. In some measure, it's because the United States has taken sides in disputes with respect to which we had traditionally maintained at least a pretense of even-handedness. We are therefore seen as part of the problem rather than part of the solution. It is because promiscuous efforts by the United States to impose military solutions on problems that force cannot resolve have left no room for American diplomacy. The resulting default on reality-based problem solving by the United States has created a diplomatic void that others are now filling. This trend toward working around the United States has been aggravated by widespread distaste for the arrogant and insulting phrasing of some U.S. policy pronouncements. The undisguised disdain of some American envoys for the United Nations, the World Court, and regional organizations and their open contempt for the views of the international communities these bodies represent has also disinclined others to work with us if they can avoid it. Washington's political marginalization in the Middle East is a predictable result of such "diplomacy-free foreign policies."

What could not have been predicted is the reputation for incompetence our country has acquired. This has touched even our armed forces, despite their well-deserved reputation as the most professional and lethal practitioners of the arts of war on the planet. Our interventions in Afghanistan and Iraq were meant to showcase this element of American power, underscore our omnipotence, and intimidate anyone tempted to resist our hegemony. Instead, these military campaigns have had the paradoxical effect of demonstrating the strategic limitations of the use of force, eroding the deterrent value of our unmatched military prowess, and proving the efficacy of asymmetric warfare as a counter to our strength. Despite the Magoo-like mutterings of the "neoconservatives" ("You've done it again, Magoo!"), when we leave Afghanistan and Iraq, we will do so much more chastened than exuberant about the potential of military power, however great, to transform the world to our advantage.

Scofflaw U.S. behavior, the ill-considered use of military power in wars of unilateral choice, and the contraction of freedom in the American homeland have indeed transformed our relationship with the world—but to our grave disadvantage. Abu Ghraib, Bagram, and Guantanamo and the practice of "extraordinary rendition" have dishonored our traditions and defiled our international reputation. Militarism has debilitated our alliances, friendships, and partnerships and corroded our ability to lead. The belligerently surly, unwelcoming face we present to would-be visitors in our embassies and at our borders puts off even the most determined admirers of our society. The elements of a garrison state we have put in place at home have enfeebled our ability to inspire others with our ideas while depriving us of theirs. Much of the world is now seriously disenchanted with the United States. Most (though not all) of these self-inflicted wounds derive from our response to the atrocities of 9/11 and our policies toward the Middle East. We have shown not only that we can shoot ourselves in the foot, but that we can reload with exceptional speed and do it again and again.

Secretary of State Condoleezza Rice famously predicted in 2006, as Israel rained American-supplied bombs on Beirut, that Lebanon's pain represented the birth pangs of "a new Middle East." She was right, but the Middle East now emerging seems to be one in which the United States no longer has convening power, political credibility, or persuasiveness. It is a region in which all countries fear our military might but in which no country—not even Israel, despite its dependence on American subventions—defers to our leadership.

In our own hemisphere too, without many noticing, a major ebb in U.S. influence has taken place. Latin America's governments may have little in common beyond a commitment to some form of democracy and social justice, but they share a determination to assert greater autonomy from the United States. To this end, they are courting investment from China, opening markets in Europe, stalling the Free Trade Agreement of the Americas, dissenting from the "Washington consensus," and crafting regional institutions and forming partnerships that not only exclude the United States but are sometimes openly antagonistic to it. Political Washington's apparent disinterest in a region it long commanded and its ideologically induced inability to respond to opportunities there (like those in a changing Cuba) have facilitated these trends. The Council on Foreign Relations' recent declaration that "the era of the United States as the dominant influence in Latin America is over" may be overstated, but it is not easily rebutted. The regional agenda in Latin America is increasingly set there, without reference to the United States.

This is true in Africa as well, where the United States has mounted a very significant continent-wide effort against HIV-AIDS but is, in most respects, substantially less engaged than China, Europe, or India. Africans have taken the lead—so far not very effectively, to be sure—in crisis management of issues on their continent like the mayhem in the Congo, the genocidal warfare in Sudan, and the collapse of democracy and decency in Zimbabwe. In doing so, they have largely sidelined the United States and other outside powers. In response, and to upgrade our capabilities in Africa, Washington unilaterally decided to create a U.S. military combatant commander for the African continent and to station him and his staff there. Logic and precedent supported this initiative.

American flag officers now sit at the head of combatant commands in most other regions of the globe. The prominent role of such uniformed American proconsuls abroad reflects the extent to which our foreign relations have become skewed toward reliance on military instruments of influence. The forward presence of American generals and admirals with transnational responsibilities, unmatched fiscal resources, and wide authority to draw on the immense capabilities of our armed forces makes them the most active and visible face of our country abroad. Since they are on the spot, moreover, they tend to be more in touch with regional trends and realities than officials in Washington. That's one reason most American ambassadors are so fond of them.

As the United States saw it, the establishment of an Africa Command would elevate Africa's symbolic importance in our foreign policy. But Africans have reacted badly to the idea. They see it as an attempt to reestablish a non-African military presence on their newly de-colonized continent and as an indication that American military adventurism might soon extend there. For the time being, at least, USAFRICOM remains in Stuttgart rather than within its area of operational responsibility.

The United States' strongest international ties, of course, have been with Europe, where continent-wide integration is in the final stages of erasing the divisions of the Cold War. The European Union is less than the sum of its parts, but it has emerged as the dominant factor in its region and adjacent areas. Increasingly, Europeans are charting their own course even on issues of great importance to the United States, like membership in NATO or how to deal with the return of Russia to assertive nationalism or that of China or India to wealth and power. The United States is, however, now valued as a participant in the Eurasian balance of power rather than as the protector of Europe against a credible external security threat. (This is so even though we have taken a second look into Putin's eyes and seen his role: He is a KGB guy playing a tsar with post-Soviet characteristics.) There are no longer many compelling reasons for Europeans to defer to Americans even if we had not given them cause to doubt our wisdom. For the first time in the five decades since they embraced American leadership of the Atlantic community, they seem comfortable ignoring Washington's views or rejecting them outright.

This is in part because the extraordinary transatlantic solidarity of 9/11 has given way to sharp differences over international law and comity, privacy and due process of law, and the desirability of multilateral approaches to transnational issues like climate change. Very few in Europe have any sympathy for claims by American politicians that 9/11 changed everything, justifying the suspension of individual rights and the separation of powers insisted upon by Enlightenment thinkers like America's own founding fathers. To a distressing extent, therefore, the Atlantic community is no longer united by shared ideals but ominously divided by emerging differences over them. Transatlantic disagreement on core values bodes ill for the prospect that these values will prevail in a world in which the center of gravity is migrating to the Asian ends of the Eurasian landmass.

Paradoxically, given the much ballyhooed shift of global wealth and power to Asia, the trend toward regional assertiveness and the decline of American influence is in some ways least obvious in the Asia-Pacific region. This reflects the realities of Chinese and Indian power in relation to the nations on their periphery. With the notable exception of Pakistan, India's neighbors have reconciled themselves to its hegemony in South Asia. The United States has recognized India's primacy there and does not seek to undermine or thwart it.

In East and Central Asia, however, Chinese hegemony remains an unwelcome conjecture, not a reality. China has repeatedly assured its neighbors that it does not and will not seek to dominate them, but none is inclined to self-insure against the risk that it might do so. In this context, the safe and easy course for most has been a carefully calibrated measure of continued association, including military cooperation, with the United States. Much of the Cold War pattern of East Asian alliances with the United States, with Japan as its lynchpin, therefore persists. From the point of view of the Asian participants in these alliances, their purpose is not, as in the past, to contain China but to ensure that China will fit unthreateningly into a regional balance bolstered by American power. Meanwhile, China itself is firmly focused on its own economic and social development. It very much wishes to avoid needless confrontations with the United States. As a result, in comparison with other regions, East Asia remains relatively disinclined to challenge American views and prone to accommodate them when possible.

This deferential stance has not, however, precluded disagreements with the United States over issues like how to deal with Myanmar [Burma] and North Korea or the development of regional groupings or institutions that exclude Washington. Such groupings are a growing phenomenon, largely centered on the Association of Southeast Asian Nations. Some of them involve various Asian-only combinations; some involve Europe. Some include Australia or India, while others exclude one or both. Washington has inadvertently accelerated the trend toward exclusion of the

United States from regional groupings in the Asia-Pacific region by erratic participation in key meetings and by sometimes tediously insisting that such meetings focus on terrorism or various Middle East–related issues with respect to which Asians do not share either America's perspectives or obsessions. Meanwhile, China and India have taken out their own insurance against American hegemony, in the form of regular trilateral meetings with Russia devoted to promoting multipolarity, respect for the United Nations Charter, and other offsets to U.S. efforts to dictate and dominate the world order.

The fact that other countries are willing to take greater responsibility for managing the affairs of their own regions, even if they have been moved to do so mainly in reaction to perceived U.S. errors of commission and omission, should probably be seen as a positive development. But it is certainly not a good thing for our government to be excluded from conversations on major regional or global issues. The risk is that our interests will be misunderstood or ignored when actions are taken that affect us. U.S. policies since the end of the Cold War—especially over the eight years of the George W. Bush administration—have tended to isolate the United States, take us out of the diplomatic game, and leave us at the mercy of decisions and arrangements that others increasingly craft in our absence. Rediscovering the diplomatic arts of persuasion is key to recovering the role and standing we have lost.

One can learn more from catastrophe and failure than from victory or success. Students of U.S. foreign policy since the catastrophe of 9/11, rejoice! There is a lot of material from which to extract lessons for future foreign policy.

A good place to start might be 9/11 itself. Among other things, the shocking attack on our homeland that day showed that, in the post–Cold War world, if the United States launches or sponsors military operations in other people's homelands, we should expect them to find a way to retaliate against ours. This caution remains relevant. Without intending to do so, we have installed a lot of incubators and created a lot of training opportunities for terrorists in Iraq, Gaza, the West Bank, and Lebanon as well as in the border regions of Afghanistan and Pakistan.

Meanwhile, we have repeatedly adjusted our military campaign plans in Iraq and Afghanistan. We have yet to adjust our diplomacy. And we have not come up with a strategy to overcome the appeal of anti-American terrorism, turn its adherents against it, slash the numbers of its recruits, or even capture its most notorious spokesmen.

Those best qualified to accomplish these tasks are mainstream Muslims, acting out of their own self-interest and in concert with us. Cultivating support in the Islamic world should, therefore, be a principal focus of U.S. foreign policy. The struggle to outlaw and suppress terrorism cannot succeed without the full cooperation of allies and friends around the world. Reinvigorating our alliances and partnerships is as essential to this task as it is to the renewal of foreign respect for American leadership in general.

In this regard, a few of the lessons that might be drawn from the global and regional trends of recent years stand out. Three have to do with rediscovering diplomacy as an alternative to militarism. Two are more substantive.

First, Woody Allen was right: Eighty percent of success is indeed just "showing up." At the moment, the U.S. military shows up a lot more than anyone else at the regional level. We need diplomatic counterparts to our regional combatant commanders. They should be forward deployed and endowed with the resources and authority to address regional as well as bilateral interests. They should have a mandate to implement strategies that integrate the political, economic, cultural, and informational, intelligence, and military elements of our national influence.

Second, our leaders at all levels and in all branches of government need to rediscover the art of listening. Listening is essential to successful relationship management. If we don't pay attention to the opinions of others, they will be—as we have seen—less likely to find our views persuasive. If we don't attend to their interests, they are unlikely to buy into ours. Diplomacy is not preaching to others about what they must do. This does not build partnership or elicit cooperation. Diplomacy is persuading others that they should serve our interests because their interests coincide with ours.

Third, as that consummate realist, Otto von Bismarck advised, "Be polite. Write diplomatically. Even in a declaration of war one observes the rules of politeness." Only small boys, hicks, and clueless speech writers think it clever to call foreign leaders or countries names. Statesmen understand that insults just deepen the commitment of those they target to the error of their ways. Sometimes negotiated solutions are the only solutions available at an affordable price. Discourtesy closes the door to negotiated solutions and locks it shut. Getting others to do things our way is difficult. Denigrating their character or putting derogatory labels on them can make it impossible.

Fourth, we need to clear the foreign policy decks as rapidly as we can. Our plunge into the quicksand of endless warfare abroad has already done great damage to our prestige and influence abroad and considerable injury at home. These wars are not sustainable. They cannot be conducted as we have been fighting them without destroying the very ideals we believe in and are fighting to preserve. We are corroding our civil liberties and mortgaging our posterity to foreign bankers. The money that might rebuild crumbling American infrastructure is being squandered on the destruction and botched reconstruction of vast areas of the Middle East. The wars there bring grief, pain, and uncertainty to America, as well as the places where they are fought. They confer no benefits. They divide Americans from each other and from the world. They divert us from urgent tasks of vital importance to our future. We have no plan for ending them, yet we cannot afford not to end them if we wish to recover our domestic tranquility and international standing.

Once we have relieved the myopic and deluded Mr. Magoo of his duties as helmsman, we can take a realistic look at where we are and chart a new course. This will require us belatedly to develop strategies to deal with the many pressing issues we have left largely unattended in recent years. These involve classic foreign policy issues of great consequence such as how to manage our relations with emerging regional orders and how to deal with rising powers like Brazil, China, India, and Russia; reemerging countries like Germany and Japan; failing states like Pakistan; or angry, isolated nations like Iran, North Korea, and Myanmar. Among the neglected issues are also many of vital importance, such as reform of the global trade, investment and monetary systems to protect our prosperity and that of the many other countries that depend on the value of our currency. Beyond this, the issues we must address include the long-overdue formulation of effective multilateral responses to transnational issues like terrorism, pandemic disease, the environment, climate change and security of food, energy, and natural resource supplies.

These are formidable challenges but there is no reason to doubt that we can meet them if we marshal the world's peoples and their resources behind a common effort. For decades, the world looked to the United States for solutions. We Americans were good at providing them. We have the capacity to do so again.

In the self-indulgent final decade of the last century, Americans saw little reason to focus on foreign affairs. In the first decade of this century, we have been long on assertive patriotism but short on realism, vision, and statesmanship. These are qualities we have historically exemplified. They enabled us to create a new order of peace, progress, and prosperity after the World War II. We have the talent and ability to define a world order for the 21st century as well. There is no other country that can make that claim, nor is there another to which the world looks for leadership. As we prepare to enter this century's second decade, we have within us the potential to rise again to the challenge of global leadership. We have the duty to do so. If the United States leads, the world will follow.

Chapter 19

On Intelligence

In early-mid December 2008, I was asked whether I would serve in the incoming Obama administration as chairman of the National Intelligence Council, the body that leads mid- and long-term strategic analysis in the U.S. intelligence community. I declined. About five weeks later, after persistent efforts to recruit me, I eventually succumbed to deeply ingrained impulses to set aside my personal interests in order to serve my country—as I earlier had for 30 years, in the U.S. Foreign Service. I asked for time, however, to manage an orderly withdrawal from the many nonprofit boards on which I served as well as the global business development firm that I chaired. I resigned from all positions on or about February 1.

In the last weeks of February, someone who had learned of my appointment from a mutual friend leaked the news. The reaction was a rapidly escalating campaign of vilification alleging that I was a lobbyist in the pay of Saudi Arabia and an "Israel hater." There was considerable irony in this charge, coming as it did from paid lobbyists for the Israel Lobby and people who make their living producing what Israelis call "hasbara"— propaganda and polemics calculated to exempt Israeli policies and actions from any and all critical examination. While "some of my best friends" may be lobbyists, I myself had never lobbied for any cause, foreign or domestic; nor has any country other than my own ever paid me to speak on its behalf. I had never received any money or favors from Saudi Arabia nor had the Saudis ever asked me to say anything on their behalf. Far from being anti-Israel, my objective has consistently been to safeguard it from its own self-destructive shortsightedness and thereby to safeguard my own country, the United States, which is closely identified internationally with Israel.

In another irony, the leader of the campaign against me was then under indictment as a spy for Israel. (The case against him was ultimately not prosecuted on technical grounds.) A few charges of political incorrectness on China-related matters were adduced based on selective misquotation of purloined emails, but they were clearly a distraction. The campaign was quite evidently organized by the right wing of what is commonly known as the Israel Lobby.

The American Israel Public Affairs Council (AIPAC) did not officially take up the case against me but actively circulated calumnious material on Capitol Hill and collaborated with other groups like the Zionist Organization of America—which is closely aligned with the set-tler movement in Israel—that officially opposed my appointment. By March 10, 2009, it had become apparent that, should I attempt actually to do the job for which I had been recruited, I would be a lightning rod for criticism of any and all intelligence analysis to which these groups objected; and I withdrew my acceptance of the position. The next day's Washington Post *contained three items about this: (1) a front-page account by Walter Pincus detailing aspects of the Lobby's campaign against me; (2) a column by David Broder saying that my resignation was America's loss; and (3) an unsigned editorial calling me a "crackpot" for imagining that there was an Israel Lobby and that it had opposed me. Those elements of the Israel Lobby that had been most active, meanwhile, began to cite my case to their donors as evidence of their effectiveness in advancing their cause. Various demagogues on Capitol Hill also claimed my scalp.*

For the record, the statement I circulated on March 10 read as follows:

You will by now have seen the statement by Director of National Intelligence Dennis Blair reporting that I have withdrawn my previous acceptance of his invitation to chair the National Intelligence Council.

I have concluded that the barrage of libelous distortions of my record would not cease upon my entry into office. The effort to smear me and to destroy my credibility would instead continue. I do not believe the National Intelligence Council (NIC) could function effectively while its chair was under constant attack by unscrupulous people with a passionate attachment to the views of a political faction in a foreign country. I agreed to chair the NIC to strengthen it and protect it against politicization, not to introduce it to efforts by a special-interest group to assert control over it through a protracted political campaign.

As those who know me are well aware, I have greatly enjoyed life since retiring from government. Nothing was further from my mind than a return to public service. When Admiral Blair asked me to chair the NIC, I responded that I understood he was "asking me to give my freedom of speech, my leisure, the greater part of my income, subject myself to the mental colonoscopy of a polygraph, and resume a daily commute to a job with long working hours and a daily ration of political abuse." I added that I wondered "whether there wasn't some sort of downside to this offer." I was mindful that no one is indispensable; I am not an exception. It took weeks of reflection for me to conclude that, given the unprecedentedly challenging circumstances in which our country now finds itself abroad and at home, I had no choice but accept the call to return to public service. I thereupon resigned from all positions that I had held and all activities in which I was engaged. I now look forward to returning to private life, freed of all previous obligations.

I am not so immodest as to believe that this controversy was about me rather than issues of public policy. These issues had little to do with the NIC and were not at the heart of what I hoped to contribute to the quality of analysis available to President Obama and his administration. Still, I am saddened by what the controversy and the manner in which the public vitriol of those who devoted themselves to sustaining it have revealed about the state of our civil society. It is apparent that we Americans cannot any longer conduct a serious public discussion or exercise independent judgment about matters of great importance to our country as well as to our allies and friends.

The libels on me and their easily traceable email trails show conclusively that there is a powerful lobby determined to prevent any view other than its own from being aired, still less to factor in American understanding of trends and events in the Middle East. The tactics of the Israel Lobby plumb the depths of dishonor and indecency and include character assassination, selective misquotation, the willful distortion of the record, the fabrication of falsehoods, and an utter disregard for the truth. The aim of this Lobby is control of the policy process through the exercise of a veto over the appointment of people who dispute the wisdom of its views, the substitution of political correctness for analysis, and the exclusion of any and all options for decision by Americans and our government other than those that it favors.

There is a special irony in having been accused of improper regard for the opinions of foreign governments and societies by a group so clearly intent on enforcing adherence to the policies of a foreign government—in this case, the government of Israel. I believe that the inability of the American public to discuss, or the government to consider, any option for U.S. policies in the Middle East opposed by the ruling faction in Israeli politics has allowed that faction to adopt and sustain policies that ultimately threaten the existence of the state of Israel. It is not permitted for anyone in the United States to say so. This is not just a tragedy for Israelis and their neighbors in the Middle East; it is doing widening damage to the national security of the United States.

The outrageous agitation that followed the leak of my pending appointment will be seen by many to raise serious questions about whether the Obama administration will be able to make its own decisions about the Middle East and related issues. I regret that my willingness to serve the new administration has ended by casting doubt on its ability to consider, let alone decide what policies might best serve the interests of the United States rather than those of a lobby intent on enforcing the will and interests of a foreign government.

In the court of public opinion, unlike a court of law, one is guilty until proven innocent. The speeches from which quotations have been lifted from their context are available for anyone interested in the truth to read. The injustice of the accusations made against me has been obvious to those with open minds. Those who have sought to impugn my character are uninterested in any rebuttal that I or anyone else might make.

Still, for the record: I have never sought to be paid or accepted payment from any foreign government, including Saudi Arabia or China, for any service, nor have I ever spoken on behalf of a foreign government, its interests, or its policies. I have never lobbied any branch of our government for any cause, foreign or domestic. I am my own man, no one else's, and with my return to private life, I will once again—to my pleasure—serve no master other than myself. I will continue to speak out as I choose on issues of concern to me and other Americans.

I retain my respect and confidence in President Obama and DNI Blair. Our country now faces terrible challenges abroad as well as at home. Like all patriotic Americans, I continue to pray that our president can successfully lead us in surmounting them.

My resignation statement accelerated the opening for discussion of subjects that had long been taboo in American politics. Since sustaining that taboo was a prime objective of the elements of the Israel Lobby that went after me, their tactical victory was, I think, a strategic defeat for them.

I addressed the problem of the politicization of intelligence publicly, a few months later.

Foregone Conclusions: Vested Interests and Intelligence Analysis[1]

June 12, 2009

Not so long ago—before I was sprayed by political skunks and had to excuse myself to avoid subjecting others to the stench of political vilification—I had occasion to spend some time thinking about intelligence, in the sense of the analysis of information relevant to statecraft. This is an important topic under any circumstance. It is all the more so in the wake of the string of disasters that persistent inattentiveness to foreign trends and events, occasional analytical misjudgments, and frequent policy miscalculations have brought us in recent years.

In broad terms, the intelligence community provides the sensory apparatus of the state, without which the inner reaches of our government are blind, deaf, numb, and heedless of threats and opportunities alike. Intelligence agencies assure situational awareness and alertness to trends. Our executive branch relies on the analytical product of the intelligence community—how it understands and communicates the information it notices—to ensure that policymaking is on sound factual and psychological ground. Once in a great while, Congress does the same. At its best, analysis can correct the conventional wisdom and the preconceptions by which we misconstrue, misperceive, or fail to notice foreign trends and events of import. At its worst, it can fortify national denial and complacency, perpetuate blind spots, attribute our own hopes, fears, and motivations to foreigners who do not share them, or reinforce ill-founded self-congratulation. It can alert us to the dangers and opportunities change brings, or it can sedate us with comforting affirmations that assume the durability of the status quo. It can protect us from harm and enable us to position ourselves to national advantage, or it can make us vul-

---

1. Remarks to Diplomatic and Consular Officers, Retired.

nerable and prone to policy pratfalls.

Intelligence analysis, of which diplomatic analysis is a subset and to which some here have contributed much, is, in short, central to our republic's formulation and conduct of successful policy. In my experience, the analysts in our intelligence community are, by and large, exceptionally able people who are dedicated to providing us with essential insights into foreign realities and capable of doing so. But, for our leaders to be able correctly to judge what we should do and how they should adjust those moral compasses and approaches they inherit from predecessors, our best informed and most free-thinking analysts must be free to reach considered judgments without censorship and without compulsion. The analytical process must strive to understand and portray reality as dispassionate examination finds it to be, not as ideology or interested parties stipulate it should or must be. It matters greatly whether our executive branch and Congress demand analysts' honest inferences or insist that they be told only what they or powerful constituencies in our body politic want to hear.

As the fate of the Department of State's China hands in the middle of the 20th century famously attests, sustaining objectivity against the pressures of political correctness has never been easy. The China hands have been far from alone; others with unwelcome expertise and insight into foreign events have met similar punishment and ostracism. To be right when what you say is politically wrong is to invite punishment from the guardians of political correctness. No surprise there. But the very notion that analysis should be *wertfrei*—value free—has come under strong attack in recent years. Three months ago, for example, an op-ed in the now mostly neo-con editorial pages of the *Washington Post* charged me with the epistemological sin of "realism," arguing that my lack of a passionate attachment to Israel rendered me incapable of correctly assessing the impact of its policies on U.S. interests. It is clear that, in the view of some, selective apology or denunciation of foreign behavior, not the prediction of it or its effects on our country and its interests, are what intelligence work should be all about.

For such polemicists, politically correct delusion is preferable to a realistic view of the external world as the basis of policy. The splendid results of the approach they have advocated are visible around the globe but nowhere more than in the stable, secular democracy that has emerged in Iraq, the shriveling of Islamic extremism our invasion and occupation of Muslim lands has catalyzed, the peace and development we have brought to Afghanistan and Pakistan, and the concord that the suspension of independent American judgment has caused to flower in the Holy Land. You don't have to be a realist to notice discrepancies between the predicted results of policies and their actual catastrophic consequences. And yet, unchastened by the facts, those who insisted on these policies continue to advocate more of the same.

The concept of analysis as polemic finds its major expression in the myriad "think tanks"— perhaps, more accurately, "belief tanks"—established in recent decades to spin trends and events to promote the ideological or other theses of their founders and supporters. It is also a key characteristic of the cliquish dialogue of the blogosphere, in which partisan commentary reinforces parochial views and fact checking or skeptical questioning more often elicit obscene ad hominem attacks than serious reflection. Paradoxically, those obsessed with particular issues have more information than ever before to draw upon, even as general civic literacy on foreign affairs and the space for civil debate on public-policy issues continue to contract.

Courses in foreign geography, history, classics, and culture are no longer part of most school curricula. Surveys show the average American to be supremely ignorant of the world beyond our shores. The 2,500 foreign correspondents fielded by the U.S. press 60 years ago have dwindled to less than 200. Our media have been systematically reduced and homogenized by mergers and acquisitions; oligopolies decide what is fit to print. Their owners defer to advertisers but show little if any commitment to journalistic fairness, balance, or depth. The coverage of foreign events in our print media shrinks daily along with the newspapers themselves. The TV news, which bears the same resemblance to news in print media as the funny papers do to serious reportage, long since became the primary source of information for the American public. It's hard to know whether it's good or bad that television itself is now being displaced from this role by the highly selective news feeds that cater to niche audiences on the Internet.

What does all this have to do with intelligence? A lot. Intelligence is simply reliable information that is relevant to decision making. To be useful, it must be accepted by those charged with making decisions, that is, politicians. Politicians are by nature responsive to pressure from activist constituencies and disinclined to challenge them. When the public at large is uninformed and apathetic, fervent minorities can, therefore, dominate discussion, shape national views, and set the parameters of what is both politically acceptable and credible. They can define the conventional wisdom and inhibit the free expression of views contrary to their own. They can even aspire to make alternative perspectives taboo—not just unspeakable but unthinkable in private as well as in public.

In this way, a relatively small group of activists can direct national policy to the advantage of the cause they espouse even when this is arguably contrary to the broader national interest or even the majority in the community of interests they purport to represent. To accommodate these political realities, we have evolved a system of foreign policy by franchise. We turn over the design of policy and the management of its implementation to those Americans most emotionally involved with the issues in dispute, least inclined to weigh them against other priorities, and most committed to one foreign side versus the other.

This makes it all the more important to sound national leadership that our intelligence community be able to provide an independent check on reality and not leave perceptions of it to definition by the many foreign-connected and domestic interests seeking to impose their views and policy preferences on our body politic.

The current global financial crisis and our difficulties in Iraq, Afghanistan, and Pakistan and elsewhere illustrate the fact that, as a nation, we have diminished margins for error. If we can no longer live by our wallets, we must learn to live by our wits. To do this, we must deal with the world as it is, not as domestic constituencies prefer or stipulate it to be. We will pay heavily in blood and treasure if we allow political correctness to preclude analysis of important foreign policy issues or to declare in advance what the conclusions of such analysis must be. This is not a theoretical issue. Let me cite a few examples.

For the past forty or more years, the achievement of a peace that could secure the future of Israel has been a core objective of U.S. foreign policy. Every president has made the pursuit of such a peace a central element of his diplomacy. To this end, over this period, the United States has transferred more than $100 billion directly to Israel and as much as another $100 billion indirectly to it. We have also spent well over $1 trillion and thousands of lives on wars that relate, at least in part, to the objective of securing peace for Israel. Yet there has never been a National Intelligence Estimate (NIE) on the prospects for Middle East peace or, for that matter, on the prospects for the state of Israel in its absence. Nor has there been such a review of either the impact of the U.S.-Israeli strategic partnership on our relations with the Arab or Islamic worlds or the role that Arab and Muslim perceptions of it may play in stimulating anti-American terrorism. There has been no independent evaluation of the perpetually unsuccessful "peace process" despite repeated charges from the peace movement in Israel that their government gives lip-service to peace while acting to stall it so as to wrest ever more land from Palestinians. Our understanding of events in the Holy Land has been left to be defined by AIPAC and other American supporters of the settler movement in Israeli-occupied Arab lands. They have brazenly—and quite successfully—insisted that the Likud Party and related right-wing factions in Israeli politics should have the right to decide U.S. policy as well as the policy of Israel.

Is it possible that the suspension of independent judgment by the United States has something to do with the utter failure of our 40-year effort to produce a just and lasting peace between Israelis, Palestinians, and other Arabs? Could it be that in this instance, as in others, foreign policy by franchise serves the interest of the operators of the franchise more than it benefits anyone else? Might our unconditional, unexamined support of the Jewish holy war for land in Palestine have something to do with the expanding holy war against us by some Arabs and Muslims? Israelis regularly ask these questions and vigorously debate them. By contrast, Americans, have until recently been effectively enjoined from asking them and hence from considering policies that might better secure Israel while also securing ourselves.

Such silencing of debate is a perversion of democracy. The Likud Lobby does not simply seek to ensure that the positions it advocates receive favorable consideration in the policymaking process, as it is fully entitled to do. It strives to block contrary views by applying odious labels to their spokespersons, distorting their records, ostracizing them, and obstructing the circulation of their views in the media. It prefers to operate in the shadows. Its characteristic mode of attack is the whisper campaign and hit-and-run; having struck, it denies that it was even on the scene. Like the Bolsheviks, the Likud Lobby falsely claims to represent a majority—in this case, a majority of the American Jewish community—when it does not. Its thought police are in fact especially vicious in their suppression of contrary opinion among the three-fourths of Jewish Americans who favor peace over continuing land grabs in the Holy Land.

The Likud Lobby should not be allowed to usurp the title, "Israel Lobby." It is pro-settler, anti-Arab, and anti–free speech. It does not care whether those it lobbies hate it as long as they fear it. Its answer to the possibility that its actions might rekindle anti-Semitism in this country is intensified intimidation of Israel's American critics, whom it conflates with the dwindling band of citizens who object to the extraordinary contributions to our nation's public life of Jewish Americans. This lobby's object is not to win debate but to preclude it. To that end, it insists that only those associated with its points of view occupy positions of public trust in our government. It is a menace not so much because of what it advocates, with respect to which reasonable men might differ, because of the profoundly anti-democratic means by which it ensures that no one, Jew or Gentile, reasonable or not, can exercise the right to differ with it.

We have seen this phenomenon in our politics before. The "China Lobby," which, in association with Senator Joseph McCarthy, advocated the interests of Chiang Kai-shek's Kuomintang by branding its opponents as treasonous and silencing them, is a case in point. Americans waited decades for a leader with the vision and guile to devise a policy that served our interests rather than Chiang's. But not all policy blind spots are the result of such anti-democratic agitation on behalf of foreign interests.

Sometimes the commitment of those in charge of a program morphs into groupthink that blocks necessary study of ground truth. That was how we marched toward tragic outcomes at the Bay of Pigs and in Vietnam. Iraq, where we have stabilized the occupation but not the country, gives every sign of being another such situation. Continued military direction of efforts to deny Afghanistan to "terrorists with global reach" provides the most recent example.

Our conflation of al-Qaeda with the Taliban has caused anti-American terrorism to metastasize. It is now eating away at Pakistan. The recent policy review produced tactical adjustments in our campaign plan but evidently left most of the assumptions underlying past policies intact and unexamined. To a great extent the adjusted policy is more of the same. This should not surprise. After all, the policy review was begun in the last administration. It was led by the U.S. military and conceived, in large measure, to vindicate past military sacrifices. Its implicit watchword was "support the troops and stand by the generals," not "figure out how we can most efficiently deny the region to terrorists with global reach."

Our military are superb at crafting campaign plans and consistently unsuccessful at designing and implementing politico-military strategy. The new campaign plan was designed from the top down on the basis of domestic political imperatives, general military doctrine, and our experience in the very different circumstances of Iraq. It was not built from the bottom up on the basis of local realities. It pays lip-service to narrowing our objectives and pursuing non-military solutions but does not, in practice, do so. For it to work, lots of very improbable things have to happen.

For the first time in thousands of years, Afghanistan would have to develop a strong central government in Kabul. Under military pressure from us, the Pashtun tribes who straddle the border have for all practical purposes withdrawn the limited allegiance they had earlier granted to Kabul or Islamabad. They would have to restore their fealty to these capitals and accept a much greater measure of direct rule from them than ever before. Pashtun and Baluchi heads of household would have to forgive outsiders who intrude on the privacy of their women or kill their kin. They would have to delegate the defense of their honor to foreigners or central government soldiers recruited from the ranks of their traditional ethnic adversaries.

In this context, consider the implications of reports that, at present, for every two members of al-Qaeda we kill with a missile fired from a drone, we cause the deaths of a hundred Afghan or Pakistani civilians, all of them part of extensive social networks built on mutual obligation for protection and revenge. If these figures are even in the ballpark, how does one describe such a policy? ("Counterproductive" seems too wishy-washy. "Immoral" comes readily to mind. Perhaps "catastrophically misguided" is an even better fit.) Yet we now plan to expand the use of lethal drones.

The drug economy that our intervention has fostered would have to be replaced by other sources of income for Afghan farmers, as yet unidentified. Pakistan would have to set aside its judgment, born of bitter experience, that India presents a mortal threat to it. Its army would have to assign higher priority to combating militant members of the religion that defines its national identity than to defending against Indian attack. Pakistanis would have to accept the growing Indian presence in their strategic rear, in Afghanistan, rather than empowering their intelligence agencies to act on their fear of encirclement. And all of this would have to be accomplished in partnership with a foreign power—the United States—that most Pakistanis, like other Muslims, continue to see as hostile to their religion and engaged in war on its believers in Iraq and Afghanistan, as well as in league with Israel in its campaign to dislodge Palestinians from what remains of their hold on Palestine.

Even without considering feminist or nuclear non-proliferation objectives, this is a policy with aims that are far too broad, with too many moving parts, pursued by predominantly military means that are ill suited to the task and abstracted from local cultural and political realities. No doubt General Petraeus will have ample time to play his program out. Still, it is not too early to begin to do the analysis needed to design a policy with narrower objectives that leverages local realities rather than trying to overturn them. We will need such a policy if the current one strikes out. I am not the only one to fear that it represents the reinforcement of failure rather than a path to success.

There are many more examples of blind spots delineated by prejudice and sustained by vested interests that impede our understanding of the world and impair our ability to formulate effective policies to deal with its problems. I think, in particular, of the Islamophobia that post–9/11 fear-mongering has now deeply etched into the American psyche. As President Obama has eloquently argued, we cannot hope to build alliances against extremism with the fifth of the human race that is Muslim if we proceed from ignorance and fear of their faith. Nor—on another subject of vital interest to Americans—can we make the transitions we must in the global monetary and financial system if we persist in the delusion that Richard Nixon's gutted version of Bretton Woods can remain forever in place. As Edmund Burke observed, "the heart of diplomacy is to yield gracefully what you no longer have the power to withhold." But to wrest advantage from doing this, one must first understand what one cannot withhold and why.

Time does not permit me to cite the many other conditions, trends, and events with respect to which our understanding of the world could use a solid boost from the intelligence community. I will save that for another occasion. I do not want to close, however, without pointing out that, despite the breakdown or near breakdown of more than a few elements of our socioeconomic system, we have not tasked our analysts to look at how other societies have succeeded or failed in addressing similar problems. Such issues range from deteriorating and poorly integrated transportation infrastructure, to collapsing pension systems, to striking an appropriate balance between the open society and security against terrorism, to managing state ownership of significant chunks of the formerly private economy, including other issues like health-care financing along the way. To take this last example, the World Health Organization rates our health-care system 37th or so in the world in terms of what it delivers. That means there are at least 36 nations that, by some measure, do better than we at supplying affordable health care to their citizens. Why do we not see it as in our interest to learn from foreign best practices in areas like this where we clearly don't know what to do?

Is it the result of some lingering belief that—despite much evidence to the contrary—we Americans have all the answers? Or is it that the various elements of our medical-industrial complex, insurance sector, trucking companies, unions, and construction companies, and so forth cherish the cushy deals they have worked out for themselves and don't want the challenges to these that a serious consideration of foreign experience might suggest? Whatever the cause, it's hard to argue that we could not benefit from a less insular approach to crafting necessary domestic reforms. Why not put our intelligence community to work at mining foreign experiences for ideas for better solutions to our domestic problems? It seems to me, at least, that domestic reform is now too urgent to be left to the self-serving reporting and skewed analysis of the disparate champions of our status quo.

In the end, the quality of American decision making reflects the vigor and openness of our democracy. On some subjects, I have argued today, our democracy has demonstrably been neither open nor vigorous. In the case of a few, analysts have been conditioned to cringe in silence, not to exercise independent judgment or voice critical challenges to the politically correct conventional wisdom. This is a dangerous weakness in our national security system that invites correction—either through introspection and reform or from further bitter experiences with failure. Intelligence is properly the critical assessor, not the designated cheerleader, of policy results. But the best intelligence in the world is of no avail if those in Congress and the executive branch who must act on it are mentally unprepared to heed it or disinclined to accept it because it contradicts their preconceptions.

To meet the challenges before us, Americans need heightened civic literacy and reinvigorated public dialogue. This means encouraging civil debate about precisely those issues that are most painfully controversial. Realism about trends and events that affect the general welfare, common defense, liberties, and domestic tranquility of our country is the essential basis of wise and moral policies. An intelligence community that is independent and protected against vested interests, not subjected to censorship and direction by them, is the essential prerequisite for this. That is not a description of our current situation. It is, however, something we cannot do without.

PART V
Perspectives on Saudi Arabia

In early 2010, I was asked to speak to a group in Florida about Saudi Arabia. I suddenly realized that I had never before formally addressed that topic to an American audience though I had, of course, answered plenty of questions about the Kingdom at conferences. I had, however, delivered a couple of papers about interesting aspects of the mysterious Kingdom to audiences in Beijing and London. And I had, I recalled, mentioned the Saudis in passing—to the members of the San Francisco World Affairs Council—in the course of expounding on the developing relationship between China and the Arabs. In light of charges by some in the "Israel Lobby" that I had "flacked" for Saudi Arabia, the fact that I'd never given a talk about it in the United States struck me as more than a little ironic.

Here, then, is the sum total of my formal remarks about the Kingdom of Saudi Arabia.

Chapter 20

Saudi Arabia and the Forces of Globalization

I don't recall the date when I wrote the paper on which this chapter is based; but I delivered the paper at a conference on globalization held in Beijing sometime in 1998. It discusses some of the factors that formed the modern Kingdom of Saudi Arabia and shaped its relations with its neighbors and the world. It places the Kingdom's history in a broader global context and sets out a benchmark for understanding conditions in the Kingdom at the end of the last century, just a few years before 9/11 imposed a different narrative.

The dominant power on the Arabian Peninsula, the Kingdom of Saudi Arabia, has long been one of the world's least accessible societies, with a famously inscrutable government. Even Saudi Arabia's smaller Gulf Arab neighbors, who share ethnic, religious, and other ties with the Kingdom but who are separated from it by their heritage as British protectorates, regard it with a mixture of envy, apprehension, and perplexity. Saudi Arabia is, after all, the only non-Western polity to have successfully barred intrusion by Euro-American missionaries and soldiers.[1] The Saudi monarchy is the only traditional ruling structure to have survived the era of colonialism intact and on its own terms.[2] Its oil wealth and the international influence

1. When Westerners finally gained access to the Kingdom of Saudi Arabia, it was under contract as "hired help," not as conquerors. Americans and Europeans were able to enter the Kingdom only so long as they evidenced respect for Saudi religious and social tradition and accepted that any attempt to propagate Western religious, ideological, or secular values would result in summary punishment and/or deportation.

2. Those non-Western monarchies that did not, like those in Mexico, Peru, India, Central Asia, Africa, China, and Turkey, fall under pressure from Western imperialism, yielded to its tutelage or influence. Swaziland and Lesotho were incorporated into the British Empire. Bhutan and other Himalayan hill states became subdivisions of British India. Thailand practiced preemptive capitulation to European (and later Japanese imperial) influence to avoid conquest or colonization. The Japanese Empire itself sought salvation in self-Westernization, before the defeat of its bid for domination of Asia subjected it to American-dictated reforms. The Shah's unsuccessful attempt to restore the Persian Empire by Westernizing Iran catalyzed the emergence of a republic in which many Western-style institutions, like a parliament, coexist uneasily with novel forms of Islamic theocracy.

derived from it have made Riyadh the fourth corner of the traditionally triangular Arab East.[3] The Kingdom was—with Israel—the only polity to have been successfully established by military conquest in the 20th century.[4] Had the East India Company and its successor the British Indian Empire not intervened to suppress piracy and preempt other powers from establishing a foothold in the Gulf, Saudi Arabia's traditional borders would almost certainly have expanded to include the smaller emirates along the coast of the Persian Gulf and these small polities would have been absorbed by their larger neighbor.

The Kingdom's decision-making processes are largely invisible or opaque to those outside the inner circle of its royal family. It continues to defer to the uniquely demanding religious doctrines and social traditions of Wahhabi Islam, which many other Muslims in the region deride as aggressively austere and intolerant. Saudi law and custom forbid the practice of religions other than Islam. Saudi universities do not offer instruction in the Hellenistic philosophical traditions that were at the center of Islamic civilization at its height (and that subsequently flowed from there to Europe, where they inspired the Renaissance).

Despite this dedication to traditional ways, the discovery of enormous reserves of oil in Saudi Arabia's Eastern Province in 1938, the rapid growth in global demand for energy, and the huge royalties from oil exports have enabled the Kingdom to manage a three decade-long program of modernization that is unprecedented in the scope of its speed, intensity, and breadth. Almost unbelievably impoverished and backward within living memory,[5] Saudi Arabia now possesses a physical infrastructure that any developed society would envy. This modernization has, moreover, been accomplished with remarkably little apparent social

---

3. Traditionally, Baghdad, Cairo, and Damascus vied for primacy in the Mashriq. Arabia was, of course, at the center of world events for a couple of decades after the initial eruption of Islam from the Hejaz. Despite the presence of the Islamic holy places, it then became a political, economic, and cultural backwater within the Dar al-Islam. Disparaging attitudes, tinged with envy, at the three points of the traditional triangle of power mentioned above reflect this earlier reality rather than the wealth, power, and commercial sophistication of the modern Kingdom and its Gulf Arab neighbors.

4. The modern Kingdom of Saudi Arabia is the third iteration of the 18th century alliance between the founder of the Al-Saud dynasty and the religious reformer, Mohammed ibn Abdulwahhab Al-Tamimi. The previous two Saudi kingdoms were overthrown by intervention from the Egyptian outpost of the Ottoman Empire, which saw both their religious extremism and territorial expansionism as threatening. The Kingdom's borders with all of its neighbors were long unsettled and undemarcated. Not until 2000, almost a century after the founding of the modern Kingdom, were its last major territorial disputes settled—through agreement with Yemen on a land and sea border, and with Kuwait on a maritime border.

5. The Gulf Arab societies did not experience the many generations of innovation in equipment and technology that elsewhere preceded the arrival of present-day technologies. By the time Arabian cities had electricity, the transistor and touch-tone phone had long since replaced the cathode ray tube and pulse telephony. By the time literacy was the norm in Arabia, the computer was ubiquitous. By the time Arabian merchants had shoes, many of them were stylish footwear from Italy. (See the charming narrative in *From Rags to Riches*, by Mohammed Al-Fahim, London, 1995.)

stress. Other cultures challenged by their sudden, humiliating encounter with superior Euro-American wealth and power have attempted, usually with disastrous results, to import Western technology without permitting contagion by the values associated with it.[6] Saudi Arabia may be the only example anywhere to date of prolonged success in such an attempt.

Saudi monarchs, principally King Fahd bin Abdulaziz (the architect of the modern Saudi political economy), have invested the Kingdom's huge revenue from oil over the past quarter century not just to promote economic progress but also to buttress Saudi society against change by reinforcing adherence to religious tradition.[7] They have built a remarkably complete, ultramodern physical base for a modern manufacturing sector and service economy while vastly expanding and modernizing their country's religious infrastructure.[8] Saudi Arabia's mud-walled villages have become vast urban agglomerations, crisscrossed with high-speed divided highways, punctuated by high-rise buildings, and made visually exciting by grand, modern adaptations of traditional Arab and Islamic architecture.[9] Mosques that were small, stuffy, and shabby have been replaced by places of worship that are vast, air-conditioned, beautiful, and adjoined by enormous parking lots. The Kingdom's relatively small nomad population is now more likely to transport camels to new pasturage on flatbed trucks than to herd them there on foot. The Saudi merchant class is as at home in London and Los Angeles as it is in Jeddah or Al-Khobar. But, by marked contrast with other developing societies, the hundreds of thousands of Saudis who have been educated abroad have not chosen to stay there. They have come home to the Kingdom (though they often maintain vacation homes in the United States, Britain, or other parts of Europe and many have a substantial portion of their capital invested abroad).

Paradoxically, the very harshness of its climate and the constraints that this

6. This is what 19th-century Chinese reformers advocated but could not achieve. They sought to preserve traditional knowledge as the basis of national culture while adopting Western knowledge for its utility. ("Zhong xue wei ti; Xi xue wei yong," as Zhang Zhidong put it.) Given the failure of this strategy elsewhere, it is hard to believe that, absent the extraordinary wealth that oil has given them, Saudis could have been successful.

7. Universal education in Saudi Arabia has entailed universal religious indoctrination and many of the universities that oil money financed are devoted to religious rather than secular education. The result has been both a vast increase in literacy and in those schooled in the fine points of Islamic theology, if not in skills more relevant to employment in the industrial and service sectors of the Kingdom's economy; those sectors remain dominated by expatriate guest workers.

8. Mecca and Medina have been modernized, and their places of worship expanded to accommodate millions of pilgrims at a time. New mosques dot the Saudi urban landscape.

9. When Saudi Arabia established its special relationship with the United States 55 years ago in February 1945, Riyadh was a mud-brick town of about 12,000 inhabitants, closed to foreigners. Today it is a sprawling automotive city, with some of the world's most notable and innovative architecture and engineering. More than 3 million people, a third or more of them non-Saudi, now live in Riyadh. Similar transformations have overwhelmed the traditional trading and religious centers of Dhahran, Jeddah, Mecca, and Medina.

placed on economic development in the pre-oil age both isolated Saudi Arabia and facilitated a misleading appearance of rapid integration into the global economy once oil was discovered. When the Kingdom was still too poor to attract direct investment or sales efforts from the industrial democracies, Saudi merchants stepped forward to represent foreign companies and make their products available to both Saudis and foreign pilgrims performing Hajj. But when oil money began to trickle into the Kingdom in the 1950s and 1960s, and then to flood into it with the dramatic rise in oil prices imposed by the oil embargoes that accompanied the 1973 Arab-Israeli War, many more goods and services became available—but the basic pattern of commerce remained unchanged. Saudi trading traditions could easily accommodate bottling, fast food, and clothing franchises, or automobile and air conditioning dealerships, or foreign-affiliated retail outlets and supermarkets, to cite a few examples. With minor adjustments, Saudi traditions were also able to facilitate the arrival and operations of foreign engineering, construction, and hotel management companies, accounting and law firms, and the like. Local agents or partners could fit all of these businesses into the well-established Arabian custom of restricting foreign business presences to agency and representation.

The influx of new commercial activities from abroad was nonetheless immense. Along with new businesses came millions of foreign workers to manage and operate them—initially largely from Europe, East Asia, and the Middle East; later, increasingly, from South Asia, the Philippines, and the Horn of Africa. High-rise construction, modern commercial architecture, an explosion of familiar brand names on neon signs, and a huge non-Arab population (most of it non-Arabic-speaking and much of it non-Muslim) transformed Saudi Arabia's urban landscapes and altered its demography. But, appearances notwithstanding, less really changed than met the eye.

Shops continued to open and close on schedules set by calls to prayer in nearby mosques. Ownership of businesses remained overwhelmingly Saudi despite the fact that few Saudis sought or obtained management or employee positions in them. (Instead, some Saudi graduates of the Kingdom's new religious universities found employment as religious vigilantes assigned to the air-conditioned malls that replaced open-air suqs as the shopping experience of choice. Others stayed at home or frequented the coffee houses and shisha parlors between visits to the mosque.)

The fact was that foreigners continued to be barred from most direct roles in the Saudi economy. They could not own land or operate businesses on their own. To enter the Kingdom or its market, they needed Saudi partners or agents. To leave the Kingdom, even for vacation, they needed the permission of their Saudi employer or partner. (Very often this employer or partner had custody of their passports.) Foreigners could not obtain a visa to enter Saudi Arabia (except as Muslim religious pilgrims) without a local patron. And, in a pattern of patrimonial commerce[10] typical of Third World societies, they were present in the Kingdom on a long-term basis only at the sufferance and pleasure of a patron, often a royal silent partner of the Saudi merchant with whom they were legally contracted.

The oil money that built Saudi Arabia's modern civilian and military infrastructure thus also built a class of ultrawealthy Saudi contractors, each backed by a specific group of individuals or sub-family within the ruling Al-Saud and each with its exclusive tie-ins to specific corporations abroad. The emergence of this class of Saudi operators of foreign franchises was aided by the education of tens of thousands of Saudis in the United States at precisely the moment in the 1960s, 1970s, and 1980s when franchise and chain store operations first achieved unchallenged dominance of North American markets. Saudis educated in the United States introduced a wide range of U.S. retailers to their country.

Saudi Arabia's sudden wealth from oil transformed it in a few years from a collection of ill-lit desert towns to a constellation of urban clusters illuminated by the neon icons of (mostly) American fast food, furniture, automotive, office machines, and other franchises. The Kingdom's merchants then sought and gradually achieved a similar presence by European couturiers and other upscale retailers, often by introducing them to franchising and other models of collaboration that Saudis had first learned from their partnerships with North American mass marketers. So Saudi Arabia became an unwitting collaborator (or source of contagion) in the phenomenon known as "globalization."

The often unstated premise on which foreign companies sought Saudi partners to sell their goods and services in the Kingdom was the global image of Saudi Arabia as a famously wealthy and relatively populous society. But the Kingdom's per capita income has been in steady decline over the past two decades, falling from equivalency with income levels in the United States at the end of the 1970s to only a fifth as much as American living standards today. Some of this decline reflects the exceptionally rapid growth of Saudi Arabia's population, which greatly surpasses its economic growth.[11] National income must now be shared among an ever-larger number of Saudis.

Some of the fall in living standards, however, reflects the slow and uneven growth of the Saudi economy. Overall, the Middle East has been generating rates of economic growth that are less than half those in East Asia. Rates of return on investment in Saudi Arabia have remained generally lower than those in the developed economies of Europe and North America, with the result that wealthy Saudis

10. "Patrimonial commerce" is my term for a pattern of business dealings in which the validity of transactions and their security depend on the approval, support, or acquiescence of a patron rather than the rule of law. Very often the patron expects a commission, annual fee, or share of equity in the enterprise in return for his protection of the transaction or the business presence and activities it creates. In some countries, patrimonial commerce involves entrepreneurial bureaucrats or bureaucracies as patrons. In Saudi Arabia, patrons are typically princes—senior members of the royal family or their sons.

11. Saudi Arabia's population was about 9.4 million in 1980. By 1998 it was 20.7 million. It is projected to reach 33.7 million in 2015 and 46 billion in 2030.

have tended to invest disproportionately abroad rather than in the Kingdom.[12] Saudi Arabia's economy remains closely linked to the multiplier effects of revenue from energy exports, primarily oil. But oil is a commodity subject to wild price swings[13] that reflect every factor constraining short-term supplies or affecting demand. When demand and therefore prices are low, the Kingdom's government has a serious cash flow problem.[14] If the Saudi government cannot pay its bills on time, its contractors cannot pay theirs either. The staffs of large merchant conglomerates have sometimes remained unpaid for six months or more. The perceived unreliability of Saudi Arabian public finance is emerging as an obstacle to the Kingdom's further integration into the global economy.

12. According to recent estimates by investment bankers, Saudis currently hold about $650 billion (equivalent to four times the Kingdom's GDP) abroad.

13. A year earlier, oil prices had been about one-fourth what they were when the paper was delivered.

14. About 78 percent of government revenue in Saudi Arabia still derives from royalties paid by the state oil company, Saudi Aramco.

Chapter 21

Saudi Arabia's Foreign and Domestic Dilemmas[1]

September 2002

In September 2002, I accepted an invitation to speak in London about the challenges the Kingdom was facing after 9/11, especially in its relations with the United States. The review of the months before 9/11 is a reminder of the centrality of the Israeli-Palestinian imbroglio to the politics of the region and its interaction with America.

Even before 9/11, the Kingdom of Saudi Arabia faced increasingly obvious foreign policy and domestic challenges. The year since then has brought many of these challenges to a head, confronting the Saudis with the urgent need to make some very difficult adjustments in both their foreign relations and their domestic compact of governance.

During the Cold War, Saudi Arabia shared with the West an overriding interest in blocking Soviet imperialism and frustrating the spread of the godless communist ideology. The United States was the logical partner for the Kingdom, not only because it was the most powerful Western country but also because it was far away and had no history of imperial ambition or ideological agendas in the region. The basic bargain of Saudi-American relations was thus simple: In return for preferred access to Saudi oil, the United States undertook to protect the Kingdom against foreign threats. (This bargain proved its worth in the defense of Saudi Arabia in the 1960s against Nasser's Egypt, in the 1980s against the Ayatollah Khomeini's Iran, and—most notably—in the 1990s against Saddam's Iraq.)

The growing American identification with Israel after the mid-1960s troubled Saudis and caused occasional flare-ups in their relations with the United States (e.g., in 1973). In normal times, however, even severe differences over Israeli-Arab

---

1. Remarks to the International Institute of Strategic Studies, London.

issues could be, and were, subordinated to the imperative of maintaining a common front in the Cold War and against regional challenges to Saudi security. By the mid-1970s, the United States had further insulated the Saudi-American relationship from the contradictions inherent in the U.S. alliance with Israel by launching active mediation of a "peace process" in the Levant. This offered the only prospect of a negotiated solution there. It made it easier for the two countries to set aside differences over substantive issues even after the common interests of the Cold War had disappeared.

The failure of the U.S.- and Saudi-led coalitions to devise and implement a war termination strategy to follow the expulsion of Iraqi forces from Kuwait at the end of February 1991 facilitated Saddam's unexpected retention of power in Iraq. This, in turn, frustrated U.S. plans to deter future aggression from either Iraq or Iran without establishing permanent garrisons in the Gulf. Saddam's defiant efforts to reassert Iraqi sovereignty engendered continuing low intensity conflict between U.S./U.K. air forces attempting to back up UN weapons inspections and Iraqi air defense units. As time went on, the Saudi public became increasingly opposed both to sanctions against Iraq and to U.S. warplanes (with token British assistance) killing Iraqis from Saudi bases. Only the fact that both activities were pursuant to U.N. resolutions made them politically justifiable to the Kingdom.

The collapse of the Israeli-Arab peace process as the millennium ended left the U.S.-Saudi relationship without a policy framework by which to finesse increasingly emotional differences over the mounting carnage of the al-Aqsa intifada, in which the number of Palestinian dead and wounded, as usual, greatly outnumbered the number of Israelis. The Bush administration demanded an end to violence by Palestinians but ignored the violence against Palestinians inherent in the Israeli military occupation and imposition of settlements.

Ordinary Saudis linked the apparent American indifference to the death and suffering of Arabs in the occupied territories with American policies that brought death and suffering to the Iraqi people. The result was rising pressure on the government of Saudi Crown Prince Abdullah to justify the traditionally close Saudi-American relationship to his citizenry. By the eve of 9/11, he had confronted President Bush with Saudi objections to U.S. policies affecting Saudi interests.

The September 11 suicide attacks on the United States by extremist Muslim terrorists, most of them Saudi nationals, led fairly rapidly to U.S. solidarity—first on the emotional level and then as a matter of policy—with Israel as a fellow victim of suicide bombings by Muslim extremists. It also provided an opportunity for an onslaught of criticism of Saudi Arabia in the American media, often by commentators whose imaginations far outran their knowledge of the Kingdom. Their attacks featured the elements of Saudi culture and society most objectionable to liberal democratic ideology—the peculiar intolerance of Saudi Islam, the alleged anti-Jewish and anti-Christian bias of the educational system, and the subordinate status of women—to paint a portrait of the Kingdom as an enemy, rather than a friend. The Christian right joined with the Zionist left to identify Saudi religious particularism with both terrorism and anti-Americanism.

The Saudi response was halting and confused, revealing the embarrassing extent to which the Kingdom has, unlike its detractors, lacked a long-term strategy directed at building public understanding and sympathy among Americans. This is not to say that Saudi Arabia has done nothing. It has opened itself somewhat to the foreign press. It has sent a series of prestigious delegations, led by leading business-men and including female spokespersons, to the United States. It has reviewed and corrected the most objectionable features of its school curriculum.

These are useful moves, ably carried out by those entrusted with them. They seem to act as an implicit acknowledgment, for the first time, of the imprudence of relying on the U.S. administration and a few powerful American friends to protect the relationship from public scrutiny or criticism. But no long-term strategy of broad Saudi engagement with the United States through public diplomacy has yet emerged. Almost by default, anti-Saudi views are gaining a currency and reaching audiences in the United States, including among U.S. officials, that would have been unimaginable a few years ago. Trends are running against the restoration of sound Saudi-American ties.

On the popular level, Saudis and Americans are now seriously estranged. Outrageous, albeit uncommon, but widely publicized harassment of Arabs and Muslims by U.S. airline and airport security personnel, as well as by immigration, customs, and law enforcement officials, has emerged as a powerful inhibition on Saudi travel to the United States. The frightening possibility of arbitrary detention without access to the legal process is a further deterrent to visitors.

Freezes of financial assets on the basis of undisclosed evidence of alleged con-nections with organizations or individuals suspected of terrorism have led to con-cern about the political risk of Muslim investment in the United States. The result has been substantial disinvestment in U.S. financial assets by Saudi nationals. The Saudi authorities have been unable to halt a woman-led boycott of U.S. products and investments in the United States, directed at registering objections to U.S. sup-port for Israel as it kills and maims Palestinians. U.S. exports to Saudi Arabia are falling rapidly.

In this context, the unconditional American embrace of Ariel Sharon's policies toward the Palestinians and U.S. threats to invade, occupy, and reform Iraq over Saudi and other Arab opposition have placed a very heavy, and possibly unsupport-able, burden on bilateral relations. Much as it would prefer a return to business as usual with the United States, Riyadh has yet to develop a strategy for accomplish-ing this. It has been forced, for the first time, to contemplate options for cutting dependence on the United States.

In the era of American hegemony, there are no obvious alternatives to the United States as the ultimate guarantor of the Kingdom's security. As they ponder their limited choices, Saudis seem, nonetheless, to be working on diluting overdependence on the United States, favoring Britain and France even as they develop new relationships with Brazil, China, Germany, Japan, and Russia.

Meanwhile, as part of Saudi Arabia's deteriorated image internationally, concerns about its political stability have reemerged. Most of the factors cited in this regard reflect the biases of Saudi Arabia's critics rather than the Kingdom's realities. The most surprising thing about Saudi Arabia in the past has been its boring stability despite the stupefying pace of its modernization. There is no reason to doubt that this will continue to be case. The principal threat to Saudi stability is, in any event, not the religious disaffection or antimonarchical Islamic republicanism posited by Likud and its American fellow travelers. It is the Kingdom's fiscal crisis.

The Saudi fiscal system, which relies almost entirely on royalties from oil production rather than taxes for its revenue, can no longer meet the rising demands of a rapidly growing population and a prospering private sector. The Saudi paradox is that the more the Kingdom's private sector thrives, the more the government must spend to provide it with the services it needs, so—in the absence of any link, in the form of taxes, between private incomes and government revenue—the nearer bankruptcy the government finds itself. Absent a tax system, moreover, Saudi Arabia lacks the financial leeway to buy its way out of its policy dilemmas, as it has sometimes been able to do in the past. Nor does the Kingdom have the cash surplus it would need to cultivate immediate alternatives to the United States as a supplier of defense goods and services.

The basic bargain of governance in Saudi Arabia has cast the government as a dispenser of largesse and charity for the needy. If the government cannot discharge these responsibilities without introducing income and other taxes, the compact of governance—the relationship between rulers and ruled—will have to be renegotiated. If Saudis were required to pay taxes, they have quietly made clear, they would expect a larger role in determining government policy. (No taxation without representation is a principle with universal appeal.)

Not having been taxed, Saudi Arabian citizens have not considered representation a worthwhile struggle. But, as fiscal circumstance compels the Kingdom to contemplate putting in a tax-based revenue system, Saudi Arabia's rulers must consider how best to empower more representative forms of government at the provincial and national levels. They will also have to justify any tax system they proclaim by significantly reducing, if not eliminating, government waste, fraud, mismanagement, and public procurement rake-offs. Saudis, like others, will pay taxes to fund the efficient conduct of government business but not to reimburse ministries for royal or bureaucratic rip-offs of their budgets.

My clear sense is that the Crown Prince and those around him are not at all intimidated by the prospect of fiscal and political reform. Indeed, they very much want to carry out such reforms. But reform under the best of circumstances is stressful. Under circumstances in which Saudi Arabia must at the same time rethink and realign its international relationships because Saudi-American relations continue to deteriorate, it could prove fatal.

As both an American and a longstanding friend of Saudi Arabia and its ruling family, I believe strongly in the importance of reknitting Saudi-American ties. As an erstwhile diplomatic professional, I have no doubt that this is do-able. Cooperative ties have served both countries well. They are vastly preferable for both to strain in the bilateral relationship. But this is not the only reason for both sides to make a serious effort to reverse current negative trends in the relationship. Prospects for the reforms the Crown Prince and others of like mind in the Kingdom want to carry out rest in no small measure on restoring the health of the Saudi-American relationship. To do this will, however, require a breadth and depth of mutual engagement and long-term commitment that, unfortunately, neither side has yet demonstrated.

Chapter 22

The Arabs Take a Chinese Wife: Sino-Arab Relations in the Decade to Come[1]

May 7, 2006

I want to speak with you this morning about foreign affairs, by which, of course, I mean failing marriages, extramarital relationships, and instances of bigamy, maybe even polygamy. It's pretty racy stuff compared to most diplomacy. Those of you who may be offended should leave now.

I will be brief. Therefore, I will be superficial. But this doesn't bother me at all. Decades ago, a wise man from the East told me that, if something is worth doing, it is worth doing superficially. I have always heeded his advice. He was, of course, from the East Coast of the United States.

The failing marriage of which I just spoke is not our relationship with the People's Republic of China, though that is indeed troubled. Some of you may have noticed signs of this during Chinese President Hu Jintao's visit to Washington in April.

For reasons best known to Karl Rove, our president declined to honor him with a state dinner. At the ceremony on the south lawn to welcome him, President Hu's national anthem was announced as that of the "Republic of China," the name of the rival Chinese regime in Taipei. The Secret Service allowed a protester to pose as a journalist, infiltrate the White House grounds, and shriek at the Chinese president for nearly three minutes before taking her into custody, despite the fact that she had been arrested for similar unjournalistic activity before. Protestors in Lafayette Square continued to make so much noise after 11 at night, when their permit to demonstrate had expired, that President Hu and his wife were unable to sleep at Blair House. When President Hu's staff complained, the White House referred them to the Washington police, who had knocked off at 10 p.m. and refused to deal

---

1. Remarks to the World Affairs Council of Northern California annual conference at Asilomar.

with the situation unless they were paid overtime.

Other things went wrong, but this is enough to give you a sense of the confused and inhospitable atmosphere that surrounded the visit. President Hu and his party went away convinced that, not content with offering him a tepid welcome, the administration had actually gone out of its way to insult him and the nation he leads.

It's really hard to believe that an operation that choreographs every presidential appearance so meticulously that it won't let a Democrat, still less a protester, any-where near our president at public gatherings around the country could screw up so badly. But it happened. And it's pretty clear that it happened mainly because we Americans now don't know quite what to make of China.

Is China a friend or an enemy? An opportunity or a menace? Should we fête its leaders or fend them off? When it became apparent that President Hu would not be coming to present, on bended knee, major concessions that would appease anti-China sentiment in Washington, many inside the Beltway questioned why he was coming at all. In an ironic echo of the arrogant attitudes that ultimately did in the Chinese Empire, these American versions of the palace eunuchs of the Forbidden City asked, if Mr. Hu wasn't leading a tribute mission and wouldn't kowtow to our emperor, why should they go at all out of their way to be nice to him? So they didn't.

I mention all this because, as some of you know, President Hu flew directly from the United States to Riyadh, the capital of the Kingdom of Saudi Arabia, where there was no confusion at all about how to treat him. He was greeted there as a friend from afar who should be treated with respect and courted as the leader of a rising power. He was, in short, welcomed in a manner calculated to make him feel welcome and to want to come back. It was a really telling contrast.

This brings me to our own relations with the Arabs. We first met them about six decades ago. We had a common enemy in the Soviet Union. They liked to sell oil, and we liked to buy it. Back then, it was just about as simple as that. We mar-ried ourselves to the Arabs and their oil. An infatuation with us on their part fol-lowed. We played along with this, even if we were somewhat distracted by the steamy affair we were even then carrying on with Israel.

As the Arab-American relationship matured, it came to embrace many dimen-sions. The elites in the Arab Gulf countries and their children oriented themselves toward the United States. Hundreds of thousands of Arab students came to live and study here. They took their kids to Disney World and had their annual phys-icals in Houston or Cleveland or other centers of VIP medical care. This was their second home. Saudis alone came to own about 100,000 houses in the United States. And they spent a lot of money here. The United States enjoyed a command-ing share of their market. Arabia became the only place outside North America where American cars dominated the market. (Like us, Arabs love gas guzzlers. Unlike us, they don't have to pay other people for the gas they guzzle.)

Basically, the Arabs give us oil, and we give them back little green portraits of dead American presidents. Until recently, they ploughed the money we paid them back into the American economy—about $800 billion in private Arab investment by the turn of this century. And everyone benefited.

Then came 9/11. A few bad actors determined to wreck this happy partnership managed to do so. Arab students here received death threats. Their parents pulled them out of school and brought them back home. Arabs found it almost impossible to get American visas. Those who did get them found they had to run a gauntlet of abusively suspicious officials—not just at the border but at every airport in the country. They stopped coming to the United States. American businesses could no longer bring Arabs to showrooms here or train them to use U.S. equipment. The American business presence in the Arab Gulf dropped to a fourth or fifth of what it had been as corporate counsel in our companies convinced management not to risk lawsuits by employees if frequent security scares in the region were to produce actual incidents. (In practice, they haven't, but that's another story.)

Mutual affection between Arabs and Americans has, in short, been succeeded by mutual fear and loathing, punctuated by occasional self-righteous American demands for major Arab behavior modification—demands that they embrace an American reform agenda of elections, women's liberation, religious pluralism. You know the list. The deterioration in mutual regard was much in evidence during the orgy of xenophobic demagoguery that killed the attempt by Dubai Ports World to buy cargo management functions in some American ports from the British company that ran them. The furor against this convinced the world that Americans just flat out detest Arabs and are not prepared to do business with them—not even in the currency we exchange for their oil.

Somewhere along the line, before we got to this unhappy moment in U.S.-Arab relations, we Americans met the Chinese. And we established a solid relationship with them, despite our differences. The major difference between us and the Chinese, of course, is that Americans like to buy and unwrap things, and Chinese like to make, pack, and ship things. Unlike us, they are unabashed in their lust for investments in the form of little green dead presidents. And they finance our budget deficits and lend us the money we have to borrow to do the inscrutable things Americans do—like make war in Iraq.

The Arabs, meanwhile, have been looking around for alternatives to dependence on the United States. They know they can't divorce us. We're too big and fat and too important as a source of income to throw out of the bed we share with them. But now they've found the Chinese and the Chinese have found them.

If you ask folks in Washington what's going on, they will tell you that the Chinese are courting the Arabs. Perhaps. But it's always hard to tell who's courting whom. Was it the dropped stuff from the purse or the strategic display of cleavage, or was it the fast talk and the foot rub that caused one thing to lead to another? Hard to tell, especially when the attraction is mutual, as it is in this case.

What do the Arabs and Chinese see in each other? Quite a bit.

The Arabs see a partner who will buy their oil without demanding that they accept a foreign ideology, abandon their way of life, or make other choices that they would rather avoid. They see a country that is far away and has no imperial agenda in their region but which is internationally influential and likely in time to be militarily powerful. They see a place to exchange their portraits of little green dead Americans for things they can unwrap and enjoy. They see a country that unreservedly welcomes their investments and is grateful for the jobs these create. They see a major civilization that seems determined to build a partnership with them, does not insult their religion or their way of life, values its reputation as a reliable supplier too much to engage in the promiscuous application of sanctions or other coercive measures, and has no habit of bombing or invading other countries to whose policies it objects.

In short, the Arabs see the Chinese as pretty much like Americans—that is, Americans as we used to be before we decided to experiment with diplomacy-free foreign policy, hit-and-run democratization, compassionate colonialism, and other neo-con conceits of the age. And they see a chance to rebalance their international relationships to offset their longstanding overdependence on the United States. They know that they can't divorce us, even if they wished to do so. They are as addicted to our money as we are to their oil. We are locked in a Catholic marriage. But they are Muslims, and they don't have to divorce us to take a second wife—hence, their romances with China and India. And these romances are taking place when international polls routinely show that, outside of Germany and our own country, China is now far more admired and trusted than the United States.

As for the Chinese, who were the first culture to recognize that gluttony, lust, and greed are what human nature is all about, well—they see oil, gas, and petrochemicals, added respect and influence for their country abroad, a new market for their goods and services, and a new set of partners in global investment. Sounds like the basis for a relationship! And it's turning out to be the basis of a relationship that is developing very rapidly, not just in terms of trade and investment—though they are booming—but more broadly.

Some years ago, the management of Saudi Aramco, the world's largest oil company and the most Americanized of all major institutions in the Middle East, saw the future and planned accordingly. Saudi Aramco sent a couple of dozen very bright Arab teenagers to China to attend high school and university. The result is a batch of Chinese-speaking Saudis who took their engineering degrees at China's best universities. Despite efforts by Arab friends of our country, like King Abdullah bin Abdulaziz of Saudi Arabia, to persuade young people to come to America for their education, there will soon be more Arab students in China than there are in the United States. Stepping up such exchanges was one of the topics President Hu discussed with King Abdullah during his stop in Riyadh.

But China's and Saudi Arabia's leaders talked about more than cultural exchange. They explored imaginative ways of collaborating to stabilize their energy relationship. In a remarkable development that passed wholly unnoticed here, Saudi Arabia agreed to do in China what it had once proposed to do in the United States—to build, own, and operate a strategic petroleum reserve. This has major advantages for the Saudis, who are always concerned that their ability to export oil might be cut off by war or political upheavals that block the Straits of Hormuz, the Bab al-Mandeb, or the Suez Canal. Storing oil forward in the market in which it is to be sold is the most effective way to protect against that.

If the Sino-Saudi agreement on this mirrors the Saudi proposal we turned down, the oil will be stored in bond and sold only when the Chinese and the Saudis agree. Because it will not have been sold, it will not count against Saudi Arabia's OPEC quota. The Chinese, meanwhile, will have the benefit of an emergency oil supply on their territory. And anyone who might want to bomb Chinese fuel reserves—for example, the U.S. Air Force or Navy in the context of a Sino-American war over Taiwan—will now have to take into account the fact that doing so could prove to be an act of war not just against China but also against Saudi Arabia, resulting in a cutoff of Arab oil supplies. So the deal enhances the national security of China not just in economic terms but also in military terms.

Why couldn't the United States accept a similar offer when the Saudis made it? Well, think about it. It would have involved allowing an Arab country to bring oil into the United States tax free, so as to store it in bond. The reaction in Washington was, "Tax breaks for Arabs? You think the Congress would go along with something like that? You gotta be out of your mind!" So the idea never got anywhere here until it found its way to China.

With the Arabs and Chinese joining hands, are they destined to live together happily ever after? I don't think so. It's not just that no marriage ever works out quite the way those who contract it imagine it will. Some of the expectations the Arabs—and, for that matter, Americans—have for China in the energy context are almost certainly wrong.

President Bush observed that the United States is addicted to imported oil. The definition of an addict is, of course, someone who can't do demand management, someone who blames the supply side for any problems he has feeding his habit. The president has us pegged. And he's quite consistent. None of his proposals deal with demand management.

But the Chinese are determined not to follow us into an addiction for imported oil. Their new energy policy, unveiled this spring, relies heavily on demand management to reduce dependence on oil imports below the levels it would otherwise attain. China's new policies treat oil as a fuel whose use should be restricted as much as possible to the transportation sector, not used to heat buildings or generate electricity.

They envisage phasing in increases in the price of oil so as to ease the pain of holding energy consumption down, promote greater energy efficiency, and reduce the burden on China's already heavily polluted environment. Their emerging policy is essentially the opposite of the one we have followed. We have imposed gas mileage regulations on auto manufacturers rather than using price signals to discourage consumption. By contrast, China's policymakers appear to believe in using the power of the market, not bureaucratic regulation, to solve as many problems as possible.

The taxes that the Chinese will levy to raise prices will pay for a unified transport policy, not just highway construction, as in our country. China hopes to develop an integrated transportation infrastructure that links roads, high-speed railroads, airfields, and water transport for maximum efficiency. In this, they are following the example of European countries, like France, but they hope to learn from European mistakes and to do even better.

The overall Chinese objective is to develop a more balanced and varied energy diet for their country, one in which renewable and nonfossil energy sources play the largest possible role. So, by 2020, China hopes to derive 15 percent of its energy from solar, wind, biomass, and other renewable sources. And it plans to build two nuclear power plants a year—a total of 30—to more than double the role of nuclear power in its economy. Meanwhile, it will explore new energy efficient and environmentally harmless ways to use coal and turn as much as it can to the use of natural gas from Central Asia and Siberia.

All in all, I think, the Arabs are going to be a bit disappointed in their expectations for Chinese dependence on oil imports from the Middle East. China won't be another United States. The Chinese market will grow but not as fast as most people now seem to expect. Not to worry. Given continued growth in U.S. demand for oil, the Arab oil producers will make out just fine. No divorce by the United States is pending. And, even if our affection has faded, no end to our addiction is in sight!

Last year, the rise in oil prices was almost entirely attributable to Americans, not Chinese, Indians, or other foreigners we prefer to blame rather than deal with our addiction. Our demand rose despite the rise in prices. Our demand is pretty inelastic. Our invasion of Iraq both removed that country as a reliable source of oil exports to the world and stimulated mounting concern about a spillover of terrorist activity to Iraq's neighbors. More recently, our threats to invade Iran have further boosted oil prices. So our addiction, compounded by our foreign policies, ensured that oil prices would rise. Al-Hamdu l'illah! ("What a blessing from God!") I suspect that we, rather than the Chinese, are likely to remain the driving force—no pun intended—in global oil markets for the foreseeable future.

This may not, however, be the case with respect to other commodities. Supplies of iron ore, copper, aluminum, and a host of other minerals and metals are increasingly short of demand in the rapidly expanding economies of China, India, and other Asian countries. Ironically, the dollars Americans exchange for imported oil are likely to fund partnerships between Arab investors and Chinese companies that will meet these demand requirements, while bidding up prices for everyone else, including us.

As I said, marriages never seem to turn out the way that those who enter them expected. But this one between the Arabs and the Chinese, which is built on the solid foundation of the addictive behavior of the American consumer, shows every sign of being destined to last. And, at the moment, it is suffused with the joy of mutual discovery. You can call it infatuation, if you want. But it's close enough to love for government work.

Chapter 23

Saudi Arabia: The End of Progress without Change[1]

February 11, 2010

This was what I was planning to say at the speaking engagement on Saudi Arabia to which I referred at the opening of this part of the book. In the end, I was unable to give the talk because all air traffic on the U.S. East Coast was shut down by a massive snowstorm.

I have been asked to speak about the Kingdom of Saudi Arabia. This is a topic I have never before addressed to an American audience. Why bother?

We Americans reserve the right to have strong opinions on the basis of little or no knowledge. There are few countries that better exemplify our assertive ignorance of foreign geography, history, and culture than Saudi Arabia. Most of us are convinced that Saudis are Muslim zealots, control the world's oil prices, and are absurdly rich, antifeminist, and undemocratic. They hate our values and want to destroy us. Talk radio confirms this. What more needs to be said?

On reflection, a lot does. Neither caricature nor a priori reasoning is a sound basis for policy. A distorted view of foreign realities precludes success at dealing with them. There is much at stake in our relationship with Saudi Arabia. We can ill afford to get it wrong.

That country is, of course, the heartland of Islam and the custodian of the world's largest oil reserves. It lies athwart transport routes between Asia, Europe, and Africa. It is at the center of a growing concentration of global capital. Under any circumstances, the Kingdom of Saudi Arabia would be important. It is all the more so in an era when we Americans are at war with ever more peoples in the Islamic world, depend on ever greater amounts of imported energy, and need ever larger foreign loans to run our government and sustain our lifestyle.

---

1. Remarks prepared for delivery to the Sarasota Institute for Lifetime Learning.

Yet Saudi Arabia is little known. It is the only society on the planet not to have been penetrated by Western colonialism. No European armies breached its borders; no missionaries; no merchants. Its capital, Riyadh, was long off limits to infidels; the holy cities of Mecca and Medina remain so today. When Westerners finally came to Saudi Arabia, we came not as the vindicators of our presumed cultural superiority but as hired help. As a result, some say that Saudis secretly see the world's peoples as divided into two basic categories: (1) fellow Saudis and (2) potential employees. Be that as it may, foreigners, Western, Asian, or Arab, who have lived in Saudi Arabia all see it as a very strange place—one that is not easy to understand and that remains at odds with many of the values non-Saudis profess.

The Kingdom has long stood apart from global norms. Its system of government draws on tribal and Islamic traditions rather than Western models. Its king presides rather than rules over the royal family and Saudi society. His responsibility is less to make decisions than to shape and proclaim consensus, while assuring a share of the national wealth to all, especially the least privileged. Saudi Arabia levies no taxes on its citizens, other than the religious tithe known as "zakat"— a 2.5 percent annual donation of private capital to charity and other public purposes. All Saudis enjoy free education and medical care from birth to death and can pursue these services at home or abroad, as they wish. The Kingdom has no parliament, though it does have elaborate informal mechanisms for consultation with its citizens on policy matters. Saudi Arabia reverses and thereby affirms a basic principle of American political philosophy: "No representation without taxation."

Unlike some other countries in the Arab Gulf, Saudi Arabia has invested its oil wealth at home, not abroad, though it has long been generous with foreign aid. (At one point, it was donating 6 percent of GDP to other, mostly Muslim, nations.) The desperate poverty of the pre-oil period is now, at most, a dim memory. Over the lifetime of elderly Saudis, the Kingdom's per capita income has risen about 100-fold. Sparsely populated mud-walled villages have grown into huge air-conditioned cities with 21st century architecture. Today, Saudis are not just literate; many have university degrees. There are more U.S. Ph.D.s in the Saudi cabinet than in our cabinet and Congress put together.

Despite rapid development, the strong family structure that characterized traditional Saudi society has remained largely intact. It is truly moving to see how lovingly children and grandchildren care for their elders in the Kingdom. Saudi Arabia's unique social stability is reflected in the fact that almost none of its citizens emigrate, though many have second homes abroad, and a few, like Osama bin Laden, have been exiled for deviant behavior.

For a long time, it was easier for journalists and academics to get a visa to Tibet than to Saudi Arabia. Perhaps this accounts for the near-total lack of institutions and scholars that study the place. In the United States, 9/11 was followed by an avalanche of polemical tracts, but there are still very few books about the Kingdom that reflect its realities rather than the authors' biases or propagandistic agendas.

Lack of personal familiarity with the Kingdom helps explain the repeated prediction by pundits that the Saudi monarchy is in jeopardy. Generations of such pundits have passed away. The Kingdom has not. When I was ambassador to Riyadh, I was so struck by the apparent social stasis that I briefly thought the national motto should be "progress without change." But in fact change is a constant in Saudi Arabia. Most of it comes from the top down.

Not all Saudis are happy with the status quo. Some are angry about the extent to which the Kingdom is opening up and reforming. Others are impatient to get on with reform. The ranks of the latter clearly include King Abdullah bin Abdulaziz Al-Saud, the current ruler. Now in his late 80s and on the throne only since 2005, he has surprised everyone with the vigor of his efforts to modernize Saudi society and to reshape its relationships with the world beyond its borders. Saudi Arabia has plenty of problems to keep the king engaged.

A lot of issues derive from the peculiar religious heritage of the Saudi state. The current Kingdom of Saudi Arabia (now more than a century old) is the third political structure to ally the House of Saud with the family of the 18th century religious reformer Shaykh-al-Islam Mohammed ibn Abd al-Wahhab Al-Tamimi. Ibn Abd al-Wahhab's writings form the doctrinal basis of so-called Wahhabism, a notoriously intolerant and socially conservative form of Islam that is often confused with other reactionary religious traditions like that of the Taliban. Saudi history has involved a sustained effort by the Kingdom's rulers to persuade its religious scholars and their puritanical followers to embrace change and to open up to the outside world. This struggle has mainly been peaceful and virtually invisible to outsiders. Sometimes, however, it has engendered violence. In 1975, for example, the late King Faisal paid with his life for instituting public education for girls and for introducing television to his nation.

Both as regent (from 1996 to 2005) and more recently as ruler, King Abdullah has been so careful to avoid drama in his promotion of change that it is truly startling to review the cumulative results of his leadership. Take women's issues, for example. In 2002, responsibility for girls' education was transferred from the religious authorities to the ministry of education. Women now make up 58 percent of the enrollment in Saudi universities. The new Princess Noura bint Abdulrahman University for Women, currently under construction in Riyadh, will enroll 40,000 students this fall.

Female participation in the labor force is rising rapidly. Twenty-nine percent of women now work outside the home. (That is a low figure compared with our own but represents a remarkable advance for the Kingdom.) One-third of civil-service positions have been reserved for women. The first woman took her seat in the Council of Ministers last year. After a bit of a kerfuffle, the Kingdom's religious scholars finally endorsed coeducation at the new King Abdullah University for Science and Technology (KAUST). That was big blow to the legitimacy of gender apartheid. A Saudi friend and I are betting that it will not be long before women in the Kingdom can drive. We plan to clean up by building the separate road system this may require. (That's a joke, I hope.)

A word about the vision embodied in KAUST. Founded by the king last September with an initial endowment of $10 billion, KAUST is an international, graduate-level research university. It sits in a two-billion-dollar campus on the Red Sea about 75 miles northwest of Mecca. On one level, it is the leading element in an effort to prepare the Kingdom for a knowledge-based economy that can complement and eventually supersede the current reliance on energy exports. But on another level, it is a powerful answer to the religious zealotry that terrorist movements like al-Qaeda espouse. Let me explain.

There is a broad consensus among the world's 1.6 billion Muslims that the modern age is ethically corrupt and that religious faith needs reinvigoration and renewal. Much like early Christian Protestants, many believe that the way to achieve this is to rediscover and reaffirm the values of their religion's earliest times. When he inaugurated KAUST, King Abdullah explained that he envisaged it as a reborn Bait al-Hikma or "House of Wisdom." The original House of Wisdom was founded in Baghdad around 760 C.E. in the second century of the Muslim era. It was where the Arabs incorporated Greek, Indian and other foreign knowledge into Islam and conceived much of modern mathematics, astronomy, medicine, chemistry, zoology, and geography. It made Islamic civilization the global leader in science and technology. The House of Wisdom prospered in an age of tolerance, when Jews and Christians served alongside Muslims as ministers of government. Though destroyed by the Mongols in 1258, the knowledge it preserved and developed eventually found its way to Europe, where it sparked the Renaissance.

Today, like mainstream Muslims, the extremists of al-Qaeda and related movements argue that Islam must return to its roots. But they portray early Islam as puritanical, xenophobic, intolerant, and oppressive of women. KAUST is a living rebuttal of this historical fallacy and the ideology of hatred derived from it. It was conceived to renew the enlightenment of the past. It stands for the principle that Islam was founded as, and can only be reborn as, the religious guide to a society open to ideas from other traditions. It represents a call for return to an Islam tolerant of foreign ways, respectful of women, dedicated to the scientific study of God's handiwork, and committed to the development of new technologies to better the human condition. KAUST is as much an instrument of religious renaissance and an answer to extremism as it is an academic institution.

This brings me to the issue of religious tolerance. In 2003, King Abdullah inaugurated what he called a "national forum for intellectual dialogue." This ongoing national dialogue is an unprecedented acceptance of religious diversity in the Kingdom. It marks an end to longstanding official discrimination against its Shiite minority. In 2007, King Abdullah made a historic call on the Pope in the Vatican, the first time a Muslim leader of his stature had done so. In 2008, he organized two unprecedented international interfaith conferences between Muslims, Jews,

Christians, Buddhists, and others at Madrid and New York. He intends this dialogue, too, to be a continuing process.

There are other major domestic reform initiatives in progress, like a complete revamping of the Saudi educational system and curriculum, experiments with elections at lower levels of government and civil society, efforts to shift the Kingdom toward reliance on alternative sources of energy, and the development of a huge new petrochemical industry to complement the production of energy in its primary form. Time will not permit me to describe these developments. My point is simply that there is a great deal more going on in Saudi Arabia than our press and pundits seem to realize.

That said, everything is, of course, relative. Sadly, to many Saudis, the history of their nation suggests that the more religiously uptight they are, the more oil comes out of the ground. The Kingdom continues in many ways to belie God's admonition in the Holy Quran that "there can be no compulsion in religion." The open practice of religions other than Islam remains banned. The status and role of women in Saudi society is controversial and far from settled. Despite efforts at "Saudi-ization," foreign workers continue to dominate the employment market, while demanding a premium to compensate for the discomfort and stress that Saudi Arabia's religiously sanctioned mores impose on them. Methods of political consultation that worked in a more cohesive and less populous Saudi Arabia can no longer produce consensus. The fiscal basis of the state continues to be oil exports, and oil is a commodity whose price fluctuates unpredictably. There is, in other words, a very long list of problems for Saudis to work out in coming years.

Let me turn briefly to Saudi Arabia's foreign relations before reviewing the state of our country's interaction with it.

In foreign even more than domestic affairs, King Abdullah's impact has been little short of revolutionary. He has overseen the negotiated settlement of the Kingdom's long-disputed borders with all of its neighbors. He brought Saudi Arabia into the World Trade Organization, ensuring that its trade and investment activities for the first time follow internationally agreed rules. In 2002, in Beirut, he led the Arab League in a historic reversal of policy toward the Israel-Palestine issue. Saudi Arabia had long insisted that it would be the last state in the region to recognize and establish relations with Israel. In Beirut, King Abdullah committed to be the first to normalize relations with Israel upon its achievement of a mutually acceptable arrangement for coexistence with the Palestinians. He persuaded all other Arab countries to promise they would do the same. To his great frustration, Israel did not respond. Since then, hope for a two-state solution that could gain acceptance for Israel in the region has dimmed.

Many of Saudi Arabia's foreign policy challenges stem from recent American policies in the region. These policies have had the effect of liberating Israel from all constraints on its settlement activities and belligerent actions against its Arab neighbors; installing Iran as the dominant political influence in both Iraq and

Lebanon; consolidating rather than eroding the Syrian-Iranian alliance; pushing Hamas into the arms of the Iranians; and raising regional tensions over Tehran's nuclear program while doing nothing effective about it. Then, there is Afghanistan, where the United States now seems to be engaged in a crusade against militant Islam—one that many in the region now fear may soon extend to Yemen. Saudi counter-terrorism specialists, who have a well-deserved international reputation for effectiveness, are convinced that the most efficient way to radicalize Muslim populations and encourage terrorism against the United States and its foreign policy partners is to invade, occupy, and humiliate them. They believe that the panicked militarism of the U.S. response to 9/11 was exactly what groups like al-Qaeda hoped for. They see no sign that the United States is about to abandon actions and policies that metastasize extremism and stimulate terrorist reprisal against Americans and our foreign friends.

No longer willing to be publicly associated with U.S. policies in the Holy Land, Iraq, Afghanistan, and elsewhere that radicalize the region and menace the Kingdom's own security, Saudi Arabia is actively attempting to reduce its historic dependence on America. To this end, it is building new relationships with countries like China, India, and Russia, while strengthening cooperation with long-standing partners in Europe and Asia like Britain, France, Germany, Japan, and South Korea. It is not that the Kingdom has given up on the United States. As the king's scholarship program for Saudi students in this country evidences, Saudi Arabia continues to reach out and seek improved relations with America. But Saudis no longer trust us to take their interests into account or to protect them from their enemies.

In December 2002, as the United States prepared to invade Iraq against the forcefully expressed advice of then–Crown Prince Abdullah, Saudi Aramco (the world's largest oil company) quietly abandoned a decades-old subsidy for the cost of shipping oil to the North American market. Within months, China replaced the United States as the Kingdom's biggest overseas market for oil. U.S. exports have remained relatively constant as the Saudi Arabian economy has boomed, dramatically reducing our market share in our largest Middle Eastern market. Ironically, the best element of the U.S.-Saudi relationship is now cooperation against terrorists. This is a task in which the Saudis have perforce learned to excel. American policies ensure an endless supply of angry young Muslim men in the region, including in Saudi Arabia.

The United States is now said to have entered a "long war." The last time we did so, in 1947 against Soviet Communism, the enemy was obvious, George Kennan gave us a strategy, and skillful American diplomacy gave us the allies we needed to pursue it. Kennan's "long telegram" from Moscow outlined a comprehensive approach to the political, economic, cultural, and military containment of the threat to our survival and our values posed by the Soviet Union. We followed his outline. Forty years later, as Kennan forecast, without our having to go to war with the USSR, our Soviet enemy collapsed of its own infirmities.

This time, our "long war" is with various Islamic extremists, tribes, sects, and societies. We're not quite sure who our enemy is. No Kennan has emerged to give us a strategy for winning without fighting or, indeed, any "strategy" at all. Instead, we are flailing about with our superbly lethal military in response to events. Lacking a strategy, we have been unable to recruit foreign partners to support one. We are now alone in Iraq. We are isolated internationally on the Israel-Palestine issue. Our NATO allies are with us in Afghanistan out of consideration for NATO, not because they think we know what we are doing. Many of them have already announced their intention to withdraw. Pakistan is with us only because all its alternatives are worse.

Saudi Arabia and America head al-Qaeda's enemies list. The Kingdom has, however, been successfully vilified in the eyes of the American elite and public. To deal effectively with Islamic extremism, we need Muslim allies. There is none more potent than the Kingdom of Saudi Arabia. Yet we have made no effort to seek its advice about how to address the challenges of Islamic extremism. We have not sought its help to legitimize an effective political, informational, cultural, and economic strategy for productive engagement with the Islamic world.

Meanwhile, however, many things now happening in the Kingdom—like the implicit message of the king's vision for KAUST—suggest that such a partnership with Saudi Arabia and Arab nations of like mind is possible. Such a partnership could be the basis for a strategy to bring victory in this latest "long war." The common interests on which to forge an alliance are clearly there. Last June in Cairo, President Obama brilliantly articulated a credible basis for sound relations with the Islamic world. His vision was persuasive, but it remains a mirage, not a reality. It is past time to implement it. An intensive effort to reset the relationship with Saudi Arabia and to craft a common antiterrorist strategy with its king would be a good place to start.

Glossary

AIPAC: American Israel Public Affairs Council.

al-Saud (with the first 'a' being long): The eponymous ruling family of Saudi Arabia.

CENTAF: U.S. Central Command's air forces.

CENTCOM: U.S. Central Command.

CINCCENT: Commander in Chief, U.S. Central Command .

CNO: Chief of Naval Operations (U.S.)

Dar al Islam: That portion of the earth ruled by some form of Islamic law, or (more minimally) in which Islam forms the clear majority culture.

GCC: Gulf Cooperation Council.

GDP: Gross domestic product.

IAF: Israeli Air Force.

IPO: Initial public offering.

JCS: Joint Chiefs of Staff (U.S.)

jihadi: Generally used here to refer to Islamist activists who use violence in pursuit of their aims (Arabic).

KAUST: King Abdullah University for Science and Technology, Saudi Arabia.

KGB: The State Security Committee of the former Soviet Union—its premier security agency.

Lebensraum: The often expansive notion of the terrain that some leaders judge an ethnic group requires in order to live a satisfactory life (German).

madrasa: Technically, this is simply the Arabic word for school. But it is frequently used, as here, to refer to schools that inculcate militant forms of Islamist ideology.

mashriq: Traditional Arabic term for the Arab East—those Arab lands east of the Mediterranean.

mujahedeen: Individuals dedicated to the pursuit of 'jihad', with this pursuit often understood to be violent. During the Cold War, many U.S. leaders considered Afghanistan's anti-Soviet mujahedeen very heroic (Arabic).

NATO: North Atlantic Treaty Organization.

NIC: National Intelligence Council (U.S.)

NSC: National Security Council (U.S.)

NCUSAR: National Council on U.S.-Arab Relations.

NEA: Near East and South Asian Affairs—a bureau in the U.S. State Department.

NIC: National Intelligence Council (U.S.)

oderint dum metuant: "Let them hate us, so long as they fear us" (Latin).

OPEC: Organization of Petroleum Exporting Countries.

PLO: Palestine Liberation Organization.

salafis: Muslim believers and social/political activists who pursue what they judge to be the "fundamental origins" of their faith (Arabic).

Schadenfreude: Enjoyment from others' troubles (German).

shariah: Islamic law (literally, "the way"; Arabic).

shisha: A water pipe through which a compacted and often scented form of tobacco is smoked (Egyptian Arabic).

Sons of Iraq: A network of militias in Sunni Arab communities in Iraq that after 2006 were established and/or financed by the U.S. with the goal of using them against Al-Qaeda's Iraqi networks.

suq: A market; often, a traditional Middle Eastern market (Arabic).

UAE: United Arab Emirates.

UNSC: United Nations Security Council.

USIA: U.S. Information Agency.

WMD: Weapon (or weapons) of mass destruction.

Made in the USA
Lexington, KY
30 March 2011